Sep. 2022

BIRNBAUM'S
Disneyland RESORT

THE OFFICIAL VACATION GUIDE 2023

Wendy Lefkon Editorial director

Jill Safro Editor

Jessica Ward Contributing Editor

Jennie Hess Contributing Editor

Tony Fejeran Designer

Alexandra Mayes Birnbaum Consulting Editor

Stephen Birnbaum Founding Editor

DISNEY EDITIONS

LOS ANGELES · NEW YORK

For Steve, who merely made all this possible.

ISBN 978-1-368-08352-2
FAC-034274-22217
First Edition, September 2022
10 9 8 7 6 5 4 3 2 1

Printed in the United States of America

Other 2023 Birnbaum's Official Disney Guides:
Walt Disney World
Walt Disney World For Kids

The Official Disney Fan Club

D23.com

CONTENTS

113 GOOD MEALS, GREAT TIMES

Whether it's a simple snack or a multi-course feast, the Disneyland Resort offers something for nearly every palate and pocketbook. Our dining and entertainment section reflects Disneyland Resort's extensive range of possibilities, from the spirited nightspots in the Downtown Disney District to theme park dinner shows, birthday celebrations, and the ever-popular meals hosted by Disney characters.

135 SPORTS & RECREATION

Perhaps you dream of catching the perfect wave, hiking along cliffs above the Pacific coast, polishing your tennis serve, or taking in a spectator sport. It's a cinch to fulfill your fondest athletic fantasies in the land of sun and surf.

WHAT'S NEW?

To spotlight the various attractions, shows, shops, and restaurants making their debut, some listings are marked with the "new" icon shown here. Look for it throughout this book. Here are a few highlights for 2023:

A Word From The Editor

Walt Disney, the man who pioneered the realm of family entertainment, was at once an artist, entrepreneur, and creative visionary. He was also a dad. And, like many of the folks who visit Disneyland each year, Walt treasured the time he spent with his kids. In fact, while his two daughters were growing up, Walt would accompany them to carnivals, zoos, and local amusement parks. It was something of a Saturday tradition for the Disney family. During these outings he'd often make the same observation: The youngsters were happily entertained, but the adults didn't have much to do. It didn't seem right that he'd be stuck sitting on a bench while the kids had all the fun. To his way of thinking, a park should appeal to the sense of wonder and exploration in guests of all ages. His bold vision became a reality on July 17, 1955, when Disneyland had its opening day in Anaheim, California.

These days, more than ever, it seems many of us long for the classic escape that's uniquely Disney. Walt's original park is as beloved as ever—and it continues to grow and evolve. Disneyland park has an exciting new attraction in a re-imagined land— Mickey & Minnie's Runaway Railway is a brand-new smile inducer deep in the heart of the newly refreshed Mickey's Toontown. This cheery realm also boasts the new CenTOONial Park, complete with a majestic tree under which guests are encouraged to dream like Walt. Of course, Disneyland park continues to delight guests of all ages with cherished classics such as It's a Small World, Pirates of the Caribbean, Haunted Mansion, Peter Pan's Flight, Fantasmic!— the park's nighttime extravaganza, plus the limited return of a twinkling processional known as the Main Street Electrical Parade.

Across the esplanade from Disneyland, Disney California Adventure is firing on all cylinders. Attractions such as Soarin' Around the World, Guardians of the Galaxy—Mission: BREAKOUT!, and Radiator Springs Racers helped put this place on the map, but they're just the tip of the iceberg. In addition to a super new land dubbed Avengers Campus, guests are treated to an array of attractions and entertainment bearing that distinctive Disney Parks stamp. Among them are Toy Story Midway Mania!, Incredicoaster, and the splashy (wildly popular) nighttime spectacle, World of Color.

When Steve Birnbaum launched this guide, he made it clear what was expected of anyone who worked on it. The book would be meticulously revised each year, leaving no attraction untested, no meal untasted, no hotel untried. First-hand experiences like these, accumulated over the years, make this book the most authoritative guide to the Disneyland Resort. Our expertise, however, was not achieved by being escorted through back doors of attractions. Instead, we have waited in lines with everyone else, always hoping to have a Disney experience like any other guest.

Of course, there's so much more to the Disneyland Resort than the theme parks. There's also a dynamic dining, shopping, and entertainment zone known as the Downtown Disney District, and three Disney hotels (with one in the midst of an exciting Pixar make-over). It all adds up to a total that is truly greater than the sum of its parts. And, though it has nearly seven decades of history under its belt, this is still just the beginning—as per its founder's wishes: "Disneyland will never be completed. It will continue to grow as long as there is imagination left in the world."

TAKE OUR ADVICE

In creating this book, we've considered every possible aspect of your trip, from planning it to plotting day-by-day activities. We realize that even the most meticulous vacation planner needs detailed, accurate, and objective information to prepare a successful itinerary. To achieve that lofty goal, we encourage the submission of factual information and insight from Disneyland staffers—but the decision to use such information is entirely at the discretion of the editor.

We have also packaged handy bits of advice in the form of "Hot Tips" throughout the book. These helpful hints come directly from the copious notes we have taken during our countless trips to the Disneyland Resort and the surrounding Anaheim area. We have also used our "Birnbaum's Best" stamp of approval wherever we deemed it appropriate, highlighting our favorite attractions, shows, and restaurants—the crowd-pleasers we feel stand head, shoulders, and ears above the rest.

You, the reader, benefit from the combination of our decades of experience and access to inside information from the Disneyland staff—that makes this guide unique. We like to think it's indispensable, but you be the judge of that 150 pages from now.

DON'T FORGET TO WRITE!

No contribution is of greater value to us in preparing the next edition of this book than your comments on its usefulness and your own experiences at the Disneyland Resort. We encourage you to send us an email at **WDI.Birnbaum.Guides@disney.com**, or drop us a note at the address below. Thank you!

Jill Safro
Birnbaum's Disneyland 2023
Disney Editions
77 W. 66th Street
3rd Floor/Suite #356
New York, NY 10023

CREDIT WHERE CREDIT IS DUE

Enormous thanks to the amazing teams of dedicated, detail-conscious Disneyland Resort cast members from Guest Communications, the Disney Resort Reservation Center, Food & Beverage, Merchandise, Resort Operations, Attractions Operations, Disney Vacation Club, Marketing, Disney Parks Synergy, and more for helping us ensure the factual accuracy of *Birnbaum's Official Guide to Disneyland Resort 2023*.

Kudos to Michelle Olveira for her outstanding fact-checking, and to copy editor extraordinaire Monique Peterson. We would also like to tip our hats to Jerry Gonzalez, Taryn Maister, Jennifer Eastwood, Winnie Ho, Monica Vasquez, Marybeth Tregarthen, Devon Munroe, Kinden Sevorwell, Kathy Crummey, Suzanne Fass, Karen McClintock, Chris Ostrander, Valerie Lee, Flossie Gillen, Alyce Diamandis, Dan Kunkel, Jilly Bean Kunkel, Amy Henning, and Christina Fontana for their editorial support and production panache.

Of course, no list of acknowledgments would be complete without mentioning our founding editor, Steve Birnbaum, whose spirit, wisdom, and humor still infuse these pages, as well as Alexandra Mayes Birnbaum, who continues to be a guiding light—to say nothing of a careful reader of every word.

THE LAST WORD

Finally, it's important to remember that every worthwhile travel guide is a living enterprise; the book you hold in your hands is our best effort at explaining how to enjoy the Disneyland Resort at the moment, but its text is not etched in stone. Details change often—especially these days! Disneyland is always changing and growing, and in each annual edition we refine and expand our material to better serve your needs. Just before the grand opening of Disneyland, Walt Disney remarked that the main attraction was still missing: people. That's where you come in.

Have a wonderful time!

— Jill Safro, Editor

GETTING READY TO GO

TO ALL WHO COME TO THIS HAPPY PLACE: WELCOME. DISNEYLAND IS YOUR LAND. So said Walt Disney on July 17, 1955. Fast-forward 68 fun-filled years, and the "Happiest Place on Earth" is as welcoming as ever, hosting millions of visitors from around the globe year in and year out. The beloved 500-acre Disneyland Resort has evolved quite a bit over time, but Walt's original theme park, Disneyland, is still at its heart. Besides this magical kingdom, guests will discover Disney California Adventure park; Downtown Disney District; a trio of on-site hotels: Disney's Grand Californian Hotel & Spa, Disney's Paradise Pier Hotel (which is currently getting a Pixar make-over), and the Disneyland Hotel; and dozens of decidedly Disney dining and shopping destinations. Of course, you will want to do and see it all, but where should you start? When should you go? And then there are the important questions of how to get there and where to stay. Maybe you want to extend your vacation—perhaps you'll include a visit to (or a stay at) the beach or one of the other nearby attractions.

That's a lot to think about. But don't worry: By the time you've read this chapter, you will have the information you need to make smart decisions. So read on, and remember—a little advance planning can go a very long way. Note that details are subject to change. For updates, visit *disneyland.com*.

When to Go

When you weigh the best times to visit the Disneyland Resort, the most obvious possibilities often seem to be weekends, Christmas, Easter, and summer vacation—particularly if there are children in the family. But there are a few good reasons to avoid these periods—the major one being that almost everybody else wants to go then, too. (While foot traffic at Disney California Adventure {aka DCA} is often lighter than it is over at Disneyland park, DCA is a whole lot busier than it was in years past.)

If you can only visit during one of these busy times and worry that the crowds might spoil your fun, there are some tactics for making optimum use of every minute and avoiding the longest of lines—notably, go to the park early to get a jump on the day (and on the crowds), use Lightning Lane service if budget allows, and remember that Disney keeps the parks open later during busy seasons. Note that "early admission" (aka "Extra Magic Hour") to Disneyland park or Disney California Adventure may happen on select days for guests at Disneyland hotels (and other select hotels) and Walt Disney Travel Company guests. Pre-purchased, 3-day-or-more Disneyland park or Park Hopper passes may net the ticket holder "Early Entry" to Disneyland on select

days. Early Entry was "on pause" at press time. For updates, use the Disneyland app or visit *disneyland.com*.

On the other hand, choosing to visit when the parks are least crowded may mean that you miss some special events—a treasured fireworks show or parade might not be listed on the entertainment schedule, and certain shows and attractions may be closed for annual refurbishment.

A lovely time to visit—when Disneyland is not always as crowded as usual—is the stretch after Thanksgiving until about a week before Christmas, when the Christmas parade takes place and carolers add festive music to the mix. Other good times to visit are the periods after summer—September through early October—and after New Year's Day.

When Not to Go: If crowds make you queasy, keep in mind that Saturday is traditionally the busiest day of the week year-round. In summer, Sunday, Monday, and Friday tend to be the next busiest. If you decide to visit Disneyland park during a weekend, opt for Sunday (it gets less busy as the day wears on). And remember that the week before Christmas through New Year's Day, Easter week, and the period from early July through Labor Day are packed.

DISNEYLAND RESORT CROWD PATTERNS

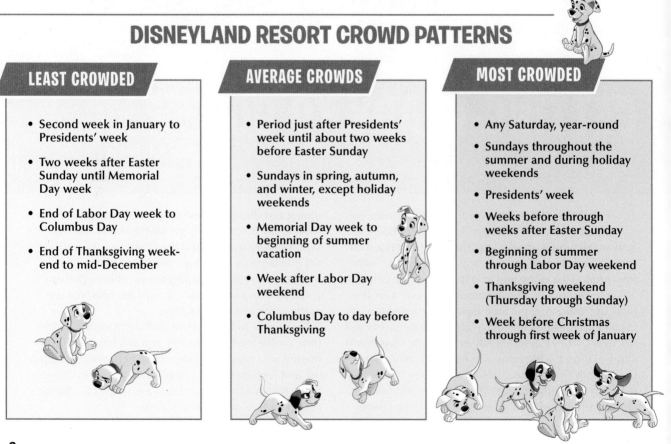

LEAST CROWDED

- Second week in January to Presidents' week

- Two weeks after Easter Sunday until Memorial Day week

- End of Labor Day week to Columbus Day

- End of Thanksgiving weekend to mid-December

AVERAGE CROWDS

- Period just after Presidents' week until about two weeks before Easter Sunday

- Sundays in spring, autumn, and winter, except holiday weekends

- Memorial Day week to beginning of summer vacation

- Week after Labor Day weekend

- Columbus Day to day before Thanksgiving

MOST CROWDED

- Any Saturday, year-round

- Sundays throughout the summer and during holiday weekends

- Presidents' week

- Weeks before through weeks after Easter Sunday

- Beginning of summer through Labor Day weekend

- Thanksgiving weekend (Thursday through Sunday)

- Week before Christmas through first week of January

Keeping Disney Hours

Operating hours tend to fluctuate based on the date and the season. For updates, call 714-781-4636, visit *disneyland.com*, or use the Disneyland Resort mobile app. All details are subject to change.

DISNEYLAND PARK: This park is typically open from about 8 A.M. to about 10 P.M. Monday through Thursday, 8 A.M. to midnight on Friday and Saturday, and 8 A.M. to 11 P.M. on Sunday. Hours are often extended in the summer months and during holiday seasons. Extra Magic Hour (when it's available) is usually offered on Tuesday, Thursday, and Saturday. This special perk allows guests of Disneyland Resort hotels to enter the park one hour early. Those bearing multi-day park passes that include "Magic Mornings" (it is stated on the ticket itself) may enter the park one hour early on Tuesday, Thursday, and Saturday mornings when the service is offered.

DISNEY CALIFORNIA ADVENTURE PARK: The theme park generally opens at about 8 or 9 A.M. and closes at 9 or 10 P.M., sometimes later. Disneyland Resort hotel guests may enter the park one hour early on Extra Magic

Hour days: Sunday, Monday, Wednesday, and Friday. For updates, use the Disneyland mobile app, or visit *disneyland.com*.

DOWNTOWN DISNEY DISTRICT: Many spots in Disneyland Resort's shopping, dining, and entertainment district open when the parks do, but some may open as early as 7 A.M. and most close at about 10 P.M. Sunday through Thursday (usually later on Friday and Saturday nights and during peak times of year).

TRANSPORTATION: The Disneyland monorail begins making its 2.5-mile loop about the time Disneyland park opens (including early entry Magic Mornings) and runs until about 15 minutes before the park closes. Trams transporting guests between parking lots and the parks begin picking up guests about an hour before the first theme park opens, and continue transporting guests back to parking areas until about an hour or so after the last park closes. If you miss the last tram, ask about alternate transportation to the Mickey and Friends parking structure (it's usually in the form of a van).

ANAHEIM WEATHER

If dry, sunny weather is your ideal, Anaheim may seem like a dream come true. Rainy days are few and far between and generally occur between the months of November and April, which is also the coolest time of year. During this season, Santa Ana winds sometimes produce short periods of dry, warm desert weather and sparkling-clear skies that unveil distant mountains usually hidden by smog. In summer, thin, low morning clouds make it logical to plan expeditions to the beach for the afternoon, when the haze burns off and the mercury rises. Mornings and nights are generally cool. The average daytime year-round temperature is about 78 degrees.

	TEMPERATURE AVERAGE		RAINFALL AVERAGE
	HIGH	LOW	
JANUARY	71	48	2.9
FEBRUARY	71	48	3.0
MARCH	73	51	2.0
APRIL	76	53	0.8
MAY	78	57	0.3
JUNE	81	61	0.1
JULY	87	65	0.3
AUGUST	89	65	0.1
SEPTEMBER	87	63	0.3
OCTOBER	82	58	1.4
NOVEMBER	76	52	1.4
DECEMBER	70	47	2.0

Holidays & Special Events

Disneyland Resort hosts special events all year long. For additional information, use the Disneyland mobile app, visit *disneyland.com*, or call 714-781-7290. Here are a few highlights to consider:

JANUARY–FEBRUARY

Three Kings Day—Día de los Reyes: Celebrate the 12th day of Christmas and some of the Latin American traditions associated with the Epiphany as part of Disney California Adventure's Festival of Holidays.

Lunar New Year: Disney California Adventure welcomes the Lunar New Year with time-honored traditions and multi-cultural festivities. Guests may follow a young lantern's quest to reunite with his family and celebrate good fortune in Hurry Home—a special 6-minute show presented before World of Color. Mulan may host a parade.

Valentine's Day: Sweethearts will certainly swoon over the romantic backdrop that Disneyland Park provides on this love-struck holiday.

MARCH–MAY

Disney California Adventure Food and Wine Festival: Enjoy savory sips and nibbles at this popular annual event featuring culinary demonstrations, spirit seminars, appearances by well-known chefs, and more. Cheers!

Easter: The parks stay open late the week before and the week after Easter (it's a very busy time to visit). One of the parks hosts an Eggstravaganza—a scavenger hunt for giant eggs—in the weeks leading up to the holiday. (Maps, which come with a character keepsake, are offered for a fee.)

JUNE–AUGUST

All-American College Band: Disney's All-American College Band performs for nine weeks during summer (usually beginning in mid-June), Tuesday through Sunday. Performances take place throughout the park.

Fourth of July: This is one of the busiest days of the year—and one to avoid if you're easily overwhelmed by crowds. The more-patriotic-than-usual day features exceptionally festive fireworks at Disneyland Park.

EARLY SEPTEMBER–OCTOBER

Halloween Festivities: At Disneyland Park, Halloween Time lets guests celebrate in many not-so-scary ways. In addition to fall color decor, the Disneyland Band and Dapper Dans celebrate with seasonal tunes. The Haunted Mansion attraction's holiday transformation gives this spot a *Tim Burton's The Nightmare Before Christmas* motif. Main Street, U.S.A., features hundreds of hand-carved jack-o'-lanterns. And Disney characters celebrate the holiday by donning Halloween costumes. (For current policies regarding guest costumes, visit *disneyland.com*.) Disney California Adventure park gets into the Halloween spirit with Oogie Boogie Bash—A Disney Halloween Party. Expect lots of spooky touches such as a Halloween-themed World of Color, a "Villainous" dance party, and a stage show with Mickey Mouse.

NOVEMBER–DECEMBER

Thanksgiving Weekend: The four days of this holiday weekend are filled with musical entertainment and the early installments of Disneyland's A Christmas Fantasy Parade and It's a Small World Holiday, and the holiday transformations of Cars Land and Buena Vista Street, all of which kick off in mid-November. The parks usually observe extended hours.

Holiday Festivities: By early November, Disneyland's Main Street is festooned with greenery and poinsettias, while more than a million lights create a wonderland that glistens from the Town Square Christmas Tree to Sleeping Beauty's Winter Castle. On two festive evenings in December, a massive choir walks down Main Street in a Candlelight Ceremony. It features a live orchestra and guest narrator who reads the story of the Nativity. There's also a holiday-themed fireworks show, "Believe . . . In Holiday Magic." It's presented throughout the holiday season. It is not to be missed.

It's a Small World is transformed into a wondrous world of holiday magic. A Christmas Fantasy Parade also takes place. Haunted Mansion Holiday extends through holiday season. Disney California Adventure has the Festival of the Holidays, a holiday World of Color, and Viva Navidad!, an energetic street party hosted by the Three Caballeros.

The Disneyland Resort celebrates Kwanzaa, Hanukkah, Diwali, and New Year's Eve in exceptionally festive fashion, too. Happy holidays!

MAGICAL MILESTONES

Walt Disney once said, "Disneyland will never be completed. It will continue to grow as long as there is imagination left in the world." Truer words were never spoken. Here's a sampling of major milestones and important dates in Disney history.

1901

Walter Elias Disney is born on December 5 in Chicago, Illinois. He spends part of his childhood in Marceline, Missouri.

1922

Walt and collaborator Ub Iwerks start Laugh-O-Gram Films, an animation studio located in Kansas City, Missouri. (The business lasts one year.)

1923

Walt and his brother Roy open the Disney Bros. Studio in Hollywood, California.

1928

The Disney studio introduces the world to the immortal Mickey Mouse with *Steamboat Willie*, the first cartoon with a synchronized soundtrack. (Walt Disney provides the voice for Mickey.)

1932

Flowers and Trees wins the Disney Studio its first Academy Award.

1937

Disney releases *Snow White and the Seven Dwarfs*, the world's first feature-length animated movie.

1940

Disney animation meets great classical music with the release of *Fantasia*.

1955

Disneyland opens its doors in Anaheim, while television's original *Mickey Mouse Club* begins a four-year run.

1967

Disneyland debuts Pirates of the Caribbean—one of the most popular and beloved attractions of all time.

1971

Walt Disney World debuts in Central Florida. It has one theme park—the Magic Kingdom—and two themed resort hotels: Contemporary and Polynesian Village.

1989

Disney animation experiences a renaissance of sorts with the release of the Studio's 28th animated feature film, *The Little Mermaid*.

2001

For the first time since its opening, the Disneyland Resort gets a new theme park: Disney California Adventure.

2003

The Many Adventures of Winnie the Pooh attraction makes its debut in Critter Country inside Disneyland park.

2004

Turtle Talk with Crush opens at Disney California Adventure park. Like, totally awesome, dude.

2006

Captain Jack Sparrow joins the merry marauders in Pirates of the Caribbean.

2008

Toy Story Midway Mania! opens at Disney California Adventure.

2012

Cars Land races onto the scene with new fan favorites, including Radiator Springs Racers and Mater's Junkyard Jamboree.

2019-2020

The Force awakens at Disneyland Park in Star Wars: Galaxy's Edge. There, guests fly in Han Solo's ship at *Millennium Falcon: Smugglers Run*, ride out an epic battle between the First Order and the Resistance, customize a lightsaber, and wet their whistles at Oga's Cantina.

2023

Mickey & Minnie's Runaway Railway chugs into a newly re-imagined Mickey's Toontown. The cheerful neighborhood unveils a charming new nature zone: CenTOONial Park—an inspirational spot where you can dream like Walt.

WEDDINGS & CELEBRATIONS

Disneyland Resort's customized Fairy Tale Weddings & Honeymoons program lets brides and grooms create an affair to remember in the parks or at one of the three Disneyland Resort hotels—either indoors or out. Couples may go the traditional route or plan a themed event with invitations, decorations, souvenirs, napkins, and thank-you notes emblazoned with their favorite Disney character couples, including Cinderella and the Prince, and Mickey Mouse and Minnie Mouse.

One special spot for tying the knot is the rose garden gazebo at the Disneyland Hotel, in a picturesque natural setting where the bride, groom, or couple may arrive in Cinderella's crystal coach. Another setting choice is the courtyard area at Disney's Grand Californian Hotel & Spa. A fantasy reception may follow (in either of the aforementioned hotels), at which the fanfare of trumpets greets the happy couple. Mickey Mouse and Minnie

Mouse may even arrive to help the newlyweds with the cake-cutting moment.

A trusty Disney wedding coordinator assists with the arrangements for the wedding and reception—everything, that is, except providing the guest's very own Prince or Princess Charming.

The bridal salon (at the Disneyland Resort Center, between the Disneyland Hotel and Disney's Paradise Pier Hotel) helps guests through the planning and prep stages, and even through those pre-ceremony jitters.

For details about creating a happy occasion in a happy location, contact the Disneyland Fairy Tale Weddings department, which coordinates events at the Disneyland Resort hotels and theme parks: *disneyweddings.com;* 321-939-4610. For info about Disneyland honeymoons, visit *disneyweddings.com*, or call Disneyland Resort Travel Sales at 800-854-3104.

Quinceañeras

Along with its popular wedding program, Disneyland Resort also offers customized quinceañera celebrations for young women who are coming of age. These popular family-oriented milestone events invite the birthday girl to become a "princess for a day" and step into the fairy-tale realms of *Beauty and the Beast* or *Cinderella*. Held in a spacious ballroom, the celebrations feature dinner, dancing, and time-honored quinceañera traditions. For more information, visit *disneyland.disney.go.com/events-tours/quinceaneras*, or call 714-520-7072.

Planning Ahead

Collect as much information as you can about the area attractions you're interested in from the sources listed below (and this book, of course). Then consider all the possibilities before making definite travel plans.

INFORMATION

For up-to-the-minute information about special events and performance times, ticket prices, theme park hours, attractions under refurbishment, and other specifics, use the Disneyland app and/or contact:

Disneyland Resort Guest Services; Call 714-781-4565, or visit *disneyland.com*. Or send a question via *disneyland.disney.go.com/en-ca/help/email*.

If you are staying at one of the Disneyland Resort hotels (see *Accommodations*), contact Guest Services at the hotel for help in planning your visit to the Disney parks and the surrounding area.

Inside the Disneyland Resort: Cast members (the friendly folks who work at Disneyland) can answer questions. Information stations in Disneyland Park include City Hall in Town Square and the Information Board near Central Plaza, on Main Street. In Disney California Adventure, the Chamber of Commerce is on the east side of the Entry Plaza and the Information Board is on Buena Vista Street, adjacent to the Red Car Trolley stop. At any Disneyland Resort hotel, visit the lobby for assistance.

For other Anaheim area information, contact these bureaus of tourism:

Visit Anaheim; Call 714-765-2800 during business hours to reach a rep, or go to *www.visitanaheim.org*.

KNOW BEFORE YOU GO

The information in this chapter is tailored to help you plan, book, and seamlessly modify your Disney vacation dreams. And we've done our best to ensure that it and all other content within this edition of *Birnbaum's Official Guide to Disneyland Resort* is as useful, comprehensive, and current as possible. That said, procedures and policies do change now and then — especially these days. So before you begin your trip, check on the latest procedural changes and updates by visiting *disneyland.disney.go.com/experience-updates*.

At press time, face coverings were optional, but encouraged, for all guests in indoor attractions, queues, and in enclosed forms of transportation. Some experiences remained on temporary pause or were being presented in a modified way. Most will return, but timing is dependent on guidance from health authorities such as the Centers for Disease Control (CDC) and appropriate government agencies.

The folks at Disneyland Resort request that you review any advisories or restrictions in place for travel to California, and do not travel to or enter Disneyland Resort unless you are free of COVID-19 symptoms, and otherwise comply with the requirements of such advisories and restrictions. If you need to reschedule your Disneyland Resort hotel reservation, please call 714-520-5050.

Things may be a little different since your last Disney visit, but rest assured that all practices are designed to offer a magical Disney experience in a safe and healthy way.

You can visit in person at 2099 S. State College Blvd., Suite 600, Anaheim, CA 92806. (They have a travel guide and a map, but no other brochures at this time.)

Long Beach Area Convention & Visitors Bureau; 301 E. Ocean Blvd., Suite 1900, Long Beach, CA 90802; *www.visitlongbeach.com*, 562-436-3645, or 800-452-7829.

Los Angeles Convention & Visitors Bureau; There were no walk-in visitor centers at press time; For more information, visit *www.discoverlosangeles.com*.

RESORT RESERVATIONS

Given the popularity of the Disneyland Resort, advance planning is essential. To get your choice of accommodations, especially for visits during the busy spring and summer seasons, make lodging reservations as far in advance as possible—at least six months ahead, if you can, since area hotels fill up rather quickly during these months. For visits at other times of the year, check with Visit Anaheim or the Anaheim/Orange County Visitor & Convention Bureau (714-765-2800), to see if conventions are scheduled when you want to travel. Some of these events can crowd facilities enough to warrant altering travel plans. To book a room at a Disneyland Resort hotel, visit *disneyland.com*, or call 714-956-6425.

TRAVEL PACKAGES

The biggest advantage to purchasing a travel package is that it almost always saves you money over what you would pay separately for the individual elements of your vacation, or it offers special options not available if you simply buy a one-day ticket. This is especially true the longer you stay. And there is the convenience of having all the details arranged in advance by someone else.

Finding the best package means deciding what sort of vacation you want and studying what's available. Do not choose a package that includes elements that don't interest you—remember, you're paying for them. And if it's Disney theming and "extras" you want, consider a Walt Disney Travel Company package.

The Walt Disney Travel Company offers packages that include a stay at a Disney hotel and a Park Hopper ticket. It's possible to add extras, such as a character breakfast in the park or a guided tour of Disneyland park, as well as admission to another Southern California attraction, such as Sea World, or LEGOLAND. Purchase extras separately.

Besides booking guests into an official Disneyland Resort hotel, the Walt Disney Travel Company also works closely with dozens of Good Neighbor hotels and motels (see pages 47–51 for details), and they are included in its packages as well. To book a vacation package at the Disneyland Resort, contact a travel agent, or call the Walt Disney Travel Company at 714-520-5060.

The Disneyland Resort is also featured in a variety of non-Disney-run package tours, including those sponsored by individual hotels and airlines (United Vacations, Alaska Airlines Vacations, Southwest Vacations, and jetBlue Vacations offer packages, for instance). AAA Vacations (800-922-8228 ext. 3) offers packages to the traveling public, too.

This book's selective guide to Anaheim-area hotels and motels can help you decide initially which property best suits your party's travel style, needs, and budget (refer to the Accommodations chapter for guidance). Pick one, then contact a travel agent or the hotel itself to make a reservation or book a Disneyland Resort package. Be sure to inquire about deposit requirements, cancellation policies, and trip insurance (we recommend opting for insurance). Happy hunting!

WHAT TO PACK

Southern California isn't so laid-back that you only need to pack shorts, T-shirts, and sneakers. Nor is it a place that demands formal attire. Casual wear will suffice in all but the fanciest restaurants, and, even there, men can usually wear sports jackets without ties. Bathing suits are an obvious must if you plan to take advantage of your hotel's swimming pool or go for a walk on a long, surf-pounded Pacific beach. It's also a good idea to bring along a bathing suit cover-up and sunglasses (and don't forget the all-important sunscreen). Tennis togs or golf gear may be necessary if you plan to hit the courts or the course. The weather in summer can be quite warm, but because Southern California air-conditioning can be exceptionally robust, you should take a lightweight sweater or jacket to wear indoors.

In winter, warm clothing is a must for evening; during nighttime visits to the parks, a heavy jacket may be a godsend. We like having hats and gloves, too. Whatever the time of year you decide to visit, always come prepared for the unexpected: Pack a light-weight shirt *and* a warm sweater or jacket—just in case.

Finally, we highly recommend packing face coverings, hand sanitizer, plus a power pack and an extra charger for your phone.

Making A Budget

Vacation expenses tend to fall into five major categories: (1) transportation (which may include costs for airfare, airport transfers, train tickets, car rental, gas, parking, and taxi service); (2) lodging; (3) theme park tickets; (4) meals; and (5) miscellaneous (recreational activities, souvenirs, toiletries, forgotten items, and expenses such as pet boarding, etc.).

When budgeting, first consider what level of service suits your needs. Some prefer to spend fewer days at the Disneyland Resort, but stay at a deluxe hotel like the Grand Californian or dine at pricier restaurants. Others may want a longer vacation with a value-priced Good Neighbor hotel and less expensive meals. The choice is up to you. (Having said that, we do feel that a great deal of the Disney experience comes from staying on Disneyland Resort property and recommend at least making room in your budget for accommodations at the somewhat more moderately priced Disneyland Hotel or Paradise Pier Hotel.)

Once you have established your spending priorities, it's time to determine your price limit. Then make sure you don't exceed it when approximating your expenses—without a ballpark figure to work around, it's easy to get carried away.

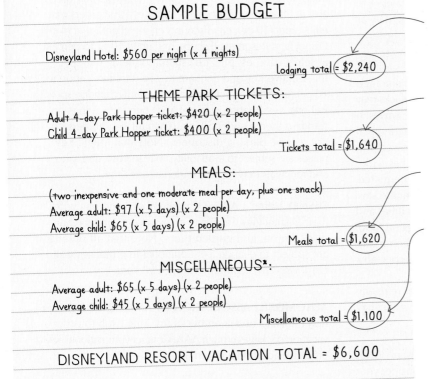

SAMPLE BUDGET

Disneyland Hotel: $560 per night (x 4 nights)

Lodging total = $2,240

THEME PARK TICKETS:

Adult 4-day Park Hopper ticket: $420 (x 2 people)
Child 4-day Park Hopper ticket: $400 (x 2 people)

Tickets total = $1,640

MEALS:

(two inexpensive and one moderate meal per day, plus one snack)
Average adult: $97 (x 5 days) (x 2 people)
Average child: $65 (x 5 days) (x 2 people)

Meals total = $1,620

MISCELLANEOUS*:

Average adult: $65 (x 5 days) (x 2 people)
Average child: $45 (x 5 days) (x 2 people)

Miscellaneous total = $1,100

DISNEYLAND RESORT VACATION TOTAL = $6,600

If you'd like a lower hotel rate, consider a stay at one of Disney's Good Neighbor hotel partners. Room rates may start as low as $129.

Don't forget: To enter a Disneyland Resort theme park, you'll need a valid ticket and a park reservation, (For details, see page 17 and visit *disneyland.com*).

Even if you plan to stick to fast food, expect to spend at least $75 (per adult) and $40 (per child) per day.

Careful packing should help cut down on miscellaneous expenses, which include forgotten toiletries such as toothpaste, hand sanitizer, and the all-important sunscreen.

This is an example of a moderately priced budget for a family of four (two adults and two kids staying at Disneyland Resort for four nights and five days during "off-peak" dates), excluding transportation costs. Theme park admission prices are likely to increase in 2023. (They always do.)

*Does not include airfare, airport transfers, or other transportation fees. See page 25 for details. Be sure to include all transportation costs (which vary widely) in your travel budget.

Money-Saving Strategies

COST-CUTTING TIPS

LODGING: The most important rule is not to pay for more than you need. Budget chains don't offer many frills, but they are usually clean and provide the essentials; many even have a swimming pool, albeit a small one. (Bigger isn't always better!)

You can also save by checking the cutoff age at which kids can no longer share their parents' room for free. Many hotels and motels allow children under age 18 to stay free. A few places have a cutoff age of 15 or 17, so it's best to find out before making a reservation. And ask about special rates or discounts, especially if you are a California resident, Disney Vacation Club member, AARP member, or are in the military.

Hostels and Recreational Vehicle (RV) parks also offer lower-priced lodging alternatives. Contact Visit Anaheim at 714-765-2800 for a listing of those areas closest to the Disneyland Resort.

FOOD: The budget-minded (and who isn't?) should plan to have meals in coffee shops or fast-food restaurants, or save your splurges for buffets and family-style eateries to get your fill and your money's worth. If you want to try an upscale place, go for lunch; the entrées are often the same as those at dinner time, but may cost a little less.

Pack a picnic and enjoy meals outside. There's a small picnic area just to the left of Disneyland Park's entrance. (It's surrounded by trees—so it's easy to miss.) Snacks may be brought into the parks, but not glass bottles, knives, or beverages containing alcohol. Refillable plastic or metal cups and bottles are permitted. Coolers are allowed, but must be no larger than 24 inches long, 15 inches wide, and 18 inches high. Loose and dry ice are not permitted. Reusable ice packs are recommended. You can also save on meals by choosing lodging with kitchen facilities and opting to eat in some of the time. The savings on food may more than cover the additional cost of accommodations. Don't forget to pack snack items, too—especially when traveling with kids.

In the Anaheim area, a number of spots offer refrigerators or kitchen facilities (look for suite hotels); some may even provide breakfast.

TRANSPORTATION: When calculating the cost of driving from your home to the Disneyland Resort, consider your car's gas mileage, the price of gasoline, and the expense of the accommodations and food en route. If you are planning to fly, don't forget about the cost of getting from

home to the airport and later to the hotel. Also factor in the cost of renting a car at your destination, if that's part of your plan. Remember to ask what your hotel charges for parking (rates tend to vary) or shuttle transportation to the Disneyland Resort—these daily charges can tack quite a bit onto a family's total vacation cost.

HOT TIP

For information on special offers for many of Anaheim's hotels, restaurants, and attractions, visit *www.visitanaheim.org* (click on the Special Offers link under the Plan Your Trip tab), or contact via telephone: 714-765-2800.

DISNEY DISCOUNTS

MAGIC KEY PASSES: Bearers of Magic Key annual passes may net savings at Disneyland Resort restaurants, select merchandise throughout the parks, Disneyland hotels, and at Downtown Disney. Dream Key Passholders may enjoy up to 20 percent discounts on merchandise at many Disneyland Resort retail shops, and up to 10 to 15 percent at select eateries, plus free standard theme park parking. Believe Key and Enchant Key Passholders get up to 10 percent off at select restaurants and merchandise spots. Believe Key-bearers also net a 50-percent savings on standard theme park parking. (Enchant Key-holders do not receive parking discounts.) Note that Magic Key passes are subject to availability, may sell out, and sales and renewals may be suspended at any time.

DISNEY VISA® CARDS: Cardmembers who pay with their Disney Visa Card may enjoy savings on merchandise, dining, and guided tours. Note that all details are subject to change. For additional information, visit *DisneyRewards.com* or *DisneyDebit.com*.

AUTOMOBILE ASSOCIATION OF AMERICA (AAA): You don't have to be a member of the Auto Club to order a vacation package through AAA. Contact your regional AAA office for additional information.

BIRNBAUM COUPONS: The coupons at the back of this book will net you savings at several spots in the Downtown Disney District. You're welcome!

Theme Park Tickets

TICKET OPTIONS

One- to Five-Day Tickets allow admission to one theme park per day, while One- to Five-Day Park Hopper tickets allow admission to both parks and allow you to "hop" between parks. Tickets generally expire 13 days after first use. Theme park reservations are required and should be made in advance with the Disneyland app or via *disneyland.com*. If you plan to park-hop, you must visit your first park before entering the second. At press time, guests could hop between theme parks starting at 1 P.M., but that may change at any time.

The main types of "Magic Key" annual passes are Dream Key, Believe Key, and Enchant Key versions. All afford the bearer shopping and dining discounts, as well as park-hopping (visiting both theme parks in one day) with theme park reservations. Two notable differences between Magic Key pass types—all of which are valid for one year after activation—are blockout dates (select dates when the passholder may not enter the Disney parks) and the number of theme park reservations that may be held at any given time.

The Dream Key pass has no blockout dates and lets the bearer hold up to 6 theme park reservations on a rolling basis. The Believe Key has blockout dates and allows up to 6 theme park reservations on a rolling basis. The Enchant Key pass has blockout dates and allows for up to 4 theme park reservations to be held on a rolling basis. Dream Key passholders get free standard theme park parking, while Believe Key bearers get half off.

There may be special passes for Southern California residents. Offers may vary and passes are limited. For details about the Magic Key program, call 714-781-4565 or go to *disneyland.disney.go.com/magic-key*.

PURCHASING TICKETS

Where to Buy Tickets: Tickets may be purchased at Disneyland Resort ticket booths, but we recommend getting them via *disneyland.com*, or the Disneyland app. This will help skirt lines and, more importantly, allow for advance theme park reservations. (You can print them, have them mailed, or pick up at Will Call. The latter options come with a fee. E-tickets may be scanned for admission, but must be displayed on an Internet-accessible hand-held device.) In past years, advance purchase tickets of 3 days or more have included one "Magic Morning," allowing access to a park one hour before posted opening time on select days. Magic Mornings were "on pause"

at press time. For updates, visit *disneyland.com*.

Tickets by Mail: Send a check or money order and ticket request (plus a $10 fee for all orders over $200) to Disneyland Ticket Mail Order Services, Box 61061, Anaheim, CA 92803. It's also possible to order by calling Ticketing & Reservations at 714-781-4400 (up to 30 days ahead). Allow 10 business days for processing.

Tickets by Phone: Allow at least 7 to 10 business days for delivery: 714-781-4565.

THEME PARK RESERVATIONS

To enter a Disney park, you need a valid ticket *and* a reservation. It's best to check for reservation availability prior to buying tickets. If your desired dates are open, buy the ticket and make reservations right way—or risk being shut out. For updates, visit *disneyland.com*.

TICKET PRICES

Although prices[†] will likely increase, the following should give an idea of what you will pay for tickets in 2023. Note that 1-Day tickets purchased in 2023 must be used by 12/30/23. The first day of use of multi-day tickets must be on or before 12/30/23. Multi-day tickets must be used within 13 days of first use or by January 12, 2024, whichever occurs first. For updates, use the Disneyland app or visit *disneyland.com*. All details are subject to change.

	ADULTS	CHILDREN*
1-Day Ticket (1 park)	$104/164	$98/154
1-Day Ticket (hopper)	$164/224	$158/214
2-Day Ticket	$255	$240
2-Day Ticket (hopper)	$315	$300
3-Day Ticket**	$330	$310
3-Day Ticket (hopper)**	$390	$370
4-Day Ticket**	$360	$340
4-Day Ticket (hopper)**	$420	$400
5-Day Ticket**	$380	$360
5-Day Ticket (hopper)**	$440	$420
Enchant Key pass		$649
Believe Key pass		$949
Dream Key pass		$1,399

† One-day prices represent the range in which you can expect to pay. Prices vary based on date. For dates, visit *disneyland.com*.
* 3 through 9 years of age; children under 3 free
** Includes one "Magic Morning" early admission to Disneyland park (when the service is offered) with advance purchase.

There is a single price (for adults and children) for Enchant Key, Believe Key, and Dream Key passes. Said passes are part of the "Magic Key" pass program that replaced traditional annual passes. For more information on Magic Key passes, use the Disneyland mobile app or website, or visit *disneyland.com*.

Customized Travel Tips

TRAVELING WITH CHILDREN

When you tell your kids that a Disneyland vacation is in the works, the challenge is keeping them relatively calm until you actually arrive at the House of Mouse.

PLANNING: Get kids involved in plotting a Disneyland trip from the outset, putting each of the kids in charge of a small part of vacation preparation—such as visiting *disneyland.com*, choosing which attractions to see and in what order to see them, and investigating which other activities you may want to include during your Southern California sojourn.

EN ROUTE: Certain resources can stave off the "Are we there yet?" chorus, such as travel games, tablets (and chargers), books, and snacks to quiet rumbling stomachs. If you drive, take plenty of breaks along the way. If you plan to fly, try to book your departure and return flight times for off-peak hours and during the off-season, when chances are better that an empty seat or two will be available (prices should be a bit cheaper, too). During takeoffs and landings, encourage toddlers to suck on bottles or pacifiers to keep ears clear, and supply older kids with chewing gum, a lollipop, or water. And don't forget toys to keep the wee ones occupied.

IN THE HOTELS: Several Anaheim-area hotels offer kids' programs. Some offer babysitting services or babysitting referrals year-round (fees apply).

IN THE THEME PARKS: The smiles that light up your kids' faces as they enter a Disney theme park should repay you a thousandfold for any fuss en route. No place in the world is more aware of the needs of little ones—or their parents—than this one.

Favorite Attractions: Fantasyland and Mickey's Toon-town (if it's open) in Disneyland Park are great places to start with small kids, who delight in the bright colors and familiar characters. In Disney California Adventure, Cars Land, Disney Junior Dance Party!, and Monsters, Inc.—Mike and Sulley to the Rescue! have big kid appeal. If you have kids of different ages in your party, you may have to do some juggling or split the group up for a few hours so that older kids won't have to spend their whole visit waiting in line for Dumbo. Some rides, like Pinocchio's Daring Journey, may be too intense for some youngsters.

Strollers: They can be rented for $18 ($36 for a double) at the Stroller Shop, located to the right of the entrance to Disneyland Park. This is the only place to rent a stroller for either park. If you leave the parks but plan to return later that day, keep the receipt and get another stroller at no additional charge.

Baby Care: Baby Care Centers feature toddler-size toilets that are quite cute—and completely functional. In addition, there are changing tables, a limited selection of formulas, baby foods, and diapers for sale, plus facilities for warming baby bottles (you can wash out your bottles here, too). A special room with comfy chairs is available for nursing mothers. The decor is soothing, and a stop here for a diaper change or feeding is a tranquil break for parent and child alike. The Baby Care Centers are located in Central Plaza, at the Castle end of Main Street, U.S.A. in Disneyland Park, and near Ghirardelli Soda Fountain & Chocolate Shop in Disney California Adventure.

Changing tables and diaper vending machines are also available in many restrooms.

Note: Parents of toddlers should pack a supply of swim diapers. They are required for children who want to spend time frolicking in hotel pools.

Where to Buy Baby Care Items: Disposable diapers, baby bottles, formula, etc., are sold at Baby Care Centers in the parks. Pack as much of your own as possible—prices can be steep and the selection is small.

HEIGHT HO!

At attractions with age and/or height restrictions, a parent who waits with a child too young or too small to ride while the other parent goes on the attraction will have expedited boarding as soon as the first parent comes off. This is known as the "rider switch" policy, and if lines are long, it can save a great deal of time. The cast member at the attraction entrance can explain what to do.

HOT TIP

Pack kid-friendly snacks, such as fruit, cereal, crackers, breakfast bars, and water. Snack stands are plentiful at Disneyland Resort, but not always handy or cost-efficient.

Lost Children: Youngsters should carry the mobile phone number for the parent or guardian who accompanies them to the parks. But even without it, when a child gets separated from his or her family or fails to show up on time, cast members (Disney employees) and Disneyland Resort's security force follow specific procedures when they encounter a lost child. Please report lost children to a cast member, and Disneyland Resort security personnel will assist you.

Kids age 13 and younger will be escorted (by a Disney cast member) to the park's Baby Care Center, while a parent or guardian is contacted via mobile phone or otherwise directed to the Baby Care location. Kids older than 13 will be taken to City Hall in Disneyland park or the Chamber of Commerce just inside the entrance area of Disney California Adventure. Lost children found in the Downtown Disney District are taken to either the Disneyland Hotel or the Baby Care Center/Lost Children location inside Disneyland Park (near the Plaza Inn on Main Street, U.S.A.)

TRAVELING WITHOUT CHILDREN

Disneyland Resort is as enjoyable for solo travelers and couples as it is for families for several reasons: Its ambience encourages interaction, and the attractions are naturally shared events.

PLANNING: Read Disneyland Resort planning literature carefully before you arrive to familiarize yourself with the area's layout and activities. Also, search for information about other places in Southern California that you intend to visit.

Food for Thought: Sightseeing takes lots of energy, and only healthy meals can provide it at a consistent level. Don't attempt to save money by skipping meals. Prices at the parks and nearby "off-property" eateries are relatively reasonable, and there are some healthy options, even in the fast-food restaurants. And don't forget to stay hydrated—running around theme parks all day is a lot of work.

Health Matters: If you visit in summer, avoid getting overheated. Protect yourself from the sun with a hat and plenty of sunscreen, rest in the shade often, and beat the mid-afternoon heat with a cold drink or a snack in an air-conditioned spot.

If you are injured or feel ill, speak to a Disney cast member or go to First Aid to see the nurse. In case of emergency, call 911. Above all, heed attraction warnings. If you have a back problem, heart condition, or other physical ailment, suffer from motion sickness, or are pregnant, skip rough rides. Restrictions are noted at attraction entrances, as well as on park guidemaps.

Lost Companions: Traveling companions can get separated. If someone in your party wanders off or fails to show up at an appointed meeting spot and cell phone communication is thwarted, head for City Hall in Disneyland park or Chamber of Commerce in Disney California Adventure park. Guests can leave and receive messages for one another during the day.

MEETING OTHER ADULTS: Downtown Disney, with its mix of eateries and bars, is a nice spot to meet and mingle with the grown-up set. While each of Disney's hotels has lounges worth visiting, the lively Trader Sam's Enchanted Tiki Bar in the center of the Disneyland Hotel is exceptionally engaging.

TRAVELING WITH DISABILITIES

The Disneyland Resort is remarkably accessible to guests with disabilities, and, as a result, it makes a solid choice as a vacation destination. But advance planning is still essential.

GETTING TO ANAHEIM

Probably the most effective means of ensuring a smooth trip is to make as many advance contacts as possible for every phase of your journey. It's important to make phone calls regarding transportation well before your departure date to arrange for any special facilities or services you may need en route.

The Society for Accessible Travel & Hospitality (SATH, 2175 Hudson St., Fort Lee, NJ 07024; *www.sath.org;* 212-447-7284) has member travel agents who book trips for travelers with disabilities, keeping special needs in mind. Membership costs about $49, or $29 for students and seniors (age 63 and older).

The following agencies specialize in booking trips for travelers with physical disabilities: TravelAble (855-500-3440; *travelablevacations.com*) and Wheel the World, (*https://gowheeltheworld.com*; 628-900-7778).

Note that the aforementioned agencies are neither run by nor endorsed by The Walt Disney Company.

Hertz (800-654-3131), Alamo (800-651-1223), and National (888-273-5262) rent hand-controlled cars at Southern California airports. Order your car at least 72 hours in advance and confirm before arrival.

Though less direct, it is also possible to access the area by public transportation. All Anaheim Resort Transportation (aka ART, the official Disneyland Resort Shuttle Bus) routes provide access to the Disneyland Resort through the Main Transportation Center (visit *www.rideart.org,* or call 888-364-2787). The same is true for many of the routes covered by the Orange County Transportation Authority, the public bus company that serves Orange County (*www.octa.net,* or 714-560-6282). All ART and OCTA buses have lifts for travelers using wheelchairs.

Scootaround rents standard and electric wheelchairs, as well as motorized scooters. Pickup and delivery is available for all hotels in the Disneyland Resort area. Visit *www.scootaround.com,* or call 888-441-7575. A company called Wheelchair Getaways of California rents wheelchair-accessible vans and has pick-up and delivery options for most area hotels. Call 866-224-1750, or visit *www.wheelchairgetaways.com.*

LODGING

Most hotels and motels in Orange County have rooms equipped for guests with disabilities, with extra-wide doorways, grab bars in the bathroom for shower or bath and toilet, and sinks at wheelchair height, along with ramps at curbs and steps to allow wheelchair access. Unless otherwise indicated, all the lodging described in the Accommodations chapter (page 41) provide guest-rooms for travelers with disabilities.

INSIDE THE DISNEYLAND RESORT

Cars displaying a "disability" placard will be directed to a section of each Disney parking lot, next to the tram pick-up and drop-off area.

Wheelchairs and Electric Conveyance Vehicles (ECVs) can be rented at the Stroller Shop outside the entrance to Disneyland Park. This is the only rental location for both theme parks. The price is $15 per day for wheelchairs, and $60 for ECVs, plus tax and a refundable $20 deposit. A few wheelchairs may be available to borrow from Disneyland Resort's three hotels; inquire at the front desk. Quantities are limited. We recommend using your own wheelchair whenever possible.

Most waiting areas are accessible, but some attractions offer auxiliary entrances for guests who use wheelchairs or other mobility devices; guests may be accompanied by up to five party members using the special entry point. The Main Street train station is not wheelchair accessible. However, guests using wheelchairs have easy access to the Disneyland Railroad in New Orleans Square, Mickey's Toontown, or Tomorrowland.

Accessibility information is provided in special brochures (see Park Resources, below). In all cases, guests with mobility disabilities should be escorted by someone in their party who can assist as needed.

In some theme park attractions, guests may remain in their wheelchair or Electric Conveyance Vehicle; in others, they must be able to transfer in and out of their wheelchair or ECV. In a few attractions, guests must leave their wheelchair or ECV and remain ambulatory during the majority of the attraction experience.

For Guests with Visual Disabilities: An audio tour and the Braille Guidebook are available upon request at City Hall in Disneyland Park and at Chamber of Commerce in Disney California Adventure. Both are free to use but require a $25 refundable deposit. A portable handheld device containing several services, including audio description, is available from Guest Relations at each theme park (a refundable deposit is required).

Trained service animals are permitted in most locations. Animals may not be permitted to ride some attractions.

PARK RESOURCES

Contact Disney Disability Services by telephone (407-560-2547) or via email (send email inquiries to disability.services@disneyland.com) for details on Services for Guests with Visual Disabilities and Hearing Disabilities; Services for Guests with Service Animals; and Attraction Access for Guests Using Wheelchairs and Electric Conveyance Vehicles (ECVs), or use the (free) Disneyland Resort mobile app or visit *disneyland.com.* Information is also available at City Hall in Disneyland and at Chamber of Commerce in Disney California Adventure.

They may wait with a non-riding member of their party or in a portable kennel. For additional information, visit *disneyland.disney.go.com/guest-services/service-animals*.

For Guests with Hearing Disabilities: Reflective captioning is available in the pre-show areas of select theme park shows and attractions—inquire at the show or attraction entrance or visit *disneyland.disney.go .com/guest-services/hearing-disabilities*.

Dozens of attractions provide hand-held captioning service. The system uses a wireless handheld receiver to display text in locations where fixed captioning systems are impractical, such as moving attractions. Receivers are available through Guest Relations and require a $25 refundable deposit. For details, visit the website referenced in the previous paragraph or check at City Hall in Disneyland Park or Chamber of Commerce inside Disney California Adventure.

Text typewriters (TTYs) are available to borrow from all three Disneyland Resort hotels. Ask about them when you check in.

Sign Language interpretation is available by request for select special events with at least 14 days advance notice. Call 714-781-4636 (select option 1, and then option 0). Guests under age 18 must have the permission of parent or guardian to call.

A portable device containing several services, including handheld captioning, may be borrowed at City Hall in Disneyland Park or Chamber of Commerce in Disney California Adventure (with a $25 refundable deposit).

DISNEYLAND RESORT TOURS

The following guided tours provide guests with a chance to explore Disneyland Park and Disney California Adventure in entertaining and informative ways. Annual Passholders and Disney Visa® Cardmembers receive a discount on select guided tours. Tours may be booked up to 30 days in advance. Availability is

limited. For details or to book a tour, call 714-781-8687 or visit *disneyland.com*, or stop by City Hall (on Main Street in Disneyland Park) or the Chamber of Commerce at Disney California Adventure. Theme park admission is required (but not included) for all guided tours. Note that many tours were "on pause" as this book went to press. For status updates, use the Disneyland mobile app, or visit *disneyland.com*.

- ***Walk in Walt's Disneyland Footsteps*** (9:30 A.M. daily): Led by a knowledgeable guide, the tour covers Walt's original theme park. In addition to your theme park ticket, expect to pay at least $109 (per person, all ages) for the 3.5-hour tour. Guests travel through Walt's original Magic Kingdom, while hearing stories of the challenges, inspiration, and fun associated with all of his creations. The tour includes a meal on Main Street, a collectible button and pin, and a visit to the Disneyland Dream Suite in New Orleans Square. All details are subject to change. For more information, visit *disneyland.com*.

- ***Disney's Happiest Haunts Tour*** (Seasonal): Journey through both parks at dusk and prepare for a night of chilling tales and eerie sights on this 3-hour walking tour. Cost is about $99 per person and includes a souvenir keepsake and a Halloween treat. Guests should be at least 40 inches tall. The tour is not recommended for guests using wheelchairs or strollers. Participating guests may ride Haunted Mansion and Big Thunder Mountain Railroad. Details (including pricing) are subject to change.

- ***Grand Circle Tour*** (Seasonal): All aboard! Get a behind-the-scenes view into Walt Disney's lifelong appreciation of trains and how they inspired some of his creations. One highlight of the 2-hour tour: a ride in a special parlor car on the Lilly Belle steam train. There is a guided walking tour and a sweet treat to enjoy, too. To participate, guests must be at least 18 years old with government-issued photo ID.

- ***Holiday Time at the Disneyland Resort*** (Seasonal): This tour shares the history of Disneyland's holiday traditions and enchanting tales of holidays from around the world, includes visits to attractions that have had holiday makeovers, and offers special seating for the holiday parade, A Christmas Fantasy. Cost is at least $99 per person and includes a pin, a warm beverage, and a gingerbread cookie. Details are subject to change.

- ***VIP Tour Services:*** A dedicated team is available to customize and guide your Disneyland Resort vacation: 714-300-7710. VIP Tour Services were available at press time, but details are subject to change.

Lightning Lane Service

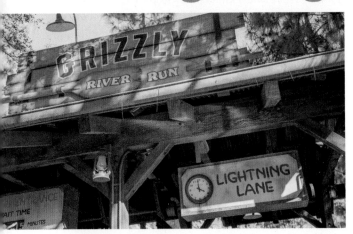

disneyland.com: An Internet-based hub for planning and managing your Disneyland visit. It's also where you can purchase Genie+ Service before you visit Disneyland Resort.

Disneyland Resort mobile app: The official app for the Disneyland Resort has planning tools, park updates, exclusive content, and more. The app lets you use (complimentary) Disney Genie Service, purchase Genie+, and pay for access to Individual Lightning Lane Entrances while inside a Disneyland Resort theme park. Be sure to download the app before you start your Disneyland theme park visit.

Disney Genie: A complimentary service that is designed to "create your best Disney day based on your interests." It's available as a feature within the official Disneyland Resort mobile app.

Lightning Lane Entrances: A fee-based alternative to traditional standby entrances, Lightning Lane Entrances offer expedited wait times at select theme park attractions. Lightning Lane Entrances fall into two categories: Disney Genie+ Service and Individual Lightning Lane selection. Fees apply for both categories.

Disney Genie+: Disney Genie+ service lets park guests select the next available arrival window for a Lightning Lane entrance at select attractions throughout the day, one at a time. A flat fee covers Genie+ Service for the day.

Individual Lightning Lane: An à la carte Individual Lightning Lane purchase, offered for the most highly demanded theme park attractions at the Disneyland Resort. At press time there was a limit of two attractions per person, per day. Fees vary.

NEW Every theme park attraction at the Disneyland Resort has a traditional "standby" line that's included with park admission. A subset of those diversions offers something called Lightning Lane service, too. The fee-based alternative to the traditional standby line offers expedited access to popular theme park attractions.

There are two ways to enter attractions via Lightning Lanes: by using "Genie+" service and by purchasing "Individual Lightning Lane" selections. Since each option offers a different set of attractions from which to choose, it's possible to combine the two if budget allows. (Though it's not necessary to purchase Genie+ to make Individual Attraction Selections or vice versa.)

DISNEY GENIE+

Genie+ lets guests enter select theme park attractions up to once per day via express "Lightning Lane" entrances rather than using the traditionally longer standby queues. How does it work? First, you need to purchase the service. That can be done as an add-on to your ticket or vacation package via *disneyland.com* (prior to arrival), or via the Disneyland app once you've entered a park for the day.

HOT TIP

The purchase of Genie+ does not guarantee attraction access. In fact, popular rides run out of Genie+ availability early in the day. That said, some folks do cancel their selections, so keep checking for availability throughout the day.

(Note that if you pre-purchase Genie+, it will be added to each day of a multi-day ticket. Same-day purchases can be done one day at a time. The latter is our preferred approach.) Genie+ costs $20 per ticket, per day and it includes PhotoPass (see page 87 for PhotoPass details). If you have questions or need help with your in-park purchase of Genie+, head to any Guest Relations location. They'll know what to do.

Next up? Enter the park for which you have a ticket and reservation. Now it's time to make the first Genie+ selection of the day! Once you have redeemed your initial selection (or the window has passed), you can use the Disney Genie Tip Board or My Day itinerary to see when you're eligible to make your next selection. Note that Genie+ selections can be made throughout the day—one at a time—until regular park closing time. All Lightning Lane selections are subject to availability and are limited to one per attraction, per day.

When your first arrival window kicks in, you can head to the attraction's Lightning Lane entrance, flash your ticket or your phone (so the bar code may be scanned), and zip on into the Lightning Lane. You can make your next Genie+ selection after your currently selected window has either started or been redeemed. You're also eligible to make an additional selection if you are holding a selection with an arrival window that's more than two hours from the time the selection was made—provided there is availability. Feeling a bit of information overload? Not to worry. The Disneyland app is an efficient way to keep track of it all. And Disney's trusty Guest Relations team is always happy to help.

INDIVIDUAL LIGHTNING LANE

Lightning Lane access to a small number of Disneyland Resort's most popular "E-ticket" attractions may be purchased on an à la carte basis. They're limited to

two purchases per person, per day and range from about $7 to $20 (prices are subject to change at any time). Be sure to check the Disneyland app on the day of your visit for current prices and attraction availability.

You can purchase up to two Individual Lightning Lane selections upon entering a Disneyland Resort theme park. Remember: Lightning Lane entry for these attractions is only available to purchase individually and not included with Disney Genie+ Service. (Individual selections can, however, be purchased separately and used along with Disney Genie+ Service.) For details, use the Disneyland mobile app, or visit *disneyland.com*.

DISNEY GENIE+ ATTRACTIONS*

The following theme park shows and attractions were included with Genie+ Service as this book went to press (details are subject to change):

DISNEYLAND PARK
- Autopia
- Big Thunder Mountain Railroad
- Buzz Lightyear Astro Blasters
- Haunted Mansion
- Indiana Jones Adventure
- It's a Small World
- Matterhorn Bobsleds
- *Millennium Falcon:* Smugglers Run
- Roger Rabbit's Car Toon Spin
- Space Mountain
- Splash Mountain
- Star Tours—The Adventures Continue

DISNEY CALIFORNIA ADVENTURE
- Goofy's Sky School
- Grizzly River Run
- Guardians of the Galaxy— Mission: BREAKOUT!
- Incredicoaster
- Monsters, Inc. Mike & Sulley to the Rescue!
- Soarin' Around the World
- Toy Story Midway Mania

* Attractions and shows may be added or removed from Disney Genie+ Service at any time. For updates, visit *disneyland.com* or check the Disneyland mobile app.

HOT TIP

At press time, attractions with Individual Lightning Lane status included Disneyland Park's Star Wars: Rise of the Resistance and Disney California Adventure's Radiator Springs Racers and WEB SLINGERS: A Spider-Man Adventure. Individual Lightning Lane status can change at any time. For updates, visit *disneyland.com*.

How to Get There

Most visitors to Disneyland Resort arrive by car. Many who live nearby own Magic Key passes and often drive there to spend a day or weekend at the resort. But for those traveling any significant distance, it tends to cost less to fly than to drive, and can save time. During your days at Disneyland Resort, you won't need a vehicle. Rent a car only for the days you plan to venture off Disneyland property, or rely on local tours to see the area sights. If you prefer to leave the driving to someone else, traveling to Disneyland by bus or train are alternatives.

BY CAR

SOUTHERN CALIFORNIA FREEWAYS: Driving just about anywhere in Orange County, or farther afield, requires negotiating a number of freeways and surface streets. But once you familiarize yourself with a few names and numbers, navigating through California becomes much more manageable.

The freeways are well marked and relatively fast, barring (common) traffic snags. That said, they can be rather frenetic. Major thoroughfares may merge with little or no notice. Monstrous traffic jams are common during morning and evening rush hours. And proper names of most roads change, depending on where you are. I-5, for instance, is called the Santa Ana Freeway in Orange County; in the Los Angeles area, it becomes the Golden State Freeway; to the south, it's the San Diego Freeway. It's a good idea to learn both the name and the route number of any freeway on which you plan to

travel. Exit signs list a route number and either a direction or city name (but not always both).

Even with GPS, it's always good to have an idea of the layout of the freeways. Several run parallel to the Pacific coast and are intersected by others running east and west. While this scheme is fairly straightforward, it is complicated by a couple of freeways that squiggle across the map.

CALIFORNIA DRIVING LAWS: Under state law, seat belts are required for all passengers; right turns at red lights are legal unless otherwise posted, as are U-turns at intersections; and pedestrians have the right-of-way at all crosswalks. By law, kids must be in car or booster seats until they reach the age of 8 or a height of 4 feet, 9 inches. And keep your hands off your phone—it's illegal to use it while driving in California.

AUTOMOBILE CLUBS: Any one of the nation's leading automobile clubs will come to your aid in the event of a breakdown en route (be sure to bring your membership card with you), as well as provide insurance covering accidents, arrest, bail bond, lawyers' fees for defense of contested traffic cases, and personal injury. They also offer trip-planning services—not merely advice, but also free maps and route-mapping assistance.

MAPS/GPS: If you don't have a GPS app on your smartphone, know that some car rental agencies provide GPS systems and maps. Of course, it's still wise to familiarize yourself with the route beforehand. Said route can be plotted via *www.bing.com/maps; www.mapquest.com;* or *maps.google.com.*

BY AIR

Anaheim lies approximately 45 to 120 minutes southeast of Los Angeles by car. Most Disneyland Resort guests who arrive by plane disembark at Los Angeles International Airport (LAX), one of the busiest in the world. It handles approximately 1,500 departures and arrivals daily of more than 59 commercial airlines. Major carriers serving Los Angeles include jetBlue, American, Delta, and United airlines.

Much closer to Anaheim, Orange County's John Wayne Airport is about a half-hour drive from Disney and is served by 7 commercial airlines and more than 200 flights a day. It is sometimes possible to find the same fare to John Wayne/Orange County Airport (SNA) as to LAX, and if

HOT TIP

Driving to Disneyland and looking for an address for the GPS? Look no further: 1313 S. Harbor Boulevard., Anaheim, CA 92802.

HOT TIP

Freeway traffic updates can help you avoid a jam. Tune to 1070 AM (in Anaheim and Los Angeles).

it's a nonstop flight, so much the better. There are not as many direct flights available, but given the proximity to the Disneyland Resort area, it's worth considering. Another airport vying for attention is the Long Beach Airport (LGB). The lovely, little airport is relatively close to Anaheim, but few airlines serve it on a nonstop basis.

HOW TO GET THE BEST AIRFARE: Airfares seem to be forever in flux, changing often. That makes it very important to shop around—or have your travel agent do so. It pays to keep these suggestions in mind:

• Check into all airlines serving your destination. See if you can get a lower fare by slightly altering the dates of your trip, the hour of departure, or the duration of your stay—or, if you live halfway between two airports, by leaving from one rather than the other or by flying into a different area airport.

• Weekend flights tend to bring higher prices. Fly midweek whenever possible. (Tuesdays and Wednesdays are usually best.)

• Purchase your tickets online. Airlines often offer lower fares or waive transaction fees when customers use their websites.

• Keep an eye on airline websites, social media sites, and newspapers for ads announcing special fares.

AIRPORT TRANSPORTATION: There are a number of shuttles and limousines available to transfer you from area airports to the Disneyland Resort.

At Los Angeles International Airport (LAX), limos, shuttles, and car services pick up passengers on the Lower/Arrival Level islands in front of each terminal on the middle island curb under the white sign marked "Passenger Pickup." For additional information about transportation to and from LAX, visit *flylax.com*.

Those who fly into John Wayne Airport, 14 miles from Disneyland, have an easier time of it. The ride into town takes half the time than from LAX. From baggage claim, head to the Ground Transportation Center. This is the spot to meet prearranged transportation, connect with Karmel Shuttle, and get a taxi. Look for coordinators who can assist you with your ground transportation needs. And be sure to inquire about a flat rate for a one-way trip to the Disneyland Resort. For more details about John Wayne Airport's ground transportation, visit *ocair.com*.

Karmel Shuttle *(karmel.com; 714-670-3480)* serves most area airports. At Los Angeles International Airport, claim luggage and call 714-670-3480 Extension 2 for pickup. Or, if you've provided a cell phone number and received a text alert upon landing, tap the "Ready to Go" link in the text from Karmel Shuttle. You will be provided with both a vehicle number and a license plate number. Be sure to match these numbers with the vehicle sent to pick you up. Then head on over to the

TO THE DISNEYLAND RESORT FROM THE AIRPORT*

	Yellow Cab	Karmel Shuttle**
Los Angeles International Airport (LAX)	Expect to pay at least $100 (plus a tip for the driver), depending on traffic.	$126 per car
John Wayne Airport (SNA)	Expect to pay at least $47 (plus tip).	$71 per car
Long Beach Airport (LGB)	Expect to pay at least $55 (plus tip).	$82 per car

* For updates and/or more information on transfers between the Disneyland Resort and area airports, visit *disneyland.disney.go.com/guest-services/getting-here/by-plane*. Prices quoted are for one-way trips.

** Price paid per person varies based on the number of passengers in the car. Solo riders pay the full price. For shared rides, the "car total" is divided evenly among passengers. Shared-ride service is available for pick-ups between 6 A.M. and 7 P.M. Private service is available 24/7. For details, visit *karmel.com*, or call 714-670-3480.

Yellow Cab and Karmel Shuttle are not owned or endorsed by The Walt Disney Company.

Lower/Arrival Level islands in front of each terminal on the middle island curb under the white sign indicating "Passenger Pickup." Follow the same procedures for John Wayne and Long Beach airport, where the pickup areas are at the airports' respective Ground Transportation Centers. (Long Beach Airport's pickup center is the island next to the covered parking structure across Douglas Drive.) Karmel offers private and shared rides.

CAR RENTALS: Several major car rental agencies have locations at LAX, John Wayne, and Long Beach airports; in Union Station; at many hotels; and elsewhere in the Anaheim area. Expect to pay somewhere between $466 and $709 a week for an intermediate car (plus tax and insurance fees), and $48 to $289 for a 3-day weekend, with unlimited mileage. Some rental companies to choose from are Avis (800-331-1212), Budget (800-527-0700), Dollar (800-800-4000), Hertz (800-654-3131), Alamo (800-651-1223), and National (888-273-5262).

It pays to call agencies and check websites to get the best available deals. Be sure to ask about any special promotions or discounts. Loss Damage Waiver (LDW) coverage is essential for your protection in case of an accident, but it can add a lot to your bill (usually at least $9 a day). Most packages that include a rental car do not include LDW. If you have your own car insurance, check with your carrier to see what is covered.

An increasing number of major credit card companies offer free collision damage coverage for charging the rental to their card, and some may provide primary coverage. That means your credit card company may deal with the rental company directly in the event of an accident, rather than compensate you after your insurance has kicked in. It's worth a call to find out.

If you are renting a car at Los Angeles International Airport (LAX), the drive to the Disneyland Resort is only 31 miles, but it'll take at least 45 minutes with light traffic, or up to two hours if the roads are congested. From John Wayne Airport (SNA), the drive takes about 25 minutes (without traffic). Expect a drive of about a half hour from Long Beach Airport (LGB)—again, that estimate does not factor in the wild card known as Southern California traffic.

HOT TIP

If you take a taxi, note whether or not the trip is metered or if there is a flat fee to your destination— and make sure you are charged accordingly.

If a car rental is needed once at the Disneyland Resort or you need a location to drop a one-way Enterprise rental, go to Disney's Paradise Pier Hotel. To confirm that this service will be offered during your visit, call 888-826-6893.

BY TRAIN

It's possible to get to Anaheim by rail from Union Station in Los Angeles by using Amtrak's Pacific Surfliner train (*www.amtrak.com*; 800-872-7245) or L.A.'s Metrolink Orange County light-rail (*www.metrolinktrains.com*; 800-371-5465). Union Station is in downtown L.A. and is served by trains from all over the country.

You can get to Union Station from Los Angeles International Airport (LAX) by cab, by bus (LAX FlyAway Bus; *www.flylax.com/flyaway*; 866-435-9529), or by L.A.'s Metro subway (323-466-3876; *www.metro.net*; the system also serves Long Beach Airport). Hertz and Budget rental car agencies have counters at Union Station; call companies directly for rates and hours.

The Anaheim train station is adjacent to Angel Stadium in Anaheim, which is about two miles from the Disneyland Resort. Yellow Cabs can be summoned from the station (714-999-9999). In addition, Hertz and Budget car rental agencies will pick up customers from the Anaheim train station; contact the companies directly for current rates and operating hours.

BY BUS

Buses make sense if you're traveling a short distance, if you have plenty of time to spend in transit, if there are only two or three people in your party, and/or if cost-control is key.

Buses make the journey from Los Angeles and San Diego, though they usually make a few stops along the way. Travel from most other destinations usually requires a change of vehicle in Los Angeles. Transfers are usually made at 1716 E. 7th St. at Alameda in downtown L.A.

The Anaheim Greyhound bus terminal is at 2626 E. Katella Ave.; *www.greyhound.com*; 800-231-2222. Yellow Cabs can get you to Disneyland from the bus terminal for about $25; 714-999-9999.

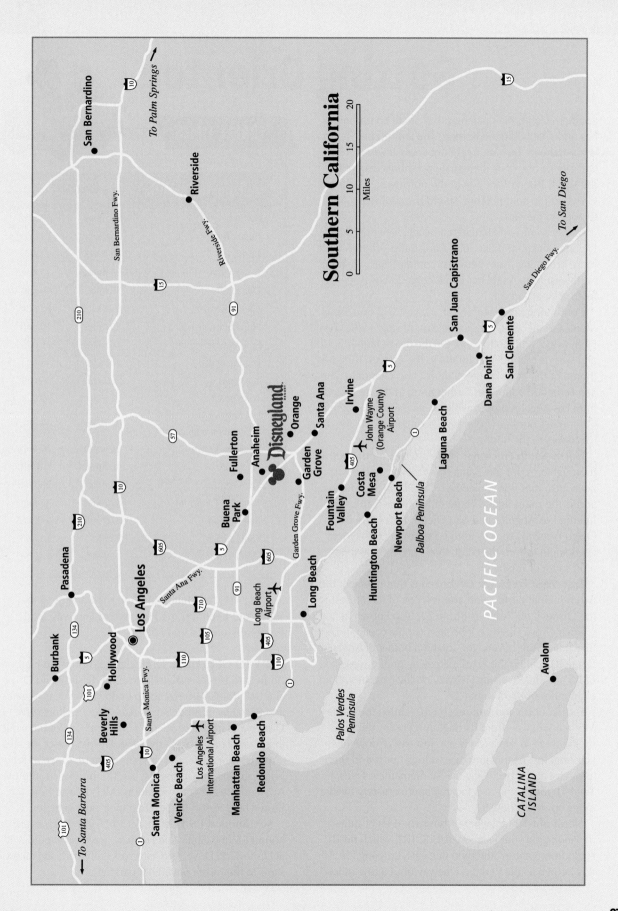

Southern California

San Bernardino

To Palm Springs

Riverside

San Bernardino Fwy.

Riverside Fwy.

Miles

0   5   10   15   20

210

Los Angeles

Pasadena

Burbank

Hollywood

Beverly Hills

Santa Monica Fwy.

Santa Monica

Venice Beach

Los Angeles International Airport

Manhattan Beach

Redondo Beach

To Santa Barbara

Palos Verdes Peninsula

Disneyland RESORT

Fullerton

Anaheim

Orange

Santa Ana

Irvine

Garden Grove

Buena Park

Garden Grove Fwy.

Fountain Valley

Costa Mesa

John Wayne (Orange County) Airport

Newport Beach

Balboa Peninsula

Laguna Beach

Huntington Beach

Long Beach

Long Beach Airport

Santa Ana Fwy.

PACIFIC OCEAN

San Juan Capistrano

Dana Point

San Clemente

San Diego Fwy.

To San Diego

Avalon

CATALINA ISLAND

27

Getting Oriented

Southern California's patchwork of small communities has undeniably blurred borders. The Disneyland Resort is in Anaheim, but you might not know if you were in that city or one of its immediate neighbors except for the signs. Buena Park lies to the northwest, Garden Grove to the south, Santa Ana to the southeast, and Orange to the east.

Farther south—in Huntington Beach, Newport Beach, Laguna Beach, and San Juan Capistrano—there's a bit more breathing room between communities. Heading northwest from Anaheim, you'll come to Los Angeles International Airport.

Continuing northwest into L.A., you will find Santa Monica to the west, and, to the east, Beverly Hills, West Hollywood, and Hollywood. On the beach farther north and west is Malibu, and inland to the east are Burbank (home of the Walt Disney Studios) and Glendale. The San Fernando Valley lies farther north and a bit inland from Los Angeles proper, while Santa Barbara, Southern California's northern boundary, is on the coast, about two hours to the north.

North–South Freeways: There are two north-south thoroughfares: I-5 (the Santa Ana Freeway in the Anaheim area) runs from Vancouver, Canada, to San Diego, and is the main inland route in Southern California, linking Los Angeles and San Diego; I-405 (the San Diego Freeway) sprouts from I-5 north of Hollywood, veers south toward the coast, then rejoins I-5 at Irvine, a bit south of Anaheim.

East–West Freeways: Of the roads that intersect the two principal north-south arteries, one of the closest to the Disneyland Resort is Route 22, also known as the Garden Grove Freeway; it begins near the ocean in Long Beach and runs beyond the southern border of Anaheim. Route 91, called the Artesia Freeway on the west side of I-5 and the Riverside Freeway on the east, lies about eight miles north of Route 22.

Farther north you will reach I-10, called the Santa Monica Freeway from its beginning point near the Pacific shore in Santa Monica to just east of downtown Los Angeles. At this juncture, it jogs north and then turns east again, becoming the San Bernardino Freeway. The I-10 thoroughfare is located approximately twelve miles north of Route 91.

North of I-10 (anywhere from two to eight miles, depending on your location) is U.S. 101, which heads south from Ventura and then due east, crossing I-405. It is known as the Ventura Freeway until a few miles

TRAVEL TIMES

To/From the Resort	Approx. Distance	Drive Time
Balboa	20 miles	40 min.
Buena Park	7 miles	12 min.
Carlsbad	60 miles	60 min.
Costa Mesa	15 miles	30 min.
Dana Point	30 miles	40 min.
Garden Grove	5 miles	10 min.
Huntington Beach	20 miles	30 min.
John Wayne Airport	16 miles	25 min.
Laguna Beach	30 miles	45 min.
Las Vegas	280 miles	5–6 hrs.
Long Beach	26 miles	30 min.
Los Angeles (downtown and airport)	31 miles	45–90 min.
Newport Beach	20 miles	30 min.
Palm Springs	100 miles	2–3 hrs.
San Diego	95 miles	90 min.
San Juan Capistrano	32 miles	45 min.
San Simeon	270 miles	5–6 hrs.
Santa Ana	7 miles	15 min.
Santa Barbara	120 miles	2–3 hrs.

east of I-405, at which point the road angles to the south and becomes the Hollywood Freeway, and eventually merges into I-5.

HOW TO GET THERE: Disneyland Resort is on Harbor Boulevard between Katella Avenue, Disneyland Drive, and Ball Road, 31 miles south of downtown Los Angeles and 87 miles north of San Diego. Many visitors drive to Disneyland from elsewhere in Southern California, while those who come from farther away fly into one of the area airports, rent a car, and drive from there. Once at their hotel, guests may prefer to use the hotel's shuttle or Anaheim Resort Transportation (ART) to and from the Disneyland Resort (rather than their own vehicle).

Southbound I-5 Exit: To get to Disneyland, southbound I-5 (the Santa Ana Freeway) travelers should exit at Disneyland Drive, turn left, cross Ball Road, and follow signs to the most convenient parking area.

Northbound I-5 Exit: Northbound travelers should exit I-5 at Katella Avenue, proceed straight to Disney Way, and then follow signs to the most convenient parking area.

From John Wayne/Orange County Airport: Take I-405 north to CA-55 north to I-5 north. Watch carefully for highway signs once out of the airport. Exit at Katella Avenue, head straight to Disney Way, then follow signs to the most convenient parking area.

From Los Angeles International Airport: Take I-105 east to I-605 north to I-5 south. Take Disneyland Drive exit toward Ball Road. Merge onto Disneyland Drive, and proceed to the most convenient parking zone (the Mickey & Friends parking structure or the Toy Story parking area).

Exit off Orange Freeway: Travelers on the 57 freeway should exit on Katella Avenue and proceed west. Turn right on Harbor Boulevard, and follow signs to the parking area.

ANAHEIM SURFACE STREETS: The Disneyland Resort is in the center of the Anaheim Resort, a 1,100-acre district. Disneyland Resort is bounded by Harbor Boulevard on the east, Disneyland Drive (a segment of West Street) on the west, Ball Road on the north, and Katella Avenue on the south.

Harbor Boulevard, near Ball Road, is the most convenient place to pick up I-5 (Santa Ana Freeway) going north to Los Angeles. Katella Avenue, past Anaheim Boulevard, is the most convenient entrance to southbound I-5 going to Newport Beach and points south.

Note: Parking rules are strictly enforced in Anaheim. Be sure to park in a designated lot, feed the parking meter often, and heed all signs.

LOCAL TRANSPORTATION: The Orange County Transportation Authority (OCTA; *www.octa.net*; 714-560-6282) provides daily bus service throughout the area, with limited service on the weekend. Several different lines stop at the Disneyland Resort, but note that public transportation, while cost-efficient, may involve considerable waiting and transferring. Tickets must be purchased at a Metrolink vending machine at any station or through the Metrolink app. Los Angeles' Union Station has ticket windows, too.

Anaheim Resort Transportation, also known as ART (*www.rideart.org*; 888-364-2787), is a multi-route guest transit system serving the Anaheim Resort area. ART Passes may be purchased online and from many area hotels, public sales outlets, and various kiosk

locations. Drivers do not sell passes. Adult fares are $6 for a one-day pass, $16 for three days, and $25 for a five-day pass. Kids ages 3 to 9 pay $2.50 for one day, $3.50 for three days, and $5.50 for five-day passes. There is no charge for baby passengers.

The Metro serves L.A. County and the major attractions of Orange County (*www.metro.net*; 323-466-3876). Cost is about $1.75 each way (75 cents for seniors). A refillable TAP (Transit Access Pass) card is required.

TAXIS: The only licensed taxi company that's officially authorized to serve Disneyland Resort is the Anaheim Yellow Cab Company (*www.californiayellowcab.com*; 714-999-9999). The fare to John Wayne Airport from the Disneyland Hotel generally runs about $47, plus tip; if you are going to LAX, figure at least $95 (or more, depending on the traffic). The fare to and from Long Beach Airport runs approximately $55, plus gratuity. Prices for town cars are usually slightly higher. Taxis can be called to pick you up at train and bus stations. Lyft and Uber car-sharing services are also authorized to pick up and drop off guests—see the Hot Tip below for more information.

HOT TIP

There are two areas for Disneyland Resort park guests to get picked up or dropped off by car (including taxis and car-sharing services). One is off Harbor Boulevard and the other is at Downtown Disney District.

For Downtown Disney District, take Magic Way from Disneyland Drive, then turn left at Downtown Drive. Follow the signs to the drop-off area. There's a 15-minute grace period—after that, standard parking rates apply. (The first hour costs $10. For more rate specifics, visit *disneyland.com*.)

For Harbor Boulevard, enter the drop-off area from the right southbound lane on South Harbor Boulevard. This spot is located between South Manchester Avenue and Disney Way.

Planning Your Itinerary

For those lucky enough to live in the Los Angeles/Orange County area, the Disneyland Resort offers the opportunity to return frequently. Seasoned visitors and first-timers alike will do well to plan each step of their visit far in advance—make the travel arrangements as soon as vacation dates are set (refer to the Trip Planning Timeline below to make sure you don't miss any crucial steps), and then study the following chapters of this book to decide how you'd like to spend each day of the trip.

How many days should you spend with the Mouse and his pals? Well, that's up to you, but to experience the Disneyland Resort at its best, we recommend a stay of at least four full days—you will have enough time to see quite a few theme park attractions, parades, and shows (plus revisit all of your favorites), lounge beside your hotel's pool, enjoy a meal with favorite Disney characters, shop for souvenirs, and enjoy a rejuvenating spa treatment. If you'd like to visit other area attractions, add on one day for each excursion. But don't try to cram too much into one visit; this is your vacation, after all.

Once you've decided how many days you're going to dedicate to Disney, it's time to decide how you'll split up your time on Disney property. We suggest starting with a day at Disneyland Park (for the original and quintessential Disney experience), followed by a visit to Disney California Adventure. On day three, return to Disneyland and hit the park's highlights, plus any attractions you missed, and save time for souvenir shopping. Day four should be focused on your preferred park and some downtime by the pool or in the Downtown Disney District. Evenings can be spent in a park, if it's open late, or in Downtown Disney's lively restaurants, lounges, and play zones. The options are plentiful.

On the following pages, we have provided full-day schedules to guide you through four days in the parks (with tips for families with young children and priorities for days when the lines are at their longest). The schedules are meant to be flexible and fun (not Disney boot camp), so take them at your own pace and plan breaks to relax: Have a Mickey Mouse ice cream bar, browse through the shops, smell the flowers, or just pick a bench and watch the crowds rush by.

Details are subject to change. Visit *disneyland.com,* or use the Disneyland mobile app for updates.

TRIP PLANNING TIMELINE

FIRST THINGS FIRST
● Check for hotel availability as far ahead as possible. Go to *disneyland.com,* or call 714-520-5050 to book Disney hotel accommodations; remember that a deposit must be paid within 21 days of the reservation.

6 MONTHS
● Unless you opted for a vacation package that includes theme park admission, it's time to buy park tickets and make park reservations. Check for theme park reservation availability *before* you buy park tickets! Link all tickets to your *disneyland.com* account as soon as possible. (For details about park reservations, see page 17 and visit *disneyland.com*). Be sure to arrange for transportation to/from the Disneyland Resort, too.

UP TO 2 MONTHS
● Find out theme park hours, attraction refurbishment schedule, and details on any special events by visiting *disneyland.com,* using the Disneyland Resort mobile app, or calling 714-781-4565.
● Make dining reservations (they're necessary at most table-service eateries at the Disneyland Resort; use the Disneyland mobile app, visit *disneyland.com,* or

call 714-781-3463), and add the info to a day-by-day trip schedule. Refer to the *Good Meals, Great Times* chapter for details on Disneyland Resort dining spots.

2 WEEKS
● Airline confirmation and travel vouchers should have arrived by now. Contact your travel agent or travel company if they haven't shown up in your inbox yet.

1 WEEK
● Confirm all reservations and finalize your day-by-day vacation schedule. We recommend making printouts of all reservations, just in case. And double-check theme park operating hours (they change often).
● Jot down important telephone numbers (doctors, family members, house sitter, etc.) in case something happens to your mobile phone during your travels.

1 DAY
● Place print-outs of any tickets you have purchased (and a valid, government-issued photo ID) in a day-bag or carry-on bag.

DISNEYLAND PARK
One-Day Schedule

🐭 Disneyland's breakfast options have expanded of late. If you don't nosh at the hotel, consider having a bite at Red Rose Taverne, Plaza Inn, or Carnation Cafe.

🐭 Take in the sights as you walk down Main Street, but don't stop to shop now (you'll have time for that later). Instead, head straight to Adventureland's Jungle Cruise and Indiana Jones Adventure* before making your way to Splash Mountain* and The Many Adventures of Winnie the Pooh in Critter Country. (If you plan to dine at the Blue Bayou, make a reservation in advance via the Disneyland app or at *disneyland.com*, or by calling 714-781-3463.)

🐭 Experience the park's newest land, Star Wars: Galaxy's Edge. Highlights include *Millennium Falcon:* Smugglers Run* and Star Wars: Rise of the Resistance**

🐭 Backtrack to New Orleans Square, and pay a visit to the Haunted Mansion* and Pirates of the Caribbean before breaking for a bite to eat.

🐭 Next, see the show at the Golden Horseshoe Saloon, then tackle Big Thunder Mountain Railroad* in Frontierland. (Don't ride Big Thunder on a full stomach.)

🐭 Explore Fantasy Faire. Then walk through the castle into Fantasyland and visit Snow White, Pinocchio, Peter Pan, and Mr. Toad. Be sure to see Alice, the Mad Tea Party, the Matterhorn,* and It's a Small World,* too.

🐭 Keep an eye on the time and try to fit the afternoon show or parade into your schedule.

(Continued on page 32)

DISNEYLAND DELIGHTS

These attractions combine to form the quintessential Disneyland park experience:

Indiana Jones Adventure
Pirates of the Caribbean
Haunted Mansion
Big Thunder Mountain Railroad
Splash Mountain
Peter Pan's Flight
Matterhorn Bobsleds
Mickey and Minnie's Runaway Railway
It's a Small World
Star Tours—The Adventures Continue
Jungle Cruise
The Many Adventures of Winnie the Pooh
Buzz Lightyear Astro Blasters
Space Mountain
Fantasmic!
Mr. Toad's Wild Ride
Star Wars: Rise of the Resistance

LINE BUSTERS

When the park is packed, the following attractions may have shorter waits: The Disneyland Railroad, Enchanted Tiki Room, Pirates Lair on Tom Sawyer Island, The Many Adventures of Winnie the Pooh, *Mark Twain* riverboat, and The Disneyland Story—Presenting Great Moments with Mr. Lincoln.

IF YOU HAVE YOUNG CHILDREN

• First, go to Fantasyland and visit each area attraction (note that some are scary for young kids) before heading to Mickey's Toontown (if it is open during your visit). Then visit Critter Country to enjoy The Many Adventures of Winnie the Pooh.
• Take tykes to King Arthur Carrousel and It's a Small World (the latter is an absolute must!).
• Ride the Jungle Cruise, then sing with the Tiki Birds in Adventureland, or enjoy a frozen treat at Tropical Hideaway before returning to your favorite rides.
• Scope out a spot on a Main Street curb up to an hour before the Magic Happens parade. For smaller crowds, watch from the viewing area near It's a Small World.

DISNEYLAND PARK One-Day Schedule

(Continued from page 31)

🐭 If it's open during your visit, head over to Mickey's Toontown, making Mickey & Minnie's Runaway Railway a priority. (The re-imagined land is expected to re-open in early 2023.)

🐭 Hop aboard the Disneyland Railroad and disembark in Tomorrowland. Enjoy the Finding Nemo Submarine Voyage, Space Mountain*, and Buzz Lightyear Astro Blasters* before heading to dinner.

Note: If the park is open late, you can board the monorail in Tomorrowland and dine in the Downtown Disney District before returning to the park.

🐭 After dinner, take the wheel of a hot rod at Autopia*, then take flight at Star Tours—The Adventures Continue*, and/or Astro Orbitor.

🐭 Take little ones back to Fantasyland to hit any attractions you may have missed earlier in the day or to repeat a favorite. This land tends to get a bit less congested as the evening hours kick in.

🐭 On nights when Fantasmic! is presented, make a point of getting to New Orleans Square and the Rivers of America in plenty of time to see it. (Check a park Tip Board, the Disneyland app, or *disneyworld.com* for the schedule.)

🐭 Stroll back to Main Street. Shop, stop for dessert, see the Disneyland Story featuring Great Moments with Mr. Lincoln, and watch the fireworks light the sky over Sleeping Beauty Castle.

🐭 If there's time, take a second spin on your favorite shows and attractions.

SEE THE CHARACTERS

There are lots of places to see Disney characters in this park. Some of the better spots include Toontown (Mickey, Minnie, Donald, Goofy, and more), Critter Country (Pooh and pals), Fantasyland's Fantasy Faire (princesses), Star Wars: Galaxy's Edge, and around Town Square on Main Street, U.S.A. Details are subject to change. For current character appearance schedules, check a park Tip Board, the Disneyland app, or *disneyland.com*. And please don't forget your camera!

TOP SHOPS

Whether you're browsing or buying, Disneyland is a shopper's paradise. Here are a few of the spots where wallets get a workout:

Candy Palace
Disneyana
Emporium
Main Street Magic Shop
Pieces of Eight
Pioneer Mercantile
Port Royal Curios & Curiosities
The Star Trader

HOT TIP

As of press time, the State of California strongly recommends that guests be fully vaccinated or obtain a negative COVID-19 test prior to entering the Disneyland Resort. Please don't travel to or enter the Disneyland Resort if you have any symptoms of COVID-19. For details about current pandemic protocols, please visit *disneyland.disney.go.com/experience-updates*.

* *Genie+ Service for Lightning Lane Entrances is available for this attraction. Details are subject to change.*
** *Individual Purchase for Lightning Lane Entrance is available for this attraction. Details are subject to change.*
Fees apply for Genie+ and Individual Purchase for Lightning Lane Entrances. To learn about how to use Lightning Lane Entrances, see page 22.

DISNEY CALIFORNIA ADVENTURE
One-Day Schedule

Begin your California adventure with an early-as-possible visit to Cars Land. Do not miss Radiator Springs Racers!** If possible, enjoy Mater's Junkyard Jamboree before moving on to Avengers Campus. Enjoy a thrilling adventure at popular Guardians of the Galaxy—Mission: BREAKOUT!* and wrangle spider-bots at WEB SLINGERS: A Spider-Man Adventure**.

Mosey through Hollywood Land, taking in Monsters, Inc.—Mike & Sulley to the Rescue!*, Mickey's PhilharMagic, and visit Disney Animation (be sure to say hello to Anna and Elsa and see an amazing interactive show called Turtle Talk with Crush). Take little ones to the energetic Disney Junior Dance Party.

Make your way over to the Grizzly Peak Recreation Area and experience Soarin' Around the World*. Then get set to get wet on the drenching Grizzly River Run* white-water raft ride. (Unless they're waterproof, leave valuables in a nearby locker or with a non-riding member of your party.) If you're up for it (and wearing proper footwear), tackle the Redwood Creek Challenge Trail.

(Continued on page 34)

ADVENTURE ACES

If you're short on time, be sure to catch as many of the following four-star attractions at Disney California Adventure as possible:

- Toy Story Midway Mania!
- Radiator Springs Racers
- Frozen—Live at the Hyperion
- Soarin' Around the World
- World of Color
- Turtle Talk with Crush
- Incredicoaster
- Mater's Junkyard Jamboree
- Guardians of the Galaxy—Mission: BREAKOUT!
- Monsters, Inc.—Mike & Sulley to the Rescue!
- The Little Mermaid—Ariel's Undersea Adventure
- Mickey's PhilharMagic
- WEB SLINGERS: A Spider-Man Adventure

IF YOU HAVE YOUNG CHILDREN

• Head to Hollywood Land for Monsters, Inc.—Mike & Sulley to the Rescue! and Mickey's PhilharMagic. Stop in at Disney Animation for Turtle Talk, Sorcerer's Workshop, and to say hello to Anna and Elsa. Then join an interactive shindig at Disney Junior Dance Party!

• Zoom into Cars Land for a wild-but-mild ride at Mater's Junkyard Jamboree.

• Amble on over to Pixar Pier. Take a spin on Jessie's Critter Carousel, do Toy Story Midway Mania!, and experience Inside Out Emotional Whirlwind.

• Over at Paradise Gardens, be sure to hit these kid-pleasers: The Little Mermaid—Ariel's Undersea Adventure and Jumpin' Jellyfish.

• Try the kid-friendly obstacle course at the Grizzly Peak area's Redwood Creek Challenge Trail.

• Finally, treat night owls to the dazzling World of Color water show. (The noisy water jets might spook some.) Warn kids that they may get a teeny bit wet.

DISNEY CALIFORNIA ADVENTURE
One-Day Schedule

(Continued from page 33)

🎧 Pick up some wine-pairing tips or sample California's finest at the Golden Vine Winery.

🎧 Explore the Pacific Wharf area before proceeding on to Pixar Pier's crowd-pleasing rides, including but not limited to Incredicoaster* and Toy Story Midway Mania!* (don't ride on a full stomach).

🎧 Work your way around Paradise Bay, making sure to stop at The Little Mermaid—Ariel's Undersea Adventure.

🎧 Be sure to catch the delightful nighttime extravaganza World of Color. Line up for a waterside viewing spot at least 45 minutes before showtime—and know that you might get a little wet if you are up close.

   Note: If you're okay with missing World of Color, visit (or revisit) a popular attraction during the show. Wait times may be a bit shorter as park guests watch the wildly popular lagoon-based water show.

LINE BUSTERS

When lines abound at Disney California Adventure, we suggest heading to the following: Jessie's Critter Carousel, Silly Symphony Swings, Redwood Creek Challenge Trail, Disney Animation, and Monsters, Inc.—Mike & Sulley to the Rescue!* The line for The Little Mermaid—Ariel's Undersea Adventure often thins later in the day. If you don't mind splitting up your party, do consider the Single Rider line at Radiator Springs Racers. The wait is usually much shorter than for the standby line.

TOP SHOPS

Shopping at this park can be an adventure in and of itself. These are some of the spots that have earned their place in the spotlight:

Big Top Toys
Elias & Co.
Off the Page
Oswald's
Rushin' River Outfitters
Sarge's Surplus Hut
Trolley Treats

SEE THE CHARACTERS

Guests have many opportunities to catch up with favorite characters at Disney California Adventure. Among the best spots to see them are Buena Vista Street (usually Mickey, Goofy, and Donald Duck), Hollywood Land (Anna, Elsa, Olaf), Avengers Campus (Ant-Man, Black Widow, Captain Marvel, Thor, Black Panther, or others), Redwood Creek Challenge Trail (Chip and Dale), Cars Land (Mater, McQueen, and Red the Fire Engine), and Pixar Pier (Woody, Buzz, and Jessie). All details are subject to change at any time. Check a park Tip Board, the Disneyland app, or *disneyland.com* for appearance schedules.

* *Genie+ Service for Lightning Lane Entrances is available for this attraction. Details are subject to change.*
** *Individual Purchase for Lightning Lane Entrance is available for this attraction. Details are subject to change. Fees apply for Genie+ and Individual Purchase for Lightning Lane Entrances. To learn about how to use Lightning Lane Entrances, see page 22.*

A Second Day in
DISNEYLAND PARK

Returning for a second or third day in each of the theme parks means more time to savor the atmosphere, try attractions you missed the first day, and revisit all the old and new favorites. Knowing that there will be a second day to play also makes for a less harried pace on day one.

🖤 Start the morning with grab-and-go breakfast at Jolly Holiday Bakery Cafe or Market House. Or enjoy the morning meal with Disney characters at the Plaza Inn (one can also share breakfast with characters outside the park at Goofy's Kitchen in the Disneyland Hotel or the Grand Californian's Storytellers Cafe). Reservations are necessary for character meals.

🖤 If you missed or would like to revisit Star Wars: Galaxy's Edge, get there early! It is a popular realm.

🖤 Head to Tomorrowland and experience Space Mountain,* Star Tours—The Adventures Continue,* Buzz Lightyear Astro Blasters,* Autopia,* and other futuristic favorites.

🖤 Navigate over to Mickey's Toontown (when it re-opens in 2023). If you haven't done Mickey & Minnie's Runaway Railway yet, now's the time!

🖤 Visit It's a Small World*, experience the Matterhorn Bobsleds*, and tour Fantasyland.

🖤 Stroll, shop, and break for lunch on (or on your way to) Main Street, U.S.A.

🖤 Ride a Main Street Vehicle up to Town Square and continue on foot toward Adventureland.

🖤 Stop at the Enchanted Tiki Room before heading to New Orleans Square. There, the priorities are Haunted Mansion* and Pirates of the Caribbean. Visit them and navigate over to Critter Country for Splash Mountain* and The Many Adventures of Winnie the Pooh.

🖤 Meander through the shops of New Orleans Square, and then stop for a leisurely dinner at a nearby eatery. River Belle Terrace, the French Market (jambalaya!) and the full-service Blue Bayou and Cafe Orleans are all solid options for a hearty meal.

🖤 Select a viewing location (in Frontierland or New Orleans Square) about 45 minutes before the evening's performance of Fantasmic! (if it is scheduled).

🖤 After the crowds disperse a bit after Fantasmic!, make your way to Big Thunder Mountain Railroad* for one last go 'round before the park closes for the evening.

🖤 Enjoy a final snack on Main Street, U.S.A. and do a bit of people-watching before heading under the train station and saying goodbye to Disneyland for the day.

* *Genie+ Service for Lightning Lane Entrances is available for this attraction. Details are subject to change.*
** *Individual Purchase for Lightning Lane Entrance is available for this attraction. Details are subject to change.*
 Fees apply for Genie+ and Individual Purchase for Lightning Lane Entrances. To learn about how to use Lightning Lane Entrances, see page 22.

A Second Day in
DISNEY CALIFORNIA ADVENTURE

If you don't have an advance reservation for a table-service meal, stop for a quick-service breakfast at PYM Test Kitchen or Fiddler, Fifer, & Practical Cafe (aka Starbucks). Then it's off to see what you missed on day one and revisit favorite attractions.

Make tracks for the wildly popular Cars Land if you haven't seen it yet, then circle back to Avengers Campus for anything you may have saved for later. The must do's in this super spot: Guardians of the Galaxy—Mission: BREAKOUT!* and WEB SLINGERS: A Spider-Man Adventure**. After exploring the area, pop over to Pixar Pier.

Thrill-seekers flip for a second go-round on the topsy-turvy Incredicoaster,* and gamers of all ages will swoon over Toy Story Midway Mania!*

Stop in at Pacific Wharf's Boudin Bakery for a tasty behind-the-scenes tour and discover how sourdough bread is made—and enjoy a free sample. Bonus!

Take a lunch break at Pacific Wharf Cafe, Lamplight Lounge, Flo's V8 Cafe, Award Wieners, or Cocina Cucamonga—or, if the park is open late, head back to your hotel to relax or splash in the pool (be sure to

keep track of your park ticket so that you can return later in the day). Another option is to spend the afternoon in the Downtown Disney District—most of its restaurants and shops open by noon (or earlier).

Your California adventure picks up again with Soarin' Around the World* (located in Grizzly Peak Airfield), followed by a visit to The Little Mermaid— Ariel's Undersea Adventure, then on to Grizzly River Run* (if you don't mind the likelihood of getting more than a tad soggy).

Stop for the parade if one is offered today, then make your way over to Hollywood Land. En route, try to catch a performance by Five and Dime.

Wander through Hollywood Land, enjoying any impromptu entertainment, take in Turtle Talk with Crush, and see Anna and Elsa inside Disney Animation. Take a tour of Monstropolis at Monsters, Inc.—Mike and Sulley to the Rescue!* and don some 3-D glasses at Mickey's PhilharMagic.

If time permits after the show, revisit some of your favorite attractions or search for last-minute souvenirs at the shops on Buena Vista Street.

If you haven't seen World of Color yet, check a park Tip Board to see if it's being presented today. If it is, be sure to catch a performance. It's sure to put a smile on your face. (Guests up front may get a little wet.)

Genie+ Service for Lightning Lane Entrances is available for this attraction. Details are subject to change.
**Individual Purchase for Lightning Lane Entrance is available for this attraction. Details are subject to change.*
Fees apply for Genie+ and Individual Purchase for Lightning Lane Entrances. To learn about how to use Lightning Lane Entrances, see page 22.

Fingertip Reference Guide

BARBERS AND SALONS

Disney's Grand Californian Hotel & Spa offers salon services at its Tenaya Stone Spa. One nearby spot at which hair may be cut or coiffed is Pure Escape Beauty Bar at the Hilton Anaheim Hotel (777 Convention Way; 714-740-4628).

CAR CARE

The Anaheim office of the Automobile Club of Southern California is located at 420 North Euclid Street; *https://travel.calif.aaa.com*; 714-774-2392. To summon emergency roadside service, call 800-400-4222.

DRINKING POLICIES

While Disneyland Park has eased its long-standing no-alcohol policy (currently offering spirited beverages at Oga's Cantina and Blue Bayou), imbibing is an option at many spots at Disney California Adventure and at many venues located within the Downtown Disney District. Alcohol may also be purchased in the lounges and restaurants of the three Disney resort hotels. The legal drinking age in the state of California is 21. (Legal proof of age is required.)

LOCKERS

Lockers of various sizes are available just outside the main entrance of the parks (our preferred location), inside Disneyland on Main Street (behind the Market House), and inside Disney California Adventure (DCA) across

HOT TIP

To avoid the sometimes maddening congestion at the Main Street locker location, consider stowing your stuff at the lockers by the picnic area, just outside Disneyland Park's turnstiles. (You'll find them on the left side of the entrance as you face the park.)

from Guest Relations. Prices are $7, $10, $12, or $15 per day, depending on the size of the locker. These storage facilities make it convenient to intersperse frolicking on the attractions with shopping; just make your purchases and stash them in a locker. Availability is limited, and during busy periods all the space can be taken well before noon. Disney California Adventure guests may stash items in lockers for free while they ride Grizzly River Run. The lockers are situated on the side of the attraction's entrance.

LOST AND FOUND

Lost and Found is located to the left of the entrance to Disneyland Park. At any given moment, a survey of the shelves might turn up mobile phones, cameras, umbrellas, strollers, handbags, hats, sunglasses, baby shoes, jewelry, and even a few crutches, false teeth, and hubcaps. (Once, a wallet containing $1,700 in cash was turned in!) The Disneyland Resort will return lost items to guests who fill out a report. If you lose something at a hotel, contact the front desk.

MAIL

Postcards are sold in gift shops throughout Anaheim, in a few shops in Downtown Disney District and the Disneyland Resort theme parks, and at the Disneyland Resort hotels. Stamps are sold at all Disney hotels, too.

Cards that are deposited in the mailboxes in the Disney theme parks are picked up and delivered to the U.S. Post Office once a day, early in the morning. All items are postmarked Anaheim, not Disneyland. (By the way, don't forget to arrange for your own mail to be held by the post office or picked up by a neighbor while you're on vacation.) Due to the heavy volume, expect delivery to take much longer than usual—don't mail your rent from Disneyland.

Post Office: The U.S. Post Office that's closest to the Disneyland Resort is Holiday Station, a half-mile away (1180 W. Ball Rd., Anaheim; 714-533-8182). It's open from 9 A.M. to 5 P.M. weekdays only.

MEDICAL MATTERS

Blisters are the most common complaint received by Disney's First Aid departments, found at the north end of Main Street, next to Lost Children in Disneyland, and at the Chamber of Commerce near the entrance of Disney California Adventure. Be sure to wear comfortable, broken-in shoes (pack a backup pair)—and carry

Band-Aids, just in case. ***In case of emergency, notify an employee and call 911.***

If you have a serious medical problem while on Disney property, call 911 and contact any Disney cast member (aka employee). He or she will get in touch with First Aid to make further arrangements. First Aid, staffed with registered nurses, will supply breathing machines and crutches for guests. It will not dispense medication to anyone under the age of 18 without the consent of a parent or chaperone.

It's always a good idea to carry an insurance card and any other pertinent medical information. Those with chronic health problems should carry copies of all their prescriptions, along with their doctor's telephone number.

Prescriptions: The pharmacy at CVS, about a mile from the Disneyland Resort, is open 24/7 (480 South Main St.; 714-938-1200). The drive-thru pharmacy at Walgreens, about three miles from Disneyland Resort, also operates 24 hours a day, seven days a week (12001 Euclid Street, Garden Grove; 714-530-1071). At the intersection of Katella Ave. and Harbor Blvd., there is another 24/7 CVS with a pharmacy that's open Monday through Friday from 9 A.M. to 8 P.M., Saturdays and Sundays from 10 A.M. until 6 P.M. (1803 S. Harbor Blvd., Anaheim; 714-817-9116).

Refrigerator Facilities: In the Disney parks, insulin and antibiotics that must be refrigerated can be stored for the day at First Aid. (It does not store breast milk for nursing mothers.) Outside the theme parks, there are refrigerators in many of the area's hotels and motels. If your room doesn't have one, a fridge can usually be supplied for a nominal charge, or the hotel or motel may be able to store insulin in its own refrigerator. Be sure to inquire before you make the reservation.

MONEY

Cash, traveler's checks, Visa, American Express, MasterCard, JCB, Discover Card, Diner's Club, Disney gift cards, and Disney Dollars are all accepted as payment for admission to the theme parks, for merchandise purchased in shops, and for meals (except at select souvenir and food carts, where it's strictly cash). Personal checks may be used to pay for park admission. Checks must be imprinted with the guest's name and address, drawn on a U.S. bank, and accompanied by proper ID—that is, a valid driver's license or passport. Department store cards are not acceptable identification for check-writing purposes. Disney hotel guests who have left a credit card number at check-in can charge most expenses in the parks to their hotel bill.

Disney Dollars: First introduced by The Walt Disney Company in 1987, Disney Dollars were discontinued in 2016. However, those already in circulation are still accepted as cash at most Disneyland Resort, Walt Disney World, and Disney Store locations. So if you happen to have Disney Dollars that you want to spend, rest assured you can still use that colorful cash. Note that change will be provided in U.S. currency, not Mickey's money.

Disney Gift Cards: Available for purchase at most merchandise locations, these may be redeemed throughout the Disneyland Resort (though there are a few exceptions at Downtown Disney, where select vendors are not equipped to accept gift cards).

Financial Services: Automated Teller Machines (ATMs) are located at each park's main entrance; in Disneyland at The Disney Gallery on Main Street, by the Fantasyland Theatre, by the Frontierland Stockade, and in Tomorrowland; in California Adventure at the Entry Plaza, in the Pacific Wharf region, at the restrooms near Goofy's Sky School, and in the Pixar Pier area of the park; in Downtown Disney by the LEGO store and Wetzel's Pretzels; and in all Disneyland Resort hotels. For details, inquire at a Guest Relations location.

Personal checks are not accepted in the parks. ATMs at the park entrances accept credit cards for cash advances. Note that the presence of a bank on Main Street is a tad deceiving: The bank offers no financial services.

American Express Cardmember Services: Many Anaheim banks sell American Express traveler's cheques, usually for a one percent fee. Foreign Currency Exchange: Foreign currency may be exchanged (at the day's current exchange rate) at City Hall in Disneyland, Chamber of Commerce at Disney California Adventure, and at the front desk at each of the three Disneyland Resort hotels. Paper currency only.

PETS

Except for certified service animals, pets are not allowed inside Disneyland or Disney California Adventure. However, non-poisonous creatures may be boarded in the Disneyland Resort Pet Care Kennel, which is located near the entrance to Disneyland Park. Reservations are not necessary (the kennel rarely reaches capacity). Pets may be boarded for the day (no overnight stays). In addition to proof of rabies and distemper vaccinations, guests have to show proof of hepatitis and leptospirosis vaccinations for dogs over four months of age. Without proof of all four vaccinations, the dog will not be permitted entrance to the kennel. At press time, it cost about $20 per day, per pet. Cash only. To ask about the kennel rates during your WDW visit, call 714-781-7662.

Disney personnel do not handle the animals, so the pet owners themselves must put their animals into the cages and take them out again. Guests are encouraged

to visit and walk their pets several times a day. Kennel attendants are not responsible for walking any of the animals in their care.

Note: During busy seasons, there may be a morning rush, starting about 30 minutes before the theme parks open, so you may encounter some delay in arranging your pet's stay. Plan accordingly.

Outside the Disneyland Resort: If you would like to board a pet in the vicinity of the Disneyland Resort, please contact the Animal Inns of America, 10852 Garden Grove Boulevard, Garden Grove, CA 92843; *www.animalinns.com*; 714-702-1484.

Some hotels and motels within the Disneyland Resort area accept well-behaved (preferably small) pets, but most do not allow guests to leave their animals in a room unattended.

To learn about other possibilities for pets, contact the Anaheim/Orange County Visitor & Convention Bureau; search "pets" at *www.visitanaheim.org*, or call 714-765-2800.

PHOTOGRAPHIC NEEDS

Disney's PhotoPass photographers will happily document your park visit. If you bought a PhotoPass package (see page 87) or purchased Genie+ service for the day (it comes with Photopass) and have questions while at Disneyland Resort, stop at the PhotoPass window just outside the entrance to Disneyland park, or call PhotoPass Guest Support at 407-560-4300. Note that there is no charge when PhotoPass photographers snap your mug using your equipment. Sweet!

Try not to use your camera or mobile phone on wet, rough, or bumpy rides. Stash it in a locker or with a non-riding member of your party. Note that selfie sticks are not permitted in any Disney theme parks.

RELIGIOUS SERVICES

Catholic: St. Justin Martyr; 2050 W. Ball Rd., Anaheim, about two miles from Disneyland; *www.saintjustin.org*; 714-774-2595. Masses are presented in English and Spanish; call or check the website for times.

Episcopal: St. Michael's Episcopal Church; 311 W. South St., Anaheim; *http://stmichaelsanaheim.org*; 714-535-4654; about seven blocks from Disneyland. Sunday services are at 11:30 A.M. (English). Call for mass times offered in Spanish.

Jewish: Temple Beth Emet; 1770 W. Cerritos Ave., Anaheim; 714-772-4720; *www.tbe-oc.org*; a few blocks from Disneyland. Services are held on Fridays at 6 P.M. and 9 A.M. on Saturdays.

HOT TIP

Disneyland's Genie+ service is a fee-based add-on to its free Genie vacation planning tool. Built into the Disneyland mobile app, Genie+ Service includes booking and redemption of Genie+ Lightning Lane selections in Disneyland and Disney California Adventure (see page 22)—plus unlimited downloads of PhotoPass images for the day, and Audio Tales that are themed to different areas of the parks. Genie+ costs $20 per person, per day. For more information, visit *disneyland.com*. Details are subject to change.

Lutheran: Prince of Peace Lutheran Church; 1421 W. Ball Road, Anaheim; *www.princeofpeaceanaheim.com*; 714-774-0993, about one mile from the Disneyland Resort. Sunday services are at 8 A.M. (traditional) and 10:30 A.M. (contemporary divine).

Non-denominational: The Kindred Community Church; 8712 E. Santa Ana Canyon Rd., Anaheim; 714-282-9941. Services are held on Sundays at 8:30 A.M. and 10:30 A.M. The church is approximately 11 miles from the Disneyland Resort; *www.kindredchurch.org.*

United Methodist: Anaheim United Methodist Church; 1000 South State College Blvd., Anaheim; 714-776-5710; *www.anaheimumc.org*; Sunday morning services are held at 10 A.M. (traditional); approximately 3.3 miles from the Disneyland Resort.

SHOPPING FOR NECESSITIES

It's a rare vacationer who doesn't leave some essential at home or run out of it mid-trip. Gift shops in almost all the hotels stock items no traveler should be without, but they usually cost more than in conventional retail shops. One good source is CVS Pharmacy at 480 South Main Street; 714-938-1200.

Inside the theme parks, aspirin, bandages, suntan lotions, and other sundries are sold; just ask a cast member to direct you to the closest shop. Some items are also available at each park's First Aid location and Baby Care Center.

SMOKING POLICY

Disneyland Resort is a smoke-free zone. Smoking (of any kind) is not permitted anywhere within the boundaries of the Disneyland Resort. This includes Disneyland and Disney California Adventure parks, Downtown Disney District, and all three Disneyland Resort hotels (including guestrooms and balconies). A $250–$500 cleaning fee will be charged for smoking in hotel rooms, on balconies, or on patios. The (enforced) smoking ban includes tobacco, e-cigarettes, and any products creating a vapor or smoke. Smoking of marijuana is prohibited. No exceptions. For more details, visit *disneyland.com.*

TELEPHONES

If you don't have a wireless phone at the ready (or charged), know that local calls from most pay phones in Southern California cost about fifty cents. Most hotels in the area charge an average rate of a dollar or more for local, toll-free, and credit-card calls made from your hotel room.

For long-distance phone calls, policies vary greatly from hotel to hotel, but charges are always higher than they'd be for direct-dial calls made from a pay phone. It makes the most sense to use a calling card whenever dialing long-distance from an in-room telephone.

Phone Cards: Disney offers AT&T prepaid phone cards in values of $10 and $20. They can be purchased at select locations at the Disneyland resort hotels.

Wireless Phones: To ensure a dose of uninterrupted magic for you and those around you, stick to texting while visiting the parks and silence your ringer. You'll be glad you did.

TIPPING

The standard gratuities around Anaheim are about the same as in any other city of its size. Expect to tip bellhops about $1 to $2 per bag. Tip cabdrivers 15 percent; outstanding shuttle or tour bus drivers, $1 to $2. Valets usually get $1 to $3 when you pick up the car. In table-service restaurants, a 15 to 20 percent gratuity is generally the norm. If you are pleased with the condition of your room, it is customary to leave a gratuity of $2 to $5 per day for the housekeeper (leave a note with the tip to avoid any confusion). Note that room service bills often include an automatic gratuity.

WEATHER

For information such as current weather forecasts, pay a visit to *www.weather.gov, www.weather.com, or www.wunderground.com.*

DID YOU KNOW?

The real estate on which Disneyland Resort stands was once occupied by groves of orange and walnut trees. Some of the original trees' descendants still call Disneyland home.

ACCOMMODATIONS

The welcome sign is always out at the Disneyland Resort hotels, where themed meals, amenities, and decor are definitely in character and add a layer of fun to a Disneyland vacation. And the resort's Disneyland Hotel and Grand Californian Hotel & Spa take staying at Disneyland to a lovely level of luxury.

In addition to the three hotels located within the Disneyland Resort, there are dozens of properties in Orange County, known as Disneyland Good Neighbor hotels, that the Walt Disney Travel Company has hand-picked to round out the Disneyland Resort area lodging options. We have selected a bunch of these recommended hotels, based on services and proximity to the Disneyland Resort, to highlight in this chapter.

If the sole purpose of your trip is to visit Disney, you should plan to stay in the Anaheim area, either on Disneyland property or at one of the surrounding hotels. Once you arrive and check in, you won't need your car again until you leave. Complimentary transportation to and from the parks is provided by monorails and trams serving the Disneyland Resort, and by buses serving neighboring hotels, motels, and inns. If struck with a bit of wanderlust, know that Anaheim is within range of a host of Southern California destinations, including movie studios, museums, beaches, and more. Whatever your vacation goals, we have provided a variety of lodging options in the Anaheim area, from old-fashioned to contemporary, simple to sublime.

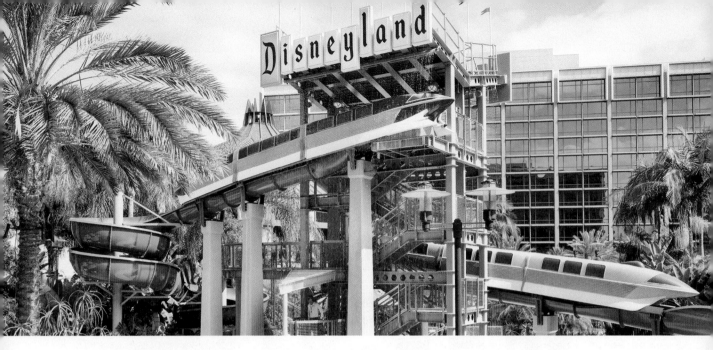

Disneyland Resort Hotels

Fans of the Disneyland Resort are faced with a difficult decision. It isn't whether or not to stay on Disneyland Resort property (that's recommended if it's within the budget), but which of the three hotels to choose. Some factors to consider:

The whimsical pool area and character meals make the classic Disneyland Hotel appeal to the kids in the family (and the kid in us all).

Meanwhile, Disney's Paradise Pier Hotel is in the midst of a massive makeover. When the dust settles, the hotel will sport a spiffy new Pixar motif. For updates about this spot's metamorphosis, visit *disneyland.com*.

The design team has really outdone itself with the Grand Californian Hotel & Spa. Located adjacent to Disney California Adventure (it has an exclusive entrance to the park), the hotel's theming and style touch every detail, right down to the floorboards.

Whichever resort hotel you decide on, one thing is certain—a stay on-property is sure to complete the overall Disneyland experience. From a resort information TV channel to wake-up calls from Mickey Mouse (or one of his pals), every detail reminds you that you are in Disney's land.

Exclusive Benefits: Some perks are reserved for guests staying at a Disneyland Resort Hotel. Perhaps the most significant of these is "Extra Magic Hour," (aka Early Entry) which allows entry into a theme park before it officially opens for the day (at no extra cost) on select mornings of their stay (with a ticket). There's even an exclusive entrance to the Disney California Adventure theme park, available only to guests staying at Disney's Grand Californian Hotel & Spa (a valid resort key card is required to use this park special entrance).

One of the most convenient perks is the ability to charge most expenses incurred at a Disney park back to the hotel room, if a credit card was provided at check-in. Purchases can be charged to the room from the time of check-in until 11 A.M. on the day of departure.

Shoppers may also enjoy having select purchases sent to their hotel's Bell Services Desk, where they can pick up their packages the next day—rather than having to tote them around the parks all day.

Other on-property perks include continuous, in-lobby (or near lobby) screenings of Disney's animated features (at all Disneyland Resort hotels), light-up "fireworks" on the headboards (at the Disneyland Hotel), and preferred access to a limited number of reservations for eateries and other guest experiences.

Check-in and Checkout: Check-in begins at 3 P.M. (4 P.M. for the Villas at Disney's Grand Californian), but guests who arrive early can check in, store their luggage at the Bell Desk, and go have fun. A photo ID is required at check-in. Checkout is at 11 A.M., and, again, all bags can be stored (for free) until guests are ready to depart.

HOT TIP

Rooms equipped for guests with disabilities are available at the three Disneyland Resort hotels, all of which are completely non-smoking. No exceptions.

Express check-out is available by leaving a credit card number at check-in.

Prices: Starting rates for standard guest rooms range from about $363 to $784. Club Level rooms range from about $820 to $1,192. Suites start from about $955 to $1,216. They fluctuate based on hotel, view, season, day of the week, etc. Self-parking costs $35 per day for registered guests at a Disneyland Resort hotel ($40 for oversized vehicles); valet parking costs $50 per day. Local calls, fitness center access, and unlimited Wi-Fi are available to all hotel guests.

Deposit Requirements: A deposit equal to one night's lodging (plus tax) is required at time of booking when making a "room only" reservation. Packages require a $200 deposit, due within 38 days of booking. The final payment is due 45 days prior to arrival. Packages booked within 30 days prior to final payment due date (45 days before arrival) don't require a deposit. If you prefer not to use a credit card to pay the deposit, call 714-520-5050 for direction.

Cancellation Policy: For a room-only booking, the deposit will be refunded if the reservation is canceled at least five days before the scheduled arrival. If you need to cancel a package, expect to be charged a $200 cancellation fee, plus insurance cost (where applicable), if the package is canceled 29 days or less prior to your scheduled arrival.

Additional Costs: Portable playpen-like cribs are available upon request (no charge). Self-parking costs $35 per day, while valet parking is available for $50 per day. Note that there is no longer an additional fee for extra guests (up to room capacity).

Discounts: Magic Key passholders may get special discounts throughout the Disneyland Resort. There may be discounts available to California residents, members of the military, and teachers, too—ask when you make your reservation. Disney Visa® Cardmembers can reap savings on merchandise, guided tours, and dining at the Disneyland Resort. For additional information, visit *DisneyRewards.com*.

Packages: The Walt Disney Travel Company offers packages that feature a stay at one of the Disneyland hotels. Call 714-520-5050.

DISNEYLAND HOTEL: This fanciful resort adjacent to the Downtown Disney District was the first hotel erected at Disneyland Resort—way back in 1955. It has had many looks over the years, and the current one proves the old adage: Everything old is new again! While the motif is a tribute to yesteryear and highlights the original mid-20th-century style of the hotel, there are some decidedly 21st-century touches, such as colorful fiber-optic "fireworks" on many of the guest-room headboards.

The pool area is popular with guests of all ages. With a nod to iconic park signage, "Disneyland" is spelled out in familiar blocks atop a platform supporting two twisting water slides. Reminiscent of the original monorail station at the Disneyland Hotel, a replica monorail train sits at each pool slide's entrance. The larger of the big slides sits 26 feet high and stretches 187 feet. The area also has a two-lane, mini slide for younger guests, as well as bubble jets in which to play. There are two hot tub spas and six poolside cabanas, too (there's a fee for cabana use).

The hotel has nearly 1,000 rooms, including 60 or so suites, located in three towers. (That number jumps up by 350 units when the new Disney Vacation Club tower is open. See the sidebar on page 44.) Most tower rooms have two queen beds, and many rooms can sleep up to five people (one of them on a daybed). The 11-story Adventure Tower looks toward Downtown Disney and Disney California Adventure on one side and the main pool on the other. The 11-story Fantasy Tower offers rooms with pool views, but only on one side; guests staying on the other side look out over city rooftops, with Disneyland Park to the right, and the best view of the fireworks. The 14-story Frontier Tower's rooms provide city and courtyard views.

A monorail stop is a short walk away in neighboring Downtown Disney District, which allows for extremely easy access to Disneyland Park (it drops guests off in the middle of Tomorrowland)—a nice convenience for folks who relish a break in their park-going with a

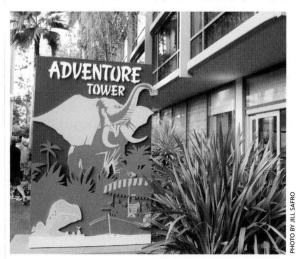

trip to one of the hotel pools, or to its Fitness Center. The workout room may be used by all registered resort guests (age 14 and above; guests under age 18 must be accompanied by an adult) and is accessed with a valid Disneyland Hotel room key.

In the lobby of the Fantasy Tower, a large shop called Fantasia sells Disney souvenirs. Goofy's Kitchen, hosted by Chef Goofy and his pals, is an extremely popular eatery open for breakfast and dinner; The Coffee House provides beverages, snacks, and quick meals for guests on the go. Room service may be offered; and Tangaroa Terrace Tropical Bar & Grill, a tiki-inspired casual dining spot, serves three meals a day with a South Seas flair, as well as a small selection of grab-and-go items. The adjoining bar, Trader Sam's, is a nice spot for drinks and appetizers. (For more about dining, see the *Good Meals, Great Time* chapter.)

The convention and meetings area, which is adjacent to Goofy's Kitchen and linked to the lobby via a photo-lined passageway, deserves a look for its Disney-related artwork, including a floor-to-ceiling collage of Disney collectibles and milestones. Created entirely from old toys, souvenirs, name tags, and other assorted memorabilia, it commemorates the colorful and unique history of the Disneyland Resort.

The hotel can provide safe-deposit boxes, currency exchange, and dining reservation assistance. An Automated Teller Machine (ATM) is on the premises. Airport buses bound for Orange County and Los Angeles airports stop at the nearby Disneyland Resort transportation area on Harbor Boulevard (aka the West Shuttle Area), as do tour buses, city, and county buses.

NEW DVC TOWER ON THE BLOCK!

The newest addition to the Disney Vacation Club (DVC) family of resorts is a pixie-dusted 12-story tower at the **NEW** Disneyland Hotel. Expected to open in 2023, the L-shaped edifice offers about 350 well-appointed villas with a Disney art and animation flair. In addition to the fresh digs, expect a new pool, outdoor bar, community hall, fitness center, and a play zone for the little ones. Note that rooms here are available to everyone when not occupied by Vacation Club members. For details about Disney's vacation ownership program, aka the Disney Vacation Club, call 800-500-3990, or visit *disneyvacationclub.disney.go.com*.

Guest rooms have 2 queen beds or one king bed, a flat-screen TV, small safe, coffeemaker, 24-hour room service, desk with a telephone, free Wi-Fi, hair dryer, iron with board, small (unstocked) refrigerator, and complimentary weekday newspaper.

Room rates start at about $490 to $740, depending on view and season; no charge for roll-aways. Club Level rooms start at about $740. Suites range from about $944 to $5,400 and up. (Note that higher rates apply to specialty suites such as the Pirates of the Caribbean Suite and the Mickey Mouse Penthouse Suite.)

Self-parking costs $35 per day ($40 per day for over-size vehicles); valet is $50 a day. Non-resort guests just visiting the hotel pay about $35 for the first hour and $10 for each extra hour to self-park (with a $75 maximum for 24 hours); $50 for the first hour and $10 for each additional hour of valet parking, with a $120 maximum. Note that all prices were correct at press time but are likely to change.

Disneyland Hotel, 1150 Magic Way, Anaheim, CA 92802; 714-956-6425 (to make reservations) or 714-778-6600 (front desk); *disneyland.com*.

DISNEY'S GRAND CALIFORNIAN HOTEL & SPA: This hotel is in a prime location—right in the middle of the Disneyland Resort. It includes 948 recently renovated studio rooms, 44 suites, 50 Disney Vacation Club villas, and 3 swimming pools. The resort has its own special entrance to Disney California Adventure park and easy access to the Downtown Disney District.

A border of trees surrounds the six-story hotel, built as a tribute to the American Craftsman tradition of the early 1900s. Cedar and redwood paneling decorates the cavernous lobby, where display cabinets filled with original art and reproductions introduce guests to that rich period of art. The lobby's great hearth fronts a perennially lit fire. Furnishings throughout the hotel feature warm colors and intricate textures.

Each deluxe guestroom and suite features a 55-inch TV, small safe, 24-hour room service, desk with a phone, Wi-Fi Internet access (no charge), USB chargers, coffeemaker (with coffee and non-dairy creamer), iron with board, and small (unstocked) refrigerator. The bathroom is equipped with a makeup mirror and hair dryer.

Most of the rooms in the hotel feature two queen beds with a sleeper chair or daybed, or a king bed and sleeper chair. The carved wooden headboards are made of quarter-sawn oak, a hallmark of Craftsman design. They feature a blossoming orange tree mural, complete with two familiar chipmunks frolicking in its branches. California-inspired artwork dots the room walls, including original designs of orange crate labels—paying homage to the history of the Disneyland Resort.

The Disney Vacation Club (DVC) villas reflect the same design as the hotel and are available to all guests when not occupied by DVC members. Each studio has a queen-size bed and queen-size sleeper sofa, plus a kitchenette with microwave, coffeemaker, and mini fridge. Larger (one-, two-, and three-bedroom) villas sleep 5 to 12 and offer dining areas, kitchens, laundry facilities, master baths with hot tub spas, and DVD players. They include a king-size bed in the master bedroom, a living room with queen-size sleeper sofa (and a sleeper chair in the one- and two-bedroom villas), and either two queen-size beds or a queen bed and a double sleeper sofa in extra bedrooms.

Guest services include 24-hour room service, laundry and dry cleaning (including same-day service), a fitness center, and a business center. The concierge level offers upgraded amenities and services. Guests can relax at the Fountain Pool and Redwood Pool (the two are adjacent) and make a splash at the Mariposa Pool, which includes a hot tub and 4 private cabanas that are available to rent throughout the day. The luxurious new Tenaya Stone Spa features an array of body treatments, facials, massage, and salon services. The Disney Imagineer-designed spa has a relaxation room with Craftsman architecture, comfy furnishings, a water feature, and a stained glass window of the rising sun. Acorn's Gifts & Goods, which sells apparel, pins, toys, collectibles, and snacks, is located in the lobby.

Among the dining options are the award-winning Napa Rose, which features fresh California cuisine and wines (plus breakfast with Disney princesses!), and Storytellers Cafe, serving three meals a day in an Old California setting and the backdrop for a breakfast hosted by Disney characters. GCH Craftsman Grill supplies coffee drinks, made-to order, and grab-and-go selections; a poolside bar is a solid choice for a light meal, snack, or refreshing beverage. The Hearthstone Lounge may double as a breakfast spot, serving coffee and pastries to hungry guests starting their Disney day.

The hotel can provide safe-deposit boxes and currency exchange. An ATM is on the premises. Tour buses, and city and county buses stop at the hotel's main entrance. Buses also stop at the nearby Disneyland Resort transportation center (aka East Shuttle Area). Guests may visit the resort's Front Desk to arrange airport transfers (fees apply).

Rates for standard guestrooms start at about $607, depending on the view, date, season, etc. Club Level (aka "Concierge") rooms start at about $1,050; suites start at about $1,000. There are no rollaway beds, but portable playpen-like cribs may be requested (no charge).

Self-parking costs $35 a day ($40 for oversize vehicles); valet parking is $50 per day. Non-resort guests pay $35 for the first hour of self-parking and $10 for each extra hour (with a $75 max); $50 for the first hour of valet parking, and $10 for each additional hour (with a $120 max). Non-registered guests who dine at Storytellers Cafe receive 3 hours free parking with validation, while Napa Rose and Tenaya Stone Spa patronage (when you spend $125 or more) includes 5 hours free parking with validation.

Disney's Grand Californian Hotel & Spa, 1600 S. Disneyland Drive, Anaheim, CA 92803; 714-956-6425 (for reservations) or 714-635-2300 (front desk); or visit *disneyland.com*.

DISNEY'S PARADISE PIER HOTEL: Long known as Disney's Paradise Pier Hotel (though that's apt to change), this property is in the midst of an extremely merry makeover! The new theme of the place matches that of its across-the-street neighbor—Pixar Pier at Disney's California Adventure Park. Woody, Jessie, Nemo, Dory, and a plethora of Pixar pals will be reflected in the resort's cheerful new motif. The decor aims to take guests on the creative journey experienced by artists who helped bring Pixar stories to life. All details are subject to change.

The hotel's two high-rise towers—one 15 stories tall, the other 14 stories—are juxtaposed to create a central atrium, which cradles the lobby and a larger-than-life sculpture. (Featuring Luxo, Jr. and Luxo Ball [aka the Pixar lamp and ball], the vibrant focal point makes for a festive photo op.) When all is said and done, each of the 481 guestrooms, including 20 suites, will be peppered with Pixar touches, one king-size bed or two queen beds, plus a twin daybed in the sitting area (a particular convenience for families). The rooms on the cabana level open onto a large recreation area that has included a sundeck, swimming pool, slide, hot tub spa, children's play area, and snack bar. If you expect to spend a lot of time in or beside the pool,

consider a Club Level room on the second floor for direct access (if available). Note that the playful Pixar theme extends to the popular rec deck.

At press time, the Mickey in Paradise shop and a grab-and-go market were the only on-site spots to purchase a snack or quick bite. (Though there are many areas to nosh nearby.) The first-floor lounge and a restaurant were "on pause," but are expected to re-open as the re-imagination process progresses. Room service, also paused at press time, is expected to return. The hotel also has an exercise room, guest laundry service, a concierge lounge, and an ATM (fees may apply). A glass-enclosed elevator provides a bird's-eye view of the resort lobby and Disney California Adventure theme park.

It may be the smallest of the Disneyland Resort hotels, but it is perennially popular. And when the "Pixar dust" settles, there will also be a new foot path conveniently connecting the hotel with a "back door" to Disney's California Adventure Park—making this park just a hop, skip, and a jump away. Note that details are subject to change. For updates, use the Disneyland mobile app or visit *disneyland.com*.

The hotel is connected to the Disneyland Hotel and Downtown Disney by a landscaped walkway. Guests (with valid admission tickets and a park reservation) can access Disneyland park by taking the monorail from the Downtown Disney District station. (The monorail transports guests to the park's Tomorrowland station.) Disneyland park's entrance is within a 10- to 15-minute walk for most pedestrians.

Standard rooms accommodate up to five guests. Rates vary depending on the view, date, season, etc. There is no charge for kids under 18 sharing their parents' hotel room; no charge for rollaways or cribs. For updates, pricing, and information about Club Level digs, visit *disneyland.com*. Self-parking costs about $35 per day ($40 for oversize vehicles); valet parking is $50.

Disney's Paradise Pier Hotel, 1717 South Disneyland Drive, Anaheim, CA 92802; 714-956-6425 (reservations) or 714-999-0990 (front desk); *disneyland.com*.

Disneyland Good Neighbor Hotels

With fewer than 2,500 hotel rooms available at the Disneyland Resort and tens of thousands of guests pouring through the parks each day, it's no wonder that a majority of visitors stay off Disney property. To make it easier for guests to narrow down their off-property choices, the folks at Disney have selected local hotels and motels that meet their standards and anointed them Disneyland Good Neighbor Hotels. Before receiving Disney's seal of approval, hotels are reportedly graded on amenities, services, decor, guest satisfaction, price, and location. All Good Neighbor hotels sell tickets to both Disney parks. *(Theme park reservations and tickets should be secured as far in advance as possible).*

Ranging from small operations to big chains, Good Neighbor hotels proliferate along Harbor Boulevard, which flanks Disneyland resort on the east. From Harbor, it's a relatively manageable walk to the Disneyland Resort. (If you're planning to walk to and from Disney's theme parks, be sure to inquire about the distance before you book your hotel.) A few hotels are on Ball Road, the Resort's northern boundary. Below Katella Avenue, which borders the resort to the south, side streets lead to the Anaheim Convention Center and major convention hotels. Divided into Superior, Deluxe, Moderate, and Suite categories, there are more than 40 Good Neighbor hotels in all. In these pages, we describe some of our favorites. For a list of Good Neighbor properties not detailed here, flip to page 52.

Prices: Expect to pay approximately $129 to $500 (plus tax), or more, per night for a hotel room for two adults and two kids (youngsters under age 18 usually stay in their parents' room for free), $70 to $250 for a motel room, and $50 to $85 for tent or RV camping. Prices drop a bit in winter; they are usually highest in the summer months and over holidays. The hotel room tax in Anaheim, California, is 15 percent.

Additional Costs: When comparing accommodation costs, do consider hidden zingers, like parking. Hotels usually charge for it (about $24 a day; more for valet service). Many also charge a fee when more than four people occupy a room. Ask about telephone rates when you check in—hotel surcharges are notoriously huge. Many hotels offer free Wi-Fi. Be sure to ask.

Savings: You may be able to save money by staying in a hotel that offers complimentary breakfast and shuttle service to Disneyland. Discounts are sometimes offered to individuals who belong to an automobile or retirement association.

HOT TIP

For additional information about the Disneyland Resort's Good Neighbor hotels, go to *https:// disneyland.disney.go.com/hotels/good-neighbor/.* To learn about any special vacation packages that may be offered during your expected visit, go to *https://disneyland.disney.go.com/vacation-packages/ good-neighbor-hotel-package.*

Individual Needs: What is absolutely essential for one vacationer—and well worth an added expense—might seem completely frivolous to another guest: room service, on-site restaurants, live music, a suite, a kitchen, concierge/Club Level service and amenities, large swimming pool, fitness center, or a place that accepts pets.

Packages: The Walt Disney Travel Company offers packages in conjunction with each of the (Disney vetted) Good Neighbor hotels representing potentially big savings for travelers. For details or to book a Good Neighbor package, contact the Walt Disney Travel Company directly at 714-520-5060, or visit *disneyland.disney.go.com/vacation-packages/good -neighbor-hotel-package.*

Note: The following establishments accept major credit cards and offer rooms for travelers with disabilities, unless otherwise indicated. Call directly to inquire about deposit requirements and cancellation policies. Rates were correct at press time, but are subject to change and should always be confirmed.

SUITE HOTELS

HYATT HOUSE AT ANAHEIM RESORT: This all-suite hotel around the corner from the convention center prides itself on its larger rooms, ranging from 355 to 790 square feet, which strongly appeal to families and those who will be staying more than a few nights. The 264 rooms and suites are decorated in neutral hues and earth tones, and range from standard to studio suites, one-bedroom or family suites. Breakfast is included, as are Wi-Fi service and a 24-hour workout room.

Suites offer either one king or two queen beds, bunk beds, sofa beds, 42-inch flat-screen TVs, and views of the Disneyland fireworks. Spacious studio and one-bedroom Kitchen Suites have a fully equipped kitchen with a refrigerator, microwave, dishwasher, stove, small appliances, and utensils.

The hotel is home to H Bar and Starbucks. There is an outdoor pool, hot tub, barbecue pit, and patio. Rates range from approximately $333 to $763 per night. Parking runs about $26 a day.

Hyatt House at Anaheim Resort, 1800 South Harbor Boulevard, Anaheim, CA 92802; 714-971-1800; *www.hyatt.com.*

CLEMENTINE HOTEL & SUITES ANAHEIM: Nestled in a garden-like setting, this residential-style hotel, formerly the Residence Inn by Marriott, is about a half-mile from Disneyland Resort. The 200 spacious suites, set inside sunny orange and yellow buildings, are offered in different room configurations, including a studio suite (one king bed and a sofa bed, which sleeps four), a one-bedroom suite (two queen beds and sofa bed, which sleeps six), and a bi-level loft suite (two queen beds, sofa bed, king bed, and two bathrooms, which sleeps eight). All rooms have a flat-screen TV, full kitchen with stove, microwave, dishwasher, a full-size refrigerator, and cooking utensils. Rates range from $252 to $499. Cribs and baby gates are available; rollaway beds are not.

Facilities include a fitness center with cardio equipment (water and towels are available), swimming pool, kiddie pool, whirlpool, and a single adaptive sport court that can be used for tennis, basketball, or volleyball (equipment may be borrowed). There is a guest laundry, mini market, fire pit and barbecue area, and playground.

Complimentary amenities include a business center with free Internet and printing services, Wi-Fi in all suites, and free parking—a huge perk. (Traditionally, this hotel has offered complimentary breakfast, but the service was temporarily suspended at press time. For updates, visit the hotel's website.) There is also a Disney planning and information desk. Pets are accepted for a flat fee of $250 per stay. Anaheim Resort Transit provides bus transportation for a fee.

Clementine Hotel & Suites Anaheim, 1700 S. Clementine Street., Anaheim, CA 92802; *www.clementinehotel.com* or 714-533-3555.

HOT TIP

If you stay in the 1300 to 1500 block of Harbor Boulevard, you can cross the street and walk to both theme parks. Of course, once you reach Disneyland property, it's another 5- to 15-minute walk to get to the theme park turnstiles.

SUPERIOR HOTELS

ANAHEIM MARRIOTT: Conveniently located next door to the Anaheim Convention Center, the Marriott is a perennial favorite among conventioneers. Guest rooms offer a residential feel and a SoCal vibe. Room amenities include a 55-inch flat-screen TV, sliding barn door entry to the bathroom, hardwood style floors, and a choice of one king-size, two double, or two queen-size beds. Wired and wireless Internet is available for a fee.

The main restaurant/lounge—nFuse—offers California cuisine with a global twist, a full-service bar, and a pleasant area with sofas, a shuffleboard court, and a pool table. For a more casual bite, Slice Pizzeria offers custom-made pizza with house-made dough. The Market Café offers a variety of food and drink options, including Starbucks drinks, grab-and-go selections, juices, sodas, and more.

The Anaheim Marriott has its own dedicated Disney Planning Desk, a fitness center, outdoor pool, and whirlpool. The hotel is a couple of (long) blocks from the Disneyland Resort—for some, it is not within walking distance. Shuttle service to the Disney theme parks is provided by Anaheim Resort Transit for a fee; transportation to area airports may also be arranged.

Room rates for two start at $129 (there is no charge for children under age 18 sharing their parents' room); suites start at about $210. Rollaway beds are $20 per stay, and cribs are free. Self-parking costs $29 per day; valet parking is $39 per day. The hotel is not pet-friendly.

Anaheim Marriott, 700 W. Convention Way, Anaheim, CA 92802; call 714-750-8000 or 800-228-9290, or visit *www.anaheimmarriott.com.*

HILTON ANAHEIM: The 14-story glass exterior of this property reflects the Anaheim convention center, a relatively short walk away, while the bustling lobby area invites the outdoors (and legions of conventioneers) inside. Hilton Anaheim, the largest hotel in the Anaheim resort area, boasts 1,572 rooms, including 93 luxurious suites, decorated in contrasting dark wood tones, with crisp white linens and warm wall coverings. Highlights include a chic lobby lounge, fifth-floor and 14th-floor Presidential Suites, a Starbucks coffee shop, and a Disneyland Resort planning desk.

The hotel's outdoor recreation area, located on the fifth floor, features a heated swimming pool, two whirlpools, and a kids' Splash Zone. Dining options include the MIX Restaurant & Lounge and the Pool Bar & Grill for outdoor dining (the latter operates on a seasonal basis). There is also a modest food court that includes Submarina (sandwiches).

Add to that a business center, FedEx shop, and Pure Escape Beauty Bar. The 25,000-square-foot Health Club & Spa at Hilton has exercise equipment, and indoor saltwater pool, basketball court, whirlpool, steam room, and sauna.

Rates for a room with two queen beds range from $175-$375 (there is no charge for kids under 18 when sharing their parents' room with existing bedding); suites start at about $293. Ask about packages. Each room has a coffeemaker (with coffee and non-dairy creamer), a safe, small flat panel TV, and free Wi-Fi for Hilton Honors members. There is no extra charge for cribs, but rollaway beds cost $35 per night. Self-parking costs $24 per day; valet parking, $35. Pets are not permitted.

Hilton Anaheim, 777 Convention Way, Anaheim, CA 92802; *www.hiltonanaheimhotel.com*; 714-750-4321 or 800-445-8667.

HYATT REGENCY ORANGE COUNTY: The hotel, in Garden Grove, is one mile south of Disneyland Resort. Its dramatic, 17-story atrium encloses palm trees and greenery and houses Starbucks, a gift shop, and an arcade. The hotel has 653 guestrooms (240 of which are suites). Rooms feature either a king-size bed or two queen beds, and modern design.

Amenities include coffeemaker, hair dryer, iron with board, 65-inch TVs, plus free Wi-Fi. The one- and two-bedroom suites also have a living room, refrigerator, and microwave. Suites can accommodate up to 8 guests.

Kids' Suites include a room for the little ones, complete with bunk beds and a TV. The parents' room has a king bed, TV, fridge, and microwave.

The hotel's recreational facilities, located on the South Tower's third-story roof, include a heated pool, a fitness center, basketball court, table tennis, a pickleball court, and a fire pit. Another pool and whirlpool are on the ground floor of the North Tower. This hotel offers a Disney planning and information desk. Transportation to and from the Disneyland Resort is provided for a fee.

Room rates start at about $199 (there is no additional charge for children under age 18 occupying their parents' room), plus $25 for each additional adult; $238 and higher for suites. There is no charge for cribs. Self-parking is $28 per day; valet parking is $36 per day.

Hyatt Regency Orange County, 11999 Harbor Boulevard, Garden Grove, CA 92840; *www.hyatt.com*; 714-750-1234.

ANAHEIM MAJESTIC GARDEN HOTEL: With its turrets and Tudor design, this 13-acre, 489-room hotel looks a bit like a castle, surrounded by grounds that incorporate three courtyards, a rose garden, and koi pond. The lobby has an exotic fish tank and free Internet service in a comfy, contemporary setting. There's a restaurant, lounge (with happy hour), and deli/gift shop.

The hotel has 463 rooms and 26 suites. The rooms—all large (490 square feet on average)—have two queen- or one king-size bed, cable TV, in-room movies, voice mail, iron, fridge, hair dryer, and coffeemaker (with coffee). Most of the rooms are designed to capture the hotel's castle theme with backdrops evoking an enchanted forest. Each suite features a sitting area with a sofa bed. Refurbished family suites offer castle bunk beds and themed rooms. Nearly all of the rooms can be connected to another to accommodate larger parties.

There is a full-service Japanese restaurant, arcade, heated pool and whirlpool, state-of-the-art fitness center, guest laundry, and conference rooms. It has a Disney planning and information desk, too. Airport transportation is available for a fee. Room rates start at $149. Self-parking is $20 per day. This property is pet-friendly. The hotel offers free and frequent shuttle service on its "Dream Machine" to the Disneyland Resort.

Anaheim Majestic Garden Hotel, 900 S. Disneyland Dr., Anaheim, CA 92802; *www.majesticgardenhotel.com*, or 714-778-1700.

SHERATON PARK HOTEL AT THE ANAHEIM RESORT: This 14-story tower is easy to spot, and the 490 rooms and six suites have balconies (some large, some small) that have a view of the pool or the Disneyland Resort (and its fireworks). Rooms offer either one king or two queen beds, refrigerator, iron, coffeemaker, and hair dryer.

The hotel features a lobby bar, Disney planning desk, Morton's The Steakhouse, Park 55 Cafe, and a snack bar. There's also a 24-hour fitness center, pool, whirlpool, and poolside watering hole.

Shuttle service to Disneyland is provided by Anaheim Resort Transportation (for a fee). Room rates run $188 to $256, depending on occupancy and season; Club Level rooms are higher. Rollaways cost about $15 extra; cribs are available free of charge. Self- and valet parking range from $21 to $25 daily. Pets may stay for $100 per stay.

Sheraton Park Hotel at the Anaheim Resort, 1855 S. Harbor Blvd., Anaheim, CA 92802; call 714-750-1811 or 866-837-4197; or visit *www.marriott.com/SNAPS*.

CAMELOT INN & SUITES: Directly across the street— and a relatively short walk away—from the Disneyland Resort, this newly renovated hotel, with its shingled roof, clock tower, turrets, and window boxes, looks like something out of a Bavarian village. Each of the 121 rooms and suites has a 49-inch TV, microwave, mini fridge, coffeemaker, safe, free Wi-Fi, hair dryer, and an iron with board. It also has a mobility scooter and stroller rental shop, and a guest laundry facility (fees apply). There is a pool (with a view of the Matterhorn Bobsleds attraction in Disneyland park), whirlpool, and terrace sundeck. Complimentary luggage storage is available in the lobby. While there's

no on-site eatery, there are many places to eat within reasonable walking distance.

Deluxe standard rooms, most with two queen-size beds, range from $199 to $329 year-round; family suites range from about $309-499 and accommodate up to six guests, but they have only one bath. All rooms have a sleeper chair. Cribs are available for free. The front desk is staffed 24/7. Adjoining rooms are usually available upon request. There's no shuttle service, but it is possible to walk to the Disneyland Resort entrance via Harbor Boulevard. Anaheim Resort Transit provides transportation to Disneyland Resort (for a fee). There is a daily fee for valet parking.

Anaheim Camelot Inn & Suites, 1520 S. Harbor Blvd., Anaheim, CA 92802; call 714-635-7275 or 800-828-4898, or visit *www.camelotinn-anaheim.com*.

SUITE HOTELS

FAIRFIELD BY MARRIOTT ANAHEIM RESORT: Fronted by palms and pines, this inviting 467-room hotel—fresh off a lobby renovation—is about a 7- to 10-minute walk to the Disneyland Resort theme park entrances. Its rooms, all accented with Disney artwork, are in two towers (one tower is nine stories high; the other, eight). Each room has a king-size bed or two queen beds, child-size sleeper sofa, smart TV, free high-speed Internet, an iron and board, a hair dryer, refrigerator, and coffeemaker (with coffee).

Other facilities include a fitness center, heated pool, whirlpool, gift shop, free Wi-Fi in the lobby and other public areas, arcade, Seattle's Best Coffee, and Pizza Hut Express. The guest rooms may be occupied by up to five people, and rates start at about $245; cribs are available. Parking costs $24 a day.

Anaheim Fairfield Inn by Marriott, 1460 S. Harbor Blvd., Anaheim, CA 92802; call 714-772-6777 or 800-228-2800, or go to *www.marriott.com*.

COURTYARD MARRIOTT ANAHEIM THEME PARK ENTRANCE: Located across the street from Disneyland Resort is the first entirely "family-geared" Courtyard. All rooms sleep up to six and feature bunk beds, two separate showers in the bathroom, and a 47-inch TV with Netflix and Pandora radio. Guestrooms at this property start at a roomy 532 square feet. Suites are available, too. This is the only four-star hotel within true walking distance of the two Disneyland theme park entrances (about a 10-minute walk, give or take). Dining options include the Bistro Restaurant & Bar, Starbucks, and a lobby lounge. There is a fitness center, two laundromats, and a gift shop. Rates for a double room start at about $322. Parking is $30 per day.

The 20,000-square-foot Surfside Waterpark has 4 super slides and 2 tot-friendly slides; a 400-gallon "drench bucket" that spills water on folks below; a 42-foot lap pool; and a hot tub perched on a sundeck. The pool deck offers a view of the Disneyland Resort fireworks.

Courtyard Marriott Anaheim Theme Park Entrance, 1420 S. Harbor Boulevard, Anaheim, CA 92802; visit *www.anaheimcourtyard.com*, or call 714-254-1442.

BEST WESTERN PLUS STOVALL'S INN: This inn is known for its fanciful topiary garden. The property features 288 guestrooms, complimentary continental breakfast, fitness center, business center, and a pair of pools (one is heated), two whirlpools, a wading pool, and a gift shop. Room configurations include two queen, one king, or two double beds, and a bathroom with a separate sink and lots of counter space.

Accommodations come with a mini refrigerator, microwave, coffee/tea maker, hair dryer, iron (with board), and TV. Room rates for up to five guests run $167 to $206. Rollaways are $15; cribs are free. Parking costs $10 a night (one car per room).

Best Western Plus Stovall's Inn, 1110 W. Katella Ave., Anaheim, CA 92802. Visit *www.stovallsinn.com*, or call 714-778-1880 or 800-854-8177, ext. 3.

CANDY CANE INN: There's a lot to like about this sweet, two-story hotel—fountain out front, relaxed ambience, wrought-iron touches, and lots of flowers. Located down the street from Disneyland Resort's entrance (a manageable walk for adults and non-toddlers), the Candy Cane Inn is family run and well maintained.

Each of the 171 rooms, most of which face a courtyard, has a fridge, safe, free Wi-Fi, coffeemaker, iron, hair dryer, and two queen beds with custom bedding. Add to that a laundry (fees apply), pool, gazebo-covered whirlpool, and fitness center. Free continental breakfast is served daily. Premium rooms have robes (to borrow), microwaves, in-room breakfast, turndown service, and 2 P.M. checkout. Sightseeing services are available, as is free shuttle service to and from the Disneyland Resort. Transportation to airports can be arranged. Parking is free.

Rates for a double room with two queen-size beds range from about $179 to $239, depending on the season. Rollaways, available in deluxe and premium rooms, are $20; cribs are free. The inn is located across the street from a shopping area with fast-food eateries.

Candy Cane Inn, 1747 S. Harbor Boulevard, Anaheim, CA 92802. Visit *www.candycaneinn.net*, or call 714-774-5284 or 800-345-7057.

HOWARD JOHNSON ANAHEIM HOTEL & WATER PLAYGROUND: This property's lush landscaping is a big reason to stay here. Flowers and trees proliferate; a central fountain anchors the four, two-story units. The hotel is close to Disneyland and local eateries. Anaheim Resort Transit offers Disneyland Resort shuttle service (for a small fee).

The 296 non-smoking rooms are spread among several buildings on seven acres. Most have two queen beds, and all have a small fridge, microwave, safe, and free Wi-Fi. The rooms are relatively spacious. Most rooms have a full balcony. Family suites are available.

There is a heated swimming pool with a hot tub, plus Castaway Cove—a splashy pirate playground featuring water slides, water cannons, toddler pool, and fountains. There are 2 guest laundries and a gift shop. Room rates range from $221 to $529, depending on the time of year. Parking is free until 3 P.M. on checkout day (there is a limit of one vehicle per room, no RVs). Rollaways cost $15 per day; cribs are free.

Howard Johnson Anaheim Hotel & Water Playground, 1380 S. Harbor Blvd., Anaheim, CA 92802; Visit *www.hojoanaheim.com*, or call 714-776-6120 or 800-422-4228.

TROPICANA INN & SUITES: This contemporary hotel is conveniently situated across from a pedestrian crosswalk that connects to the Disneyland Resort (it is about a 10-minute walk, but the time varies depending on the pace). Each of its 197 rooms has a 43-inch flat-screen TV, coffeemaker (with coffee), mini fridge, small safe, microwave, hair dryer, iron, and free Wi-Fi. Standard rooms have two queen beds and a single sleeper chair. Guests may use a computer in the lobby free of charge. Some rooms have a view of the Disneyland Resort's fireworks presentations.

The inn is home to a cafe/shop combo known as The Cove on Harbor Market and Coffee House. It sells food, drinks, souvenirs, and sundries. There are many eateries in the area (some within easy walking distance). Anaheim Resort Transportation provides shuttle service for a fee. The daily parking fee is $17. (There is a limit of one vehicle per room.)

The inn also has a heated Junior Olympic pool, whirlpool spa, and a guest laundry (fees apply). Guest room rates are about $199 to $329. Suites sleep up to 8 guests and range from $309 to $499. Some suites have kitchens.

Tropicana Inn & Suites, 1540 S. Harbor Boulevard, Anaheim, CA 92802; *www.tropicanainn-anaheim.com*; 714-635-4082 or 800-828-4898.

The Rest of the Best

Here's a roundup of the remaining Good Neighbor hotels. They have amenities and rates similar to those described in this chapter. However, some are a bit far from the Disneyland Resort.

Note: The various properties that boast Good Neighbor status are subject to change during the year; visit *disneyland.com* for updates.

SUPERIOR HOTELS

- **Delta Hotels by Marriott Anaheim Garden Grove**, 12021 Harbor Blvd., Garden Grove; 714-867-5555
- **JW Marriott Anaheim Resort**, 1775 S. Clementine St., Anaheim; 714-294-7800

DELUXE HOTELS

- **Cambria Hotel and Suites Anaheim Resort**, 101 E. Katella Ave., Anaheim; 714-520-3200
- **Courtyard by Marriott Anaheim Resort**, 2045 S. Harbor Blvd., Anaheim; 714-740-2645
- **Desert Palms Hotel & Suites Anaheim Resort Convention Center**, 631 West Katella Ave., Anaheim; 714-535-1133
- **Hampton Inn & Suites by Hilton Anaheim/Garden Grove**, 11747 Harbor Blvd., Garden Grove; 714-703-8800
- **Hampton Inn & Suites by Hilton Anaheim Resort Convention Center**, 100 W. Katella Ave., Anaheim; 714-533-1500
- **Hilton Garden Inn Anaheim/Garden Grove**, 11777 Harbor Blvd., Garden Grove; 714-703-9100
- **Holiday Inn Hotel & Suites**, 1240 S. Walnut St., Anaheim; 714-535-0300
- **Hotel Lulu Anaheim Resort**, 1850 S. Harbor Blvd., Anaheim; 714-750-2801
- **Hyatt Place at Anaheim Resort**, 2035 S. Harbor Blvd., Anaheim; 714-750-4000
- **Radisson Blu Anaheim**, 1601 S. Anaheim Blvd., Anaheim; 657-276-0145
- **Sonesta Anaheim Resort Area**, 1915 S. Manchester Ave., Anaheim; 714-748-7777
- **SunCoast Park Hotel Anaheim**, 1640 S. Clementine St., Anaheim; 714-598-0600

MODERATE HOTELS

- **The Anaheim Hotel**, 1700 Harbor Blvd., Anaheim; 714-772-5900
- **Anaheim Portofino Inn & Suites**, 1831 S. Harbor Blvd., Anaheim; 714-782-7600
- **Best Western Plus Anaheim Inn**, 1630 S. Harbor Blvd., Anaheim; 714-774-1050
- **Best Western Plus Park Place Inn & Mini Suites**, 1544 S. Harbor Blvd., Anaheim; 714-776-4800
- **Best Western Plus Pavilions**, 1176 W. Katella Ave., Anaheim; 714-776-0140
- **Best Western Plus Raffles Inn & Suites**, 2040 S. Harbor Blvd., Anaheim; 714-750-6100
- **Castle Inn & Suites**, 1734 S. Harbor Blvd., Anaheim; 714-774-8111

- **Clarion Hotel Anaheim Resort**, 616 W. Convention Way, Anaheim; 714-750-3131
- **Cortona Inn & Suites**, 2029 S. Harbor Blvd., Anaheim; 714-971-5000
- **Four Points by Sheraton Anaheim**, 1221 S. Harbor Blvd., Anaheim; 714-758-0900
- **Grand Legacy at the Park**, 1650 S. Harbor Blvd., Anaheim; 714-772-0440
- **Motel 6 Anaheim Maingate**, 100 W. Disney Way, Anaheim; 714-520-9696

SUITE HOTELS

- **Anaheim Marriott Suites**, 12015 Harbor Blvd., Garden Grove; 714-750-1000
- **Doubletree Suites by Hilton**, 2085 S. Harbor Blvd., Anaheim; 714-750-3000
- **Element by Westin Anaheim Resort Convention Center**, 1600 S. Clementine St., Anaheim; 714-326-7800
- **Embassy Suites by Hilton Anaheim-North**, 3100 E. Frontera St., Anaheim; 714-632-1221
- **Embassy Suites by Hilton Anaheim-South**, 11767 Harbor Blvd., Garden Grove; 714-539-3300
- **Holiday Inn Express & Suites Anaheim Resort Area**, 1411 S. Manchester Ave., Anaheim; 714-844-2801
- **Home2 Suites by Hilton Anaheim Resort**, 1441 S. Manchester Ave., Anaheim; 714-844-2811
- **Homewood Suites by Hilton Anaheim Resort Convention Center**, 2010 S. Harbor Blvd., Anaheim; 714-750-2010
- **Homewood Suites by Hilton Anaheim–Main Gate Area**, 12005 Harbor Blvd., Garden Grove; 714-740-1800
- **Hyatt House at Anaheim Resort Convention Center**, 1800 S. Harbor Blvd., Anaheim; 714-750-4000
- **Residence Inn by Marriott Anaheim/Resort Area**, 11931 Harbor Blvd., Garden Grove; 714-591-4000
- **Residence Inn by Marriott Anaheim Resort/Convention Center**, 640 W. Katella Ave., Anaheim; 714-782-7500
- **SpringHill Suites by Marriott Anaheim Maingate**, 1160 W. Ball Road, Anaheim; 714-215-4000
- **SpringHill Suites by Marriott Anaheim Resort Convention Center**, 1801 S. Harbor Blvd., Anaheim; 714-533-2101
- **Sonesta ES Suites Anaheim**, 1855 S. Manchester Ave., Anaheim; 714-748-7700

DISNEYLAND PARK

When you wish upon a star, your dreams come true. That's how the song goes, and it's always possible in Disneyland—Walt Disney's own dream come true. He envisioned "a place of warmth and nostalgia, of illusion and color and delight." The result: a place where imagination is given free reign, grins and giggles are encouraged, and everyone can see the world through a child's eyes.

The undisguised pleasure on the faces of park-goers reveals that they have fallen under the spell of a turreted pink castle; the oompah of a band marching down Main Street, U.S.A.; the pleasant clip-clop of a horse-drawn trolley; a cheerful greeting from Mickey and Minnie; and a fireworks spectacle more fantastic than an elaborate, pyrotechnic dream.

Those who first entered Disneyland as wee ones now return with their own kids—and grandkids—to find the park of their memories unchanged in spirit and heart. Shows and attractions have come and gone since it opened back in 1955 and whole new "lands" have been added, while many beloved classics endure. The newest neighborhood, Star Wars: Galaxy's Edge, promises high-flying intergalactic adventures for generations to come. Of course, the overall enchantment that guests experience when they walk through the portals of "the happiest place on earth" remains constant. That may well be Disneyland park's most enduring accomplishment. Enjoy!

"TO ALL WHO COME TO THIS HAPPY PLACE: WELCOME."

—WALT DISNEY

DISNEYLAND PARK

MAIN STREET, U.S.A.
1 Disneyland Railroad Station
2 Main Street Cinema
3 Main Street Vehicles
4 The Disneyland Story,
   Presenting Great Moments
   with Mr. Lincoln

ADVENTURELAND
5 Enchanted Tiki Room
6 Indiana Jones™ Adventure
7 Jungle Cruise
8 Treehouse

CRITTER COUNTRY
9 Splash Mountain
10 The Many Adventures
   of Winnie the Pooh
11 Davy Crockett Explorer
    Canoes

MICKEY'S TOONTOWN
12 Mickey & Minnie's
   Runaway Railway
13 Disneyland Railroad Station
14 Donald's Boat
15 Gadget's Go Coaster
16 Goofy's Playhouse
17 Mickey's House
18 Minnie's House
19 Roger Rabbit's Car Toon Spin

FRONTIERLAND
20 Big Thunder
   Mountain Railroad
21 Golden Horseshoe Saloon
22 *Mark Twain* Riverboat
23 Rafts to Tom Sawyer Island
24 Sailing Ship *Columbia*

NEW ORLEANS SQUARE
25 Disneyland Railroad Station
26 Haunted Mansion
27 Pirates of the Caribbean

TOMORROWLAND
28 Astro Orbiter
29 Autopia
30 Disneyland Monorail
31 Disneyland Railroad Station
32 Star Wars Launch Bay
33 Space Mountain
34 Star Tours—
   The Adventures Continue
35 Buzz Lightyear Astro Blasters
36 Finding Nemo Submarine Voyage

FANTASYLAND
37 Alice in Wonderland
38 Casey Jr. Circus Train
39 Dumbo the Flying Elephant
40 It's a Small World
41 King Arthur Carrousel
42 Mad Tea Party
43 Matterhorn Bobsleds
44 Mr. Toad's Wild Ride
45 Peter Pan's Flight
46 Pinocchio's Daring Journey
47 Sleeping Beauty Castle Walk-through
48 Snow White's Enchanted Wish
49 Storybook Land Canal Boats

STAR WARS: GALAXY'S EDGE
50 Star Wars:
   Rise of the Resistance
51 *Millennium Falcon:*
   Smugglers Run

Getting Oriented

Disneyland Park's layout—a basic hub-and-spokes configuration—is simple, but it was quite innovative when the park opened in 1955. The design makes getting around easy, though it's not altogether effortless, since the numerous nooks, crannies, and alleyways can be a bit confusing at first.

The hub of the park's wheel is Central Plaza, which fronts Sleeping Beauty Castle. From it extend five spokes leading to nine "lands": Main Street, U.S.A.; Adventureland; Frontierland; New Orleans Square; Critter Country; Fantasyland; a newly re-imagined Mickey's Toontown; Tomorrowland; and Star Wars: Galaxy's Edge. As you face Sleeping Beauty Castle, the first bridge to your left takes you to Adventureland; the next one, to Frontierland and New Orleans Square. To your right, the first walkway goes to Tomorrowland, and the next one—known as Matterhorn Way—leads to Fantasyland and Toontown. If you cross the Castle's moat and walk through the archway, you will reach Fantasyland. Critter Country occupies its own cul-de-sac, extending north from New Orleans Square. Star Wars: Galaxy's Edge is just beyond Critter Country (and may be accessed from there, as well as from Fantasyland and Frontierland).

Study the map at left to familiarize yourself with the park layout. When you arrive, check a park Tip Board, which includes details about times and locations of the day's entertainment, as well as how to see favorite Disney characters. Entertainment information is offered via the Disneyland Resort app, too.

PARKING

Guests are directed to park vehicles in the Mickey & Friends and Pixar Pals parking structures or the Toy Story lot on Harbor Boulevard. If one parking area is full, a cast member will direct you to one that isn't. Courtesy tram service transports guests from the parking decks, while buses service the Toy Story lot.

Parking areas open an hour before the park does—but getting a space can take a while if there are a lot of folks also hoping to get a head start on the day. Guests using wheelchairs will be directed to a special parking area and have access to ramps in the tram-loading area.

Parking Fees: Guests arriving in regular passenger vehicles pay about $30 to park for the day. (The fee for oversize vehicles is $35, and the cost for buses and trucks with extended trailers is $40.) Preferred parking starts at $45. You may leave the lot and return later the same day at no additional charge. (Hold on to your parking stub as proof of payment.) Prices are subject to change. Note that there is a courtesy shuttle to the parks from the Toy Story parking lot; the Mickey and Friends Parking Structure is within walking distance.

Lost Cars: Even if you take careful note of where you parked, you might have trouble remembering the exact spot when you return later. If this happens, contact a cast member and tell them approximately when you arrived for the day. With that information, parking lot personnel can usually help locate the vehicle.

GETTING AROUND

The Disneyland Railroad's five narrow-gauge trains make a loop around the park, stopping at Main Street, U.S.A., New Orleans Square, and Tomorrowland. It takes approximately 20 minutes to come full-circle on the train. Horse-drawn streetcars, horseless carriages, and an old-time motorized fire engine make trips up and down Main Street, U.S.A.

To travel outside Disneyland Park, consider taking the monorail, which glides between Tomorrowland and Downtown Disney. From the Downtown Disney District, you can walk to any of the three on-property hotels: Disney's Paradise Pier Hotel, the Disneyland Hotel, and Disney's Grand Californian Hotel & Spa.

The Grand Californian Hotel & Spa is a short walk to the Disneyland entrance and has its own entrance to Disney California Adventure. (The gate is reserved exclusively for Grand Californian Hotel guests—you will have to flash a valid Grand Californian room key to use it.) Note that the theme parks require separate admission, unless you have a Park Hopper ticket; see page 57 for ticket pricing and structures.

Park Primer

BABY FACILITIES

The Baby Care Center, on Main Street, U.S.A., by First Aid, provides changing tables, high chairs, toddlers' toilets, and a nursing area. Bottles can be warmed here, and diapers, formula, and food are sold. There are no napping facilities or babysitting services.

FIRST AID

First Aid is at the north end of Main Street, next to the Baby Care Center. A nurse is on duty during park operating hours. *In case of emergency, notify an employee and call 911.* The center can store medications that require refrigeration and provide containers for hypodermic needle disposal.

GUIDED TOURS

Several tours originate from the Guided Tour Gardens, just left of City Hall. They include the ever-popular *Walk in Walt's Disneyland Footsteps* and the *Grand Circle Tour*, which focuses on Disney trains. There are also seasonal tours: *Disney's Happiest Haunts* for the Halloween season, and *Holiday Time at the Disneyland Resort*. Park admission is required for all tours. For more details, flip to page 21. (Some tours were "on pause" as this book went to press.)

HOURS

Disneyland park is usually open daily, year round. Monday through Thursday hours are usually from about 8 A.M. to 8 P.M., Friday and Sunday from about 8 A.M. to 11 P.M., Saturday from 8 A.M. to 12 A.M., with extended hours during the summer and holiday periods. Park-hopping is allowed after 1 P.M. All details are subject to change. For updates, visit *disneyland.com*, or call 714-781-4565.

During the inevitably busy spring break, summer, and Christmas holiday seasons, it's especially wise to arrive early so that you can visit the most popular attractions before the lines get long. If you arrive at Disneyland too late, the parking structure and surrounding lots could be more crowded than usual; this is almost always the case in the summer and the last week of December.

INFORMATION

Cast members at City Hall on Main Street, Guest Relations kiosks (Fantasyland and New Orleans Square), and the Central Plaza Information Board can answer questions. Be sure to get a park guidemap as you enter. They're free.

Information Board: A valuable planning resource, the Central Plaza Information Board (aka the Tip Board) is on Main Street, U.S.A. It lets you know how long the waits are for most shows and attractions, what is not operating that day, and where and when park entertainment will take place—as do the Disneyland app and *disneyland.com*. Cast members can answer questions and provide info about eateries and hotels in the Disneyland Resort. They can help locate favorite Disney characters, too.

LOCKERS

Storage lockers are outside the main entrance (on the left) and on Center Street (about halfway up Main Street). Inside-the-park lockers cost about $7 or $10 per day, depending on size. Items may be stored during park hours only. You'll also find a kiosk from which to rent smartphone power packs. The cost is $30 per day and includes unlimited pack-swapping, plus power cords for iPhones and Android devices. The lockers outside the park cost $7, $10, $11, $12, and $15 per day (depending on size).

LOST & FOUND

Disneyland's Lost & Found is located on the left side of the Disneyland park entrance. If you realize that you've lost something after you have gotten home visit *https://disneyland.disney.go.com/guest-services/lost-and-found/*.

LOST CHILDREN

Report lost children at City Hall or the Baby Care Center and alert the nearest Disney employee to the problem. To expedite reunions, supply kids with a copy of your mobile number before you visit the park.

MONEY MATTERS

Cash and traveler's checks are accepted at all food and shopping spots at Disneyland Resort. American Express, Visa, MasterCard, JCB Card, and Discover Card are accepted at shops and eateries (though it may be cash only at some vending carts).

PHOTO BY JILL SAFRO

Main Street's City Hall can assist with some foreign currency exchange. Disneyland Resort hotel guests may charge most in-park purchases to their hotel bill if they gave a credit card number at check-in.

Disney gift cards are accepted at the three Disneyland Resort hotels, Disney California Adventure, Downtown Disney, and Disneyland park. They are also accepted at most venues in Walt Disney World (Florida), and at all U.S. Disney Store locations.

There are four Automated Teller Machines (ATMs) within Disneyland park. The first one you'll encounter is near the Disneyana shop at the Bank of Main Street building. (Though one might expect the Bank to be, well, a bank, it is not. It's a shop.)

PARK RESERVATIONS

To enter a Disneyland Resort theme park, guests must have valid park admission *and* a park reservation for the day. Park reservations can (and should) be made in advance via the Disneyland app or *disneyland.com*. We recommend checking for reservation availability before purchasing tickets, as reservations do sell out.

SAME-DAY RE-ENTRY

All Disneyland park guests have their picture taken upon initial entry to the park. (The photo links with their ticket.) This makes for speedy and convenient re-entry, with the presentation of said park ticket. If you'd like to visit two parks on one day, you'll need to purchase the "hopper" option prior to entering the first park. (Disneyland and Disney California Adventure are within walking distance of each other, which allows for hassle-free hopping between the parks.)

SMOKING RULES

Disneyland Resort is a smoke-free zone. Smoking (of any kind) is not permitted anywhere within Disneyland Resort boundaries—this includes all of Disneyland Park, Disney California Adventure, Downtown Disney, the Disneyland hotels, and the esplanade between the parks. The ban includes tobacco, e-cigarettes, and any products creating a vapor or smoke. Smoking of marijuana or illegal substances is prohibited. No exceptions.

STROLLERS & WHEELCHAIRS

Strollers ($18 for singles; doubles $36) and wheelchairs ($15 with a $20 refundable deposit and a credit card) may be rented outside the park entrance. Electric Conveyance Vehicles (ECVs) cost $60 for the day, with a $20 deposit and major credit card. Wheelchairs and ECVs are limited. Misplaced strollers may be replaced at the park entrance and at The Star Trader shop in Tomorrowland.

SECURITY CHECK

All guests are subject to a thorough security check before entering Disneyland Resort. Bags are screened and guests must pass through a metal detector. For a complete rundown of the current Park Rules, visit *disneyland.com/parkrules*.

Expect car trunks to be searched when entering Disney parking facilities.

Guests checking into a Disneyland Resort hotel must present valid government-issued photo ID.

TICKET PRICES

Although prices[†] will likely increase, the following should give an idea of what you will pay for tickets in 2023. Note that 1-Day tickets purchased in 2023 must be used by 12/30/23. The first day of use of multi-day tickets must be on or before 12/30/23. Multi-day tickets must be used within 13 days of first use or by January 12, 2024, whichever occurs first. For updates, use the Disneyland app or visit *disneyland.com*. Details are subject to change.

	ADULTS	CHILDREN*
1-Day Ticket (1 park)	$104/164	$98/154
1-Day Ticket (hopper)	$164/224	$158/214
2-Day Ticket	$255	$240
2-Day Ticket (hopper)	$315	$300
3-Day Ticket**	$330	$310
3-Day Ticket (hopper)**	$390	$370
4-Day Ticket**	$360	$340
4-Day Ticket (hopper)**	$420	$400
5-Day Ticket**	$380	$360
5-Day Ticket (hopper)**	$440	$420
Enchant Key pass		$649
Believe Key pass		$949
Dream Key pass		$1,399

† One-day prices represent the range in which you can expect to pay. Prices vary based on date. For dates, visit *disneyland.com*.
* 3 through 9 years of age; children under 3 free
** Includes one "Magic Morning" early Disneyland Park admission on Tuesday, Thursday, or Saturday with advance purchase. (Magic Mornings were "on pause" at press time, but expected to return.)

There is a single price (for adults and children) for Enchant Key, Believe Key, and Dream Key passes. Said passes are part of the "Magic Key" pass program that replaced traditional annual passes. There is a limited number of Magic Key passes available and sales may be suspended at any time. For more information on Magic Key passes, use the Disneyland mobile app or visit *disneyland.com*.

Main Street, U.S.A.

This pretty thoroughfare represents Main Street America in the early 1900s, complete with the gentle clip-clop of horses' hooves on pavement, melodic ringing of streetcar bells, and strains of nostalgic tunes such as "Bicycle Built for Two" and "Coney Island Baby."

The sounds of brass bands, a barbershop quartet, and ragtime piano fill the street. An old-fashioned steam train huffs into a handsome brick depot. Rows of picturesque buildings line the street. Authentic gaslights, which once lit up Baltimore and St. Louis, flicker at sundown in ornate lampposts lining the walkways, and the storefronts—painted in a palette of pastels—could not be more inviting. Walt Disney was a master of detail: throughout Main Street, even the doorknobs are historically correct.

To make the buildings appear taller, a set designer's technique called forced perspective was employed. The first floor is seven-eighths scale (this allows guests to enter comfortably); the second story is five-eighths scale; and the third, only half size. The dimensions of the whole are small enough for the place to seem intimate and comforting, yet the proportions appear correct. (Forced perspective was also used to make the Matterhorn and Sleeping Beauty Castle seem taller than they are.)

The following attractions are listed in the order in which you'll encounter them while walking from the entrance up Main Street, U.S.A. toward Sleeping Beauty Castle.

CITY HALL: Before strolling up Main Street, U.S.A., stop briefly at the Information Center at City Hall, on the west side of Town Square, to find entertainment schedules, make dining reservations, or get advice to help you plan your Disneyland day. City Hall is also an excellent meeting place if members of your party separate and plan to regroup later in the day.

FIRE DEPARTMENT: Next door to City Hall, this was Walt Disney's home away from home during the construction of Disneyland. His private apartment, on the top floor, looks just the same as when Walt called it home. It's decorated with antiques and items he and his wife Lillian picked up during their travels around the world. A light flickers in the window in Walt's memory. The apartment is not open to the public, but guests are welcome to visit the firehouse. Youngsters love—and are welcome—to climb on the fire wagon parked inside the firehouse. It's a realistic copy of a truck from the early 1900s and provides a great photo opportunity.

DISNEYLAND RAILROAD: Walt Disney loved trains so much he actually built a one-eighth-scale model of one, the Carolwood Pacific, in the backyard of his home. So it was only natural that his first theme park include a railroad—five narrow-gauge steam trains have circled

Disneyland Park since it opened in 1955. Two of the locomotives were constructed at the Walt Disney Studios, while three had other lives before finding a permanent home at Disneyland.

Guests who ride the train between Tomorrowland and Main Street, U.S.A., are in for a few surprises. In 1958 Walt Disney added a diorama of the Grand Canyon, depicted from its south rim on a seamless, handwoven canvas that is 306 feet long and 34 feet high, and is covered with 300 gallons of paint. The accompanying music is the "On the Trail" section of American composer Ferde Grofé's Grand Canyon Suite.

The Disneyland Railroad experience was recently enhanced a bit. It now travels across an elevated trestle, affording panoramic views of five waterfalls

gracing the Rivers of America. Disneyland veterans may also take note of some old Frontierland friends during the journey.

THE DISNEYLAND STORY, PRESENTING GREAT MOMENTS WITH MR. LINCOLN: The Disneyland Opera House makes the perfect backdrop for a tribute to the "happiest place on earth," and the man who created it, one Walter Elias Disney. A unique collection of art, models, and mementos—as well as a film—marks more than 60 years of Disneyland magic. After taking a walk down Disney memory lane, guests may pay a visit to the 16th president of the United States. Yes, Abraham Lincoln is here (in realistic, Audio-Animatronics form). After a brief presentation about the Civil War, "Mr. Lincoln" stands up and delivers a stirring discourse about liberty, the American spirit, and the challenges facing the nation. It's remarkably *au courant* for an 18th-century allocution.

PHOTO BY JILL SAFRO

MAIN STREET VEHICLES: Main Street's motorized fire wagon, horseless carriages, and horse-drawn street-cars lend the thoroughfare a real touch of nostalgia, while at the same time giving guests a lift from one end of the street to the other. The fire truck is modeled after those that might have been discovered on an American Main Street in the early 1900s, except that it has seats where the hose was meant to be carried.

The horse-drawn streetcars, inspired by those in 19th-century photographs, carry up to 30 passengers each. Most of the horses that pull the cars are Belgians (characterized by white manes and tails and lightly feathered legs) and Percheron draft horses.

PHOTO BY JILL SAFRO

PRESS A PENNY!

The art of pressing pennies—believed to have started in Austria in 1818—took the U.S. by storm when it was introduced at the 1892–1893 World's Columbian Exposition in Chicago. About a century later, Disneyland introduced guests to the joy of smushing a penny into shiny souvenir! The first two machines proved so popular, Disney has been adding new ones ever since. Now it's possible to press pennies (plus dimes and quarters) into more than 150 different Disney-themed souvenirs. (In case you're wondering, the first Disneyland penny press machine yielded (appropriately) an image of Mickey Mouse, while the second featured the beloved bruin and Disneyland darling, Big Al.) Most of the pressed-coin machines feature images from the area in which they are located—it's fun to discover them while wandering in the park.

How does it work? Simply place your penny (plus two quarters) into the machine, press the button, and *presto*: the coin is squeezed between ollers, flattened into an oval, and engraved with a Disney design of your choosing. (If you prefer to press a dime or quarter, the fee is 75 cents.) In true old-time fashion, these machines do not accept credit or debit cards. Coins only, please.)

While some guests get rather crafty with their coins (turning them into key chains, jewelry, belts, wind chimes, and more), others preserve them in a scrapbook or Disney-branded souvenir book (available for purchase at many shops throughout the Disneyland Resort).

Note: Coin-press machines are available at Disney California Adventure, Downtown Disney District, and the three Disneyland Resort hotels, too. They're easily located by using the Disneyland Resort app, visiting *disneyland.com*, or by asking a cast member.

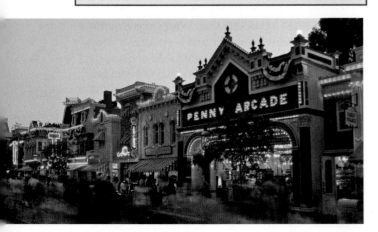

MAIN STREET CINEMA: This small, standing-room-only movie theater features classic, early Mickey Mouse cartoons. The six animated shorts, which play continuously throughout the day, were originally aired before feature films. The addition of several benches has made this cinema an even-more-pleasant place to soak up some Disney nostalgia.

PENNY ARCADE: This place is more of a candy shop than an arcade, but the air of nostalgia remains. Those who have frequented it in the past will be happy to find Esmeralda front and center, ready as always to tell your fortune. The arcade still has Mutoscopes, machines that feature hand-cranked moving pictures and require a penny to operate.

PHOTO BY JILL SAFRO

Save some change for the arcade's penny presses. You insert a penny (plus a few other coins to pay for the service), and the penny will be flattened and imprinted with the image of Sleeping Beauty Castle or the face of one of the Disney characters.

CENTRAL PLAZA: Main Street, U.S.A., ends at Central Plaza, the hub of the park, and four of the park's lands are directly accessible from here. At its center stands the Walt and Mickey Partners statue. It's one of the park's most popular picture spots.

One of Disneyland's Information Centers is located here, near the entrance to Adventureland. Besides the info desk, there is a handy Information Board, (aka Tip Board) updated frequently, that posts wait times for many attractions, which attractions offer Lightning Lane service, what (if anything) is not operating that day, and where and when park entertainment will take place.

Adventureland

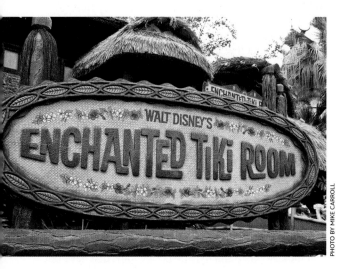

PHOTO BY MIKE CARROLL

For someone who grew up in Marceline, Missouri, around the turn of the 20th century, as Walt Disney did, the far-flung regions of the world must have seemed most exotic and exciting. So it's not surprising that when he was planning his new park, he designated one area, called Adventureland, to represent all the (then) remote and mysterious corners of the world.

The original South Seas–island ambience all but disappeared with the opening of the Indiana Jones Adventure in 1995, and Adventureland became a 1930s jungle outpost. Today, the entrance to the Jungle Cruise is a walk-through headquarters, with old photographs and radios playing big band music interrupted by news flashes about Professor Jones's latest exploits and discoveries. Shops here sell wares that are meant to appeal to modern-day adventurers.

WALT DISNEY'S ENCHANTED TIKI ROOM: Introduced in 1963, this was the first of the park's Audio-Animatronics attractions and the precursor of more elaborate variations, such as "Great Moments with Mr. Lincoln" and the above-mentioned Dr. Jones. Housed in a vaguely Polynesian complex situated at the entrance to Adventureland, the 15-minute show was given a spiffy face-lift not too long ago.

The stars are four feathered emcees (José, Michael, Pierre, and Fritz), backed up by a company of pastel-plumed parrots and an eclectic chorus of orchids, carved wooden tiki poles, tiki drummers, singing masks, bird-of-paradise flowers, macaws, Amazon parrots, toucans, fork-tailed birds, cockatoos, and several other species.

The 225 performers all sing and drum up a tropical storm with so much animation that it's hard to resist a smile. Their repertoire includes "In the Tiki, Tiki, Tiki Room," "Let's All Sing," and "Aloha to You."

JUNGLE CRUISE: The spiel delivered by the skipper on this seven-minute river adventure has its share of corny jokes, but your navigator may turn out to be a natural comic with a funny delivery. Just remember that the cornball humor is part of the fun.

As jungle cruises go, this one is as much like the real thing as Main Street, U.S.A., is like life in an actual small town—long on loveliness and short on the visual distractions and minor annoyances that constitute the bulk of human experience. There are no venomous vipers and no Montezuma's revenge. And the Bengal tiger and king cobras at the ancient Cambodian ruins, and the great apes, gorillas, crocodiles, alligators, hippos, elephants, and lions in the water and along the shores represent no threat to passersby—though according to maintenance crews, mechanical critters are almost as much trouble as real ones.

Movie buffs should note that Bob Mattey, who helped develop these jungle creatures, also worked on the giant squid for the Disney film *20,000 Leagues Under the Sea*, the man-eating plants in many Tarzan movies, and the menacing mechanical shark in *Jaws*.

The large-leafed upright tree in the Cambodian ruins section of the attraction is a Sacred Fig (Ficus religiosa), the same species of tree under which Buddha received enlightenment in India many centuries ago.

This classic attraction was recently refreshed by Disney Imagineers. Expect an increased wildlife presence, surprise scenarios, and, of course, a ton of tomfoolery.

TREEHOUSE: The 80-foot-tall, 150-ton *Disney-odendron semperflorens grandis*, or "large, ever-blooming Disney tree," cradled the original Swiss Family Treehouse from 1962 to mid-1999, and until recently, embraced another lofty dwelling: Tarzan's Treehouse (inspired by the book by Edgar Rice Burroughs and Disney's 1999 animated feature *Tarzan*). Overlooking the Jungle Cruise and the Temple of the Forbidden Eye (the setting for the Indiana Jones attraction), its moss-and-vine-covered "high-rise apartment" sheltered Tarzan, his adoptive mom, Kala (the ape), and Jane until September of 2021.

At press time, changes were afoot for this towering tree. What's next for the esteemed Disneyland artifact? A new theme and backstory! For details and updates, use the Disneyland app or visit *disneyland.com*.

F.Y.I. The *Disney-odendron semperflorens grandis* is entirely human-made, with concrete roots and steel limbs. And its 300,000 leaves were all attached by hand.

BIRNBAUM'S ★BEST★ INDIANA JONES™ ADVENTURE: G+ Hidden deep within the dense jungles of India, the Temple of the Forbidden Eye was built long ago to honor the powerful deity Mara. According to legend, Mara could "look into your very soul" and grant the "pure of heart" one of three gifts:

unlimited wealth, eternal youth, or future knowledge. But legend also issues a rather stern warning: "A terrible fate awaits those who gaze upon the eyes of Mara!" Dr. Jones would only comment, "Records indicate that many have come, but few have returned."

Now you can take an expedition through the ancient temple ruins in this attraction based on the George Lucas/Steven Spielberg films. The experience, including the pre-show and queue area, can take more than an hour (without a Genie+ selection; see page 22), though the ride itself lasts about 3½ minutes. You follow the jungle path through Dr. Jones's cluttered encampment, then enter the temple via the path marked by his original team. In the queue area, a newsreel tells of Jones's latest expedition. What it does not reveal is that Indy has entered the temple and disappeared.

Following in his footsteps, you will see warning signs that indicate there still may be booby traps that have not yet been disarmed. (The fun is in ignoring the warnings and letting the spikes fall where they may.) Inside the temple, guests board 12-passenger vehicles reminiscent of 1930s troop transports. One person sits by the wheel and serves as the expedition driver, but not until all are securely fastened in their seats for the twists and turns ahead. Hold on to your hat!

The search for Indiana Jones is on, and an encounter with the fearsome Mara is unavoidable. The trip reveals a world of mummies, glowing fires, falling lava, worrisome snakes, and poisonous darts.

Surprises lurk around every bend, and escape is only temporary (just as in the movies), as you suffer an avalanche of creepy crawlies, traverse a quaking suspension bridge, and find yourself on a collision course with a giant rolling boulder that threatens to flatten everything in its path. At the end of the ride, Indy himself is waiting for you, with a flippant parting remark, such as "That wasn't so bad" or "Next time you're on your own" or "Tourists. Why'd it have to be tourists?"

Thanks to the creative wizardry of Disney Imagineers, no two rides are exactly the same, so each time you enter the Temple of the Forbidden Eye, the overall experience may be slightly different. Hang on!

Note: Pregnant women and guests who suffer from heart conditions, motion sickness, sore necks or backs, and have other physical concerns should avoid this wild and exceptionally bumpy attraction. Guests must be at least 46 inches tall to board; children under age 7 must be accompanied by a person who is at least 14 years old. Spooked by snakes? There are more than a few in here. They may not be real, but they're still rather creepy.

New Orleans Square

Though New Orleans Square did not figure in the Disneyland layout until 1966, it's certainly among the park's most evocative areas. This would be true even if it were home to just the superb Haunted Mansion and Pirates of the Caribbean. But there's also its picturesque site near the shores of the Rivers of America, and its architecture, a pastiche of wrought iron, pastel stucco, French doors, and beckoning verandas.

Not to be missed are the pleasant open-air dining spots; the charming Blue Bayou restaurant overlooking the moonlit lagoon inside Pirates of the Caribbean; the unique assortment of boutiques; and the music—lively jazz and Dixieland, performed in traditional New Orleans style.

As you relax on a warm evening, snacking on beignets and mint juleps, images of Disneyland-as-amusement-park may start to evaporate. Just as Main Street, U.S.A., makes the theme park a great place to shop, New Orleans Square makes it a fine spot to spend a few relaxing hours. Those perpetual click-click sounds emanating from the railroad station are the Morse code version of the actual dedication speech given by Walt Disney on the opening day of Disneyland back in 1955. It begins: "To all who come to this happy place; welcome."

The attractions that are described on the following pages are listed in the order in which you'd encounter them while strolling from east to west in Disneyland's New Orleans Square.

BIRNBAUM'S ★BEST★ PIRATES OF THE CARIBBEAN: The most swashbuckly adventure you'll find at Disneyland, this 16-minute boat ride takes guests through a series of sets portraying a rowdy

pirate raid on a Caribbean village. Bursting with cannon fire, stolen loot, a gluttonous feast, and a raucous band of unruly mercenaries, Pirates of the Caribbean has been a fan favorite for more than half of a century. It was the last attraction built under Walt Disney's direct creative supervision.

The experience begins with a peaceful voyage through a bayou, where will-o'-the-wisps glow just above the grasses. Fireflies twinkle nearby, while stars spangle the twilight-blue sky overhead. The attention to detail nearly boggles the mind. The Audio-Animatronics cast includes plastered pigs whose legs actually twitch in their soporific contentment, singing marauders, and wily wenches. The observant will note a couple of familiar rapscallion residents. Yep, that beloved scally-wag Captain Jack Sparrow has dropped anchor here, as has his nefarious nemesis, Captain Barbossa. And there's a new pirate in town—the famous redhead resident of this attraction has teamed up with the local marauders! Redd hopes to help the townspeople "unload" their valuables at the Mercado Auction.

While it's by no means the most politically correct attraction, the theme song, "Yo-Ho, Yo-Ho (A Pirate's Life for Me)," manages to transform some rather blatant buccaneering into a rousing time for all. A must—again and again.

BIRNBAUM'S ★BEST★ HAUNTED MANSION: G+ In a British radio interview, Walt Disney once explained how sorry he felt for those homeless ghosts whose hauntable mansions had fallen

HOT TIP

Haunted Mansion Holiday kicks off in early September and runs through the New Year. It features Jack Skellington from *Tim Burton's The Nightmare Before Christmas*, as well as holiday decor galore. Silly, seasonal sight gags abound.

to the wrecker's ball. Feeling that these lost souls sorely needed a place of their own, he offered this Haunted Mansion, unquestionably one of Disneyland's top attractions. From its stately portico to the exit corridor, the special effects are piled on to create an eerie, but never terrifying, mood. Just frightfully amusing.

Judicious applications of paint and expert lighting effects heighten the shadows that play ghoulishly on the walls outside. The jumble of trunks, chairs, dress forms, and other assorted knickknacks in the attic are left appropriately dirty, and extra cobwebs, which come in convenient liquid form, are strung with abandon. The eerie music and the slightly spooky tones of the Ghost Host often set small children to whimpering, and soon their Mickey Mouse ears have been pulled tightly over their eyes. Still, the spirits that inhabit this house on the hill—999 in all—are a tame lot for the most part, though they are always looking for occupant number 1,000. Any volunteers?

What makes the seven-minute attraction so special is the attention to, and abundance of, details—so many that it's next to impossible to take them all in during the first, or even the second or third, time around. In the Portrait Chamber—a room full of fearsome-looking gargoyles that adjoins the chandeliered and lace-curtain-adorned foyer—it's fun to speculate on whether the ceiling moves up or the room moves down. (It's one way here and the opposite way at the Haunted Mansion's counterpart at Walt Disney World's Magic Kingdom park.)

Once seated in your Doom Buggy, look for the bats' eyes on the wallpaper, the tomb-sweet-tomb plaque, and the rattling suit of armor in the Corridor of Doors. Can you spot a Hidden Mickey in the haunted dining room? And keep your eyes peeled for the infamous "Hatbox Ghost" in the attic scene. Absent from the manse for decades, he's made a creepy comeback!

Then there are the dead plants, withered flowers, and broken glass in the Conservatory, where a hand reaches out of a half-open casket; the terrified cemetery watchman and his mangy mutt in the Graveyard; the ghostly teapot that pours spectral tea; the ectoplasmic king and queen on the teeter-totter; the bicycle-riding spirits; the transparent musicians; and the headless knight and his supernatural Brunhilde. Nice stuff all.

The mansion was constructed in 1963, based on the historic Evergreen House in Baltimore, Maryland; the attraction opened in 1969. The signature song "Grim Grinning Ghosts" was composed especially for the Haunted Mansion attraction.

Frontierland

PHOTO BY JILL SAFRO

This is the America experienced by the pioneers as they pushed westward: rough wilderness outposts and dense forests, and rugged mountains delineating the skyline.

The sights in Frontierland are just about as pleasant as they come in Disneyland park, and the atmosphere just as inviting.

FRONTIERLAND SHOOTIN' EXPOSITION: This rustic shooting gallery, set in an 1850s town in the Southwest Territory, is completely electronic. Eighteen rifles are trained on Boothill, a mining town complete with a bank, jail, hotel, and stables. They fire invisible infrared beams that trigger silly results whenever they strike the little red targets. The most challenging target is the moving shovel, which, when struck, causes a skeleton to pop out of a grave. There are nearly 100 targets on which to test your marksmanship.

Note: Park admission does not include use of the Frontierland Shootin' Exposition. Pay a buck for about 25 shots—then fire away. Pricing and other details are subject to change.

BIRNBAUM'S **★BEST★** **BIG THUNDER MOUNTAIN RAILROAD:** G+ Hold on to your hats and glasses, because this here's the wildest ride in the wilderness! Inspired by peaks in Utah's Bryce Canyon and Arizona's Sedona, Big Thunder Mountain is entirely a Disney creation. The name comes from an old Indian legend about a sacred mountain in Wyoming that thundered whenever anyone

tried to excavate its gold. The now classic attraction took five years of planning and two years of construction, and it cost about as much to build as the rest of the original Disneyland attractions put together.

As roller coasters go, this one is relatively tame. It's short on steep climbs and precipitous drops that put hearts in throats and make stomachs protest, but long on tight curves that provoke giggles of glee. Adding to the appeal of this thrill ride is the scenery that the runaway mine train passes along the way: a pitch-black bat cave, giant stalactites and stalagmites, a waterfall, a natural-arch bridge that affords fine views over the Big Thunder landscape, and mine walls ready to cave in.

The queue area sets the scene of the quaint mining town, with two hotels, a newspaper office, dance hall, saloon, and general store. If you listen closely, you may hear a local barmaid flirting with a miner to the tune of "Red River Valley" or "Listen to the Mockingbird."

As you approach the ride's loading area, notice the brownish stone walls on each side of you. They were made from a hundred tons of real gold ore from the former mining town of Rosamond, California, which also yielded the 10-foot-tall stamp mill designated "Big Thunder Mine 1880."

Note: Pregnant women and guests who have heart conditions, weak backs, are prone to motion sickness, or other limitations should not ride. Guests must be at least 40 inches tall to experience Big Thunder Mountain Railroad. Kids under age 7 must be accompanied by a guest age 14 or older.

PHOTO BY JILL SAFRO

MARK TWAIN RIVERBOAT: One of the original Disneyland attractions, this five-eighths-scale vessel circumnavigates Tom Sawyer Island. Along the way, it passes the River Belle Terrace, the Royal Street Veranda, piney Critter Country, a waterfall, abandoned railroad tracks, and lovely dense woods filled with alders, cottonwoods, maples, and willows that might have been found along the Missouri frontier more than a century ago. Moose, elk, and (real) ducks complete the scene. The 14-minute ride offers a pleasant respite from the crowds. And if you manage to get one of the few chairs in the bow, the *Mark Twain* also provides a rare opportunity to rest your weary feet.

GOLDEN HORSESHOE SALOON: Tongue-in-cheek humor and Western flair are the key ingredients in the acts featured at this venue. The hall itself is resplendent with chandeliers, polished floors and banisters, and a long brass railing. Walt Disney kept a private box here, just to the left of the stage, on the upper level.

Performance times vary. Check a park Tip Board, use the Disneyland app, or visit *disneyland.com* for schedules.

There is no assigned seating inside; all of the seats are good, though those up front or on the balcony are perhaps the best in the house.

SAILING SHIP COLUMBIA: A full-scale replica of the 10-gun, 3-masted "Gem of the Ocean," the *Columbia* operates seasonally and on busy days at Disneyland. The original ship, built in Plymouth, Massachusetts, in 1787 and christened the *Columbia Rediviva* ("freedom reborn"), was the first American craft to circumnavigate the globe. (Back then, that took about three years to do!)

Disney's *Columbia*, dedicated in 1958 and renovated in 1984, was the first ship of its kind to be built in more than a century. It circumnavigates the Rivers of America in 15 minutes. It has a steel hull and a deck planked with Douglas fir, and measures 110 feet from stem to stern, with an 84-foot mainmast. Usually moored at Fowler's Harbor, opposite the Haunted Mansion, the sailing ship towers majestically above the treetops of Frontierland.

Below Decks: The *Columbia's* maritime museum, found below the main deck, celebrates the dedication and sacrifice of the brave explorers who filled in the final details of the world's map. It has historical displays and re-creates the living conditions of 18th-century sailors, based on reports in the ship's log and in letters between the captain and the owners.

PIRATE'S LAIR ON TOM SAWYER ISLAND: Yes, you read that right—there has been a pirate invasion in Frontierland. Tom Sawyer Island has been transformed into a pirate-y paradise, complete with hidden treasure, creepy caves, and shipwrecks.

The only way to reach the island is by pirate-piloted raft. Once there, guests have many areas to investigate. Among them is Smuggler's Cove, which incorporates the island's beloved bridges and invites guests to man the bilge pumps in an effort to raise sunken treasure. Then there's the Castle Rock lookout point, with its spyglasses and peepholes (perfect for spying on scallywags or fellow park guests); Will Turner's Blacksmith Shop offers a glimpse at some of his works in progress; Dead Man's Grotto is a dark and labyrinthine set of caves sporting some spooky yet snazzy special effects. Purists are pleased by the preservation of Tom and Huck's Tree House. (Tom Sawyer Island is the only attraction designed by Walt Disney himself.)

Small signs point to places of interest on the island. Time spent here is worthwhile and could unexpectedly encompass some of your happiest moments in Disneyland.

Note: Tom Sawyer Island closes early to allow for Fantasmic! preparation. Check at the dock for excursion times, particularly the last raft departure of the day.

Critter Country

Lush, shady forests of pines, locusts, white birches, coastal redwoods, and evergreen elms surround Critter Country, one of the most pleasant corners of Disneyland. In 1972, this land debuted as Bear Country, the backwoods home of the since-departed Country Bear Playhouse. From 1956 through 1971, the area was called the Indian Village and was considered part of Frontierland.

In 1989, the zone welcomed foxes, frogs, geese, rabbits, crocodiles, and many of the other critters that make up the Audio-Animatronics cast of Splash Mountain. To make the furry residents feel at home, Disney Imagineers rechristened the area Critter Country. Observant guests will spot scaled-down houses, lairs, and nests tucked into hillsides and along the river.

PHOTO BY JILL SAFRO

BIRNBAUM'S ★BEST★ SPLASH MOUNTAIN: G+ The fourth peak in Disneyland's mountain range of thrill rides—along with Big Thunder Mountain, the Matterhorn, and Space Mountain— Splash is unlike the others, where passengers ride roller-coaster-style cars down tubular steel tracks. In this 9-minute ride, they board hollowed-out logs and drift on a waterborne journey through backwoods swamps and bayous, down waterfalls, and finally (here's where the speed picks up) over the top of a super-steep spillway at the peak of the mountain into a briar-laced pond five stories below.

Originally inspired by Disney's 1946 film *Song of the South*, Splash Mountain will soon celebrate Mardi Gras in jubilant fashion—thanks to a splashy new *Princess and the Frog* make-over (expected to happen soon). The theme may be new, but rest assured: the classic essence of the Splash Mountain experience shall endure.

It can be a challenge for a first-time rider to take in all the details, since the tension of waiting for the big drop is all-consuming. It's more than a tad terrifying at the top, but once back on the ground, it seems most riders just can't wait for another trip—even though they may get drenched. (Water-wary guests are sometimes seen wearing rain ponchos on this attraction. On the other hand, if you would like to get soaked, try to sit up front; seats in the back may receive a slightly smaller splash.)

PHOTO BY KEITH GROSHANS

HOT TIP

If you want to get totally soaked on Splash Mountain, sit in the front of the log; the spray has less of a dampening effect in the back. Though nobody stays dry! We highly recommend stashing electronics and other non-water-proof items in a nice dry locker or with a non-riding member of your party.

By the second or third time around, it's possible to relax a bit, enjoy the interior scenes, and take in the spectacular views of the park from the top of the mountain. At this point, you may even manage to keep your eyes open for the duration of the final fall—or at least part of it.

Splash Mountain's stars and supporting cast of about 103 mechanical performers number almost as many as those in Pirates of the Caribbean attraction, which has 119 Audio-Animatronics characters.

Comparisons to Pirates of the Caribbean are particularly apt, as Splash Mountain was designed to be a "How do we top this?" response to the popular, long-running pirate adventure. Splash Mountain broke new ground on several counts. In addition to its impressive number of Audio-Animatronics characters, it also boasts one of the world's tallest and sharpest flume drops (52½ feet at a 47-degree angle). That drop makes for one of the fastest rides ever operated at Disneyland Park.

Notes: Guests must be at least 40 inches tall to ride Splash Mountain. Kids under age 7 must be accompanied by a guest age 14 or older. Most seats are arranged single-file. If you'd like to ride side-by-side with a timid tyke, request seating in the back of the log.

DAVY CROCKETT EXPLORER CANOES: Part attraction, part workout, the Davy Crockett Explorer Canoes requires teamwork and elbow grease to make the trip around the Rivers of America. The 25-foot-long canoes hold 20 passengers at a time and they are definitely not on a track. Modeled after boats used by early Native Americans and European explorers, the canoes are powered entirely by handheld paddles. Though the helmsman and the sternman guide the rowing, guests' contributions are vital when it comes to completing the 2,400-foot voyage. Small children must wear (provided) life jackets while in a canoe.

Note: The Davy Crockett Explorer Canoes operate on select days, and it closes at dusk. Check at the landing for excursion times.

THE MANY ADVENTURES OF WINNIE THE POOH: There's a cuddly critter in town, and he goes by the name of Winnie the Pooh. In this whimsical attraction, everyone's favorite honey-lovin' cub treats Disneyland park guests to a wild and whimsical 3½-minute tour of his home turf.

The attraction features a most unlikely form of transportation: beehives. They whisk (and bounce) guests through the Hundred Acre Wood, where the weather's most blustery. The wind is really ruffling the feathers of one of the locals. It seems Owl's treehouse has been shaken loose and just may topple to the ground—and onto the beehives below.

Similar sight gags abound, from a bubble-blowing Heffalump (hey, this is Disneyland) to a treacherous flood that threatens to sweep Tigger, Piglet, and the rest of the gang away. When the Pooh bear saves the day, it's time to celebrate—and everyone is invited to the party.

Note that, like many other Fantasyland attractions, this Critter Country ride has a few scenes that take place in near darkness. Some timid youngsters may find these moments a bit unsettling. (If your kids can handle the likes of Mr. Toad's Wild Ride and Pinocchio's Daring Journey, they should be within their comfort level while in the Hundred Acre Wood.)

Fantasyland

Walt Disney called Fantasyland a timeless land of enchantment. We couldn't agree more. The skyline, dominated by the peak of the Matterhorn, bristles with chimneys and weather vanes, turrets and towers. At the center of it all, as if deposited here by an itinerant carnival, is the regal King Arthur Carrousel.

Note: Parents of young children should be aware that many of Fantasyland's attractions—while tame—have moments that take place in the dark. (In fact, they are often referred to as "dark rides.") These include Peter Pan's Flight, Mr. Toad's Wild Ride, Alice in Wonderland, Snow White's Enchanted Wish, Pinocchio's Daring Journey, and Storybook Land Canal Boats.

SLEEPING BEAUTY CASTLE: Rising above the treetops at the end of Main Street, U.S.A., it could be a figment of your imagination or a mirage created by Tinker Bell's pixie dust. Closer inspection proves this architectural confection is as real as the ducks gliding across the moat that surrounds it. A composite of medieval European castles, primarily in the French and Bavarian styles, Sleeping Beauty Castle, the gateway to Fantasyland, is constructed of concrete, with towers that rise 77 feet above the moat. Trimmed in 22-karat gold leaf, it appears shiny even on gray days. The structure seems larger than it really is due to its designers' use of forced perspective, down to the bricks.

From the Central Plaza, you're actually looking at what was originally intended to be the back of the castle; Walt Disney decided it was prettier that way and had the builders turn it around. The drawbridge, lowered when the park first opened in 1955, is like a real one—though it has been raised (and lowered again) only once since that day. The historic event took place in 1983, at the re-dedication ceremony for Fantasyland.

One of the two graceful trees to the right of the drawbridge bears hundreds of tiny yellow flowers in spring, and the other is covered with lavender flowers for several weeks in early summer.

CASTLE WALK-THROUGH: This classic Disneyland experience features additional scenes and enhanced special effects. The show, which features a series of dioramas, tells the story of *Sleeping Beauty*—including the magic of fairies Flora, Fauna, and Merryweather and the sinister spells of the evil Maleficent.

Guests enter the walk-through from the right, on the Fantasyland side of the castle. Note that it is rather dark

PHOTO BY JILL SAFRO

inside (which may spook tots) and there are some stairs to climb. Guests who are unable to do stairs or navigate the narrow passageways of the castle may experience the walk-through "virtually" in a special room on the ground floor.

FANTASY FAIRE: Once upon a time . . . in a storybook village nestled beside Sleeping Beauty Castle, folks of all ages were invited to mix and mingle with Disney characters and enjoy a live (and lively!) stage show. That time is now, and the guest list includes you. The Royal Hall and The Royal Theatre are the highlights of Fantasyland's newest neighborhood.

THE ROYAL HALL: Behind the richly detailed facade of this regal residence, you'll find a gorgeous gothic interior fit for a princess. A rotating group of royals is always on hand to greet guests. Expect favorites such as Belle, Cinderella, Snow White, and more.

THE ROYAL THEATRE: Bring your funny bone to this theatre—the antics on stage are meant to make you chuckle. The show features a madcap and original retelling of a classic and beloved Disney tale. The action recently regaled tales from *Beauty and the Beast* and *Tangled*. The theatrical yarns are presented by Mr. Smythe and Mr. Jones, Renaissance bards with vastly vaudevillian vigor, and a multitasking cast. It's fun for the whole family. Tales change periodically. Shows typically last about 22 minutes. The Royal Swing Big Band Ball may be offered on select evenings.

PIXIE HOLLOW: Where do Disney fairies live? In Pixie Hollow! Disneyland guests may enter the world of Tinker Bell and her friends. As guests walk along the garden path, they feel as though they are shrinking down to fairy size as the landscape gets larger and larger. This miniature realm is extra sparkly on summer nights, when it glows with the "magic" of pixie dust. You will find it between Sleeping Beauty Castle and the entrance to Tomorrowland.

SNOW WHITE WISHING WELL & GROTTO: Tucked off Matterhorn Way, at the eastern end of the moat around

Sleeping Beauty Castle, this is one of those quiet corners of the park easily overlooked by some guests. (Though not everyone, as it is a popular spot to "pop the question.") If you stand by the wishing well, you might hear Adriana Caselotti, the original voice of Snow White, singing the lovely melody "I'm Wishing," written for Walt Disney's Oscar-winning 1937 film.

F.Y.I.: Coins tossed into the well go to children's charities—so your wish will help fulfill other wishes.

BIRNBAUM'S ★BEST★ PETER PAN'S FLIGHT: "Come on, everybody, here we go! Off to Never Land!" This attraction is one of the park's loveliest—and consistently one of the most popular. Based on the story by Sir James M. Barrie about a boy with an immunity to maturity and an affinity for flying—by way of Disney's 1953 animated feature—the ride's effects soar to celestial heights. Pirate ships embark from the Darling kids' nursery and carry travelers through the clouds and into a starry sky.

Water ripples and gleams softly in the moonlight; the lava on the sides of a volcano glows with an intensity that mimics the real thing. After an ephemeral few minutes, the ships drift back into reality, an unloading area that is all the more jarring after the magic of the trip through Never Land.

Of the approximately 350 miles of fiber optics throughout Fantasyland, the majority is used in this attraction. The twinkling London scene is actually an enlarged model of an authentic map of the city.

Peter Pan's Flight is atop the popularity list with guests of all ages and usually has a line consistent with its status. Head here first thing in the morning, or late in the day (after little ones have gone to bed).

BIRNBAUM'S ★BEST★ MR. TOAD'S WILD RIDE: Based on the 1949 Disney animated film *The Adventures of Ichabod and Mr. Toad*—which was inspired by Kenneth Grahame's novel *The Wind in the Willows*—this simple, zany attraction is housed in an English manor bristling with ornate chimneys that really smoke. The wild, low-tech ride is experienced from the perspective of the eccentric but lovable Mr. Toad.

Of course, he is as inept a driver as you'd expect a toad to be. During the excursion, you crash through the fireplace in his library, burst through a wall full of windows, careen through the countryside, charge headlong into a warehouse full of TNT, lurch through the streets of London, then ram into a pub and veer out again. During the 2-minute journey, you'll also be berated by

DID YOU KNOW?

There is a shadow of Sherlock Holmes (complete with pipe and cap) in the second-story window of the Constabulatory building inside the Mr. Toad's Wild Ride attraction.

a judge in court, nearly collide head-on with a railroad train, and be banished to a fiery inferno (Yes, you read that right.) Some effects may be too intense for tots.

ALICE IN WONDERLAND: This Fantasyland staple has been revamped and revitalized. It features a new Alice figure, animated flowers, and a rolling hedgehog. It is Alice in *Wonderland*, after all.

Traveling in oversize caterpillars, visitors fall down the rabbit hole and embark upon a bizarre adventure in that strange world known as Wonderland. They come face-to-face with Tweedledum and Tweedledee, a garden filled with singing roses, the Cheshire Cat, the Queen of Hearts and her playing-card soldiers, the White Rabbit, and other characters from Lewis Carroll's beloved story *Alice's Adventures in Wonderland*.

At the conclusion of the nearly four-minute journey, a giant un-birthday cake explodes (thanks to a dynamite "candle"), providing a suitable finish to this sweet and surreal interlude. It's understandably popular with the under-age-7 demographic.

MAD TEA PARTY: The sequence in Walt Disney's 1951 release *Alice in Wonderland* in which the Mad Hatter hosts a tea party for his "un-birthday" is the theme for this ride—a group of colorful oversize teacups whirling wildly on a spinning tea table. Festive Japanese lanterns hang overhead. One of the park's original attractions, this dizzying ride lasts only 1½ minutes—but it may feel a bit longer!

Note: The teacups may look mild, but it's a good idea to let a reasonable interval pass after eating before you take one for a spin.

BIRNBAUM'S ★BEST★ MATTERHORN BOBSLEDS: G+ Though it's 100 times smaller than the actual peak, Disney's version of the Matterhorn is still a credible reproduction. The use of forced perspective makes the snowy summit look

much loftier than the approximately 147 feet it does reach. Even the trees and shrubbery contribute to the illusion. Those at the timberline are far smaller than the ones at the bottom.

The ride itself, like the Space Mountain and Big Thunder Mountain Railroad attractions, has to be counted among the most thrilling at Disneyland. At the time the Matterhorn Bobsleds were dedicated, in 1959, they were considered an engineering novelty because their dispatch system allowed more than one car to be in action at once. The ride was also the world's first tubular steel roller coaster. This classic is also considered Disney's first thrill ride. The old favorite has enhanced snowcaps, lighting, and visual effects.

The somewhat jolting adventure begins with a climb into the frosty innards of the mountain, then makes a speeding, twisting, turning descent through a cloud of fog and past giant icicles and ice crystals. The wind howls as you hurtle toward a brief encounter with the Abominable Snowman (take note of the effects!). The speed of the downhill flight away from the creature seems greater than it really is because much of the journey takes place inside tunnels. Splash-down is in an alpine lake.

Note: Pregnant women and guests who suffer from weak backs (the seats are hard and the ride is bumpy), heart conditions, motion sickness, or other physical limitations should not take the ride. Guests must be at least 42 inches tall. Children under age seven must be accompanied by an adult.

PHOTO BY JILL SAFRO

STORYBOOK LAND CANAL BOATS: This 7-minute cruise through Monstro the Whale and past miniature scenes from Disney's animated films is not one of Disneyland's major attractions, yet few who take the trip would deny that the journey is one of the park's sweetest. No detail was spared, from the homes of the Three Little Pigs, to the Old English village of Alice in Wonderland (where the White Rabbit boasts his very own mailbox), to the London park that Peter Pan and Tinker Bell flew over with Wendy, John, and Michael Darling on their journey to Never Land.

Other storybook locales include the marketplace where Aladdin met Princess Jasmine, the Seven Dwarfs' home and jewel mine, and Cinderella's castle. At the end of the cruise, the boat drifts past Geppetto's village, Prince Eric and Ariel's castle, King Triton's castle—and *Frozen's* Kingdom of Arendelle.

IT'S A SMALL WORLD: **G+** The background music for this attraction is cheerful and singsong, sometimes maddeningly so. It does grab your attention, starting with the cheery facade, embellished with stylized representations of the Eiffel Tower, the Leaning Tower of Pisa, Big Ben, the Taj Mahal, and other landmarks. The 30-foot-tall clock with the loud ticktock and the syncopated swing is frosting on the architectural cake. The whirring of gears that marks every quarter hour alone warrants a trip to the attraction's plaza.

Boats carry guests into a land filled with more than 300 Audio-Animatronics dolls representing children (and popular Disney characters) from 100 regions of the world. It's a pageant for the eyes, even if the ears grow weary. (If you find yourself humming "It's a Small World" for the next several hours, you can blame Richard M. and Robert B. Sherman, the Academy Award–winning composers of the music for *Mary Poppins,* among many other renowned Disney scores.)

Topiary (sculpted shrub) figures in the shapes of a giraffe, elephant, rhinoceros, lion, horse, and other friendly beasts bid guests farewell at ride's end.

Note that It's a Small World is transformed inside and out between Thanksgiving and New Year's to become as close to a winter wonderland as you're likely to find in Southern California. The dolls even sing "Jingle Bells" along with "It's a Small World."

PHOTO BY MIKE CARROLL

CASEY JR. CIRCUS TRAIN: One of the key sequences in the film *Dumbo*, in which an engine named Casey Jr. pulls a circus train up a steep hill, became the inspiration for this 3½-minute train ride that circles Storybook Land. The Storybook Land Canal Boats are better for viewing the landscaping and miniature details there, but it's worth a ride inside one of the wild-animal cage cars. Each train has two of them—plus a real caboose. Listen as the engine chugs, "I think I can" and then, "I thought I could" as it negotiates the hill.

DUMBO THE FLYING ELEPHANT: As beloved a symbol of Fantasyland as Sleeping Beauty Castle, this attraction reminds all who see it of the baby elephant immortalized in Disney's 1941 feature film. In it, Dumbo discovers that his large ears actually enable him to fly. A mechanical marvel, Dumbo the Flying Elephant is full of filigreed metalwork, with a system of cogs, gears, and pulleys. Brass pipes spew water from the base, and music is supplied by a vintage band organ housed in a small, ornate structure nearby. That tiny figure atop the ride is Dumbo's trusty sidekick, Timothy Mouse.

PHOTO BY JILL SAFRO

SNOW WHITE'S ENCHANTED WISH: As guests enter this classic attraction, they gaze upon the pages of a storybook. It sets the stage for what's to come: "Once upon a time, a lovely princess named Snow White had a wish"—and it warns that the cruel Queen aims to thwart Snow's wish for happiness. It's a rather ominous start to a primarily pleasant adventure.

The two-minute journey begins with a visit to the Seven Dwarfs' unkempt cottage, where they're enjoying a dance party with Snow White (that's Grumpy playing the pipe organ!). From there, the story takes a very brief but dark tone, as the ride vehicle whisks through the dark Enchanted Forest and past the dreaded Queen—who is clearly up to no good. The mood quickly lightens as Dopey, Doc, and their diminutive comrades head off to work. Heigh-ho, heigh ho, it's off to the diamond mine everyone goes.

After passing through that brief-but-happy scene, ride vehicles visit a darkened chamber where the evil Queen engages with her magic mirror and morphs into a wicked witch before your very eyes. She's next seen laboring over a bubbling cauldron, perfecting the poison apple into which Snow White promptly bites. A mirror shatters! A storm hits the Forest! And then, *poof*—it all ends in true storybook fashion: Snow White awakens, and with her Prince and their seven sidekicks, is set to live happily ever after. Her wish has come true.

Note: While dark moments in this attraction can be too intense for some children, recent enhancements make the adventure a little less scary.

PINOCCHIO'S DARING JOURNEY: Based on Disney's 1940 animated feature, this is a 3-minute morality play of sorts, with Jiminy Cricket serving as host and guide. Pinocchio, who is the creation of the toymaker Geppetto, pays a somewhat scary visit to Pleasure Island and soon discovers the right way to live.

As the ride vehicles move from the cheerful land of popcorn and Ferris wheels to the seamy world of Tobacco Road, Pleasure Island hues are replaced by drab shades of brown and gray. Here, little boys are turned into donkeys and sold to work in the salt mines.

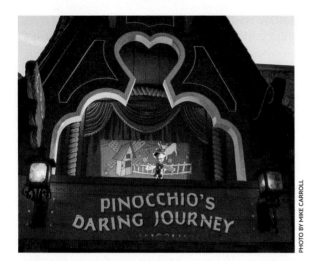

PHOTO BY MIKE CARROLL

Pinocchio escapes that fate, nearly becomes supper for Monstro the Whale, and winds up back home in the care of his dad, Geppetto—another happily-ever-after ending. The final scene, in which the Blue Fairy turns into a cloud of sparkles and then disappears, leaving a smattering of sparkly pixie dust on the floor, is partially accomplished via fiber optics.

KING ARTHUR CARROUSEL: Guests come upon this graceful park landmark as they stroll toward the Sleeping Beauty Castle passageway into Fantasyland. One of the few attractions in the park that is an original rather than a Disney adaptation, the carrousel contains 68 horses—all movable, as Walt Disney wished. Carved in Germany over a century ago, no two are alike, and they are as pampered as the live Belgian horses on Main Street, U.S.A. The ornamentation on them is gold, silver, and copper leaf. The nine hand-painted panels on top of the carrousel's main face tell the story of Princess Aurora, aka Sleeping Beauty.

PHOTO BY JILL SAFRO

HOT TIP

Select a member of your party to serve as the Lightning Lane coordinator—someone who will keep an eye on the clock so you don't miss a Genie+ return window or Individual Attraction Selection.

LIGHTNING LANE ATTRACTIONS

Long lines got you down? Not to worry—many major Disneyland attractions offer Lightning Lane Access (fees apply). The Disneyland park attractions listed here may change and Lightning Lane service may not be offered at all times during the year.

Lightning Lanes may be accessed two ways: by using Genie+ and by the à la carte method known as Individual Lightning Lane Access (which carries its own fee and is limited to two attractions per guest, per day).

The following attractions fall into the Genie+ category (one daily fee covers them all, except for Star Wars: Rise of the Resistance. At press time, Rise was designated as an "Individual Purchase" attraction and comes with a separate fee (it's not included with Genie+). For more about the Lightning Lane attraction access system, see page 22 and visit *disneyland.com*. Details are subject to change.

ADVENTURELAND
• Indiana Jones Adventure

CRITTER COUNTRY
• Splash Mountain

FANTASYLAND
• Matterhorn Bobsleds • It's a Small World

FRONTIERLAND
• Big Thunder Mountain Railroad

MICKEY'S TOONTOWN
• Roger Rabbit's Car Toon Spin

NEW ORLEANS SQUARE
• Haunted Mansion

TOMORROWLAND
• Space Mountain • Autopia
• Star Tours—The Adventures Continue
• Buzz Lightyear Astro Blasters

STAR WARS: GALAXY'S EDGE
• *Millennium Falcon:* Smugglers Run
• Star Wars: Rise of the Resistance (available for Individual Lightning Lane purchase)

Mickey's Toontown

Disneyland lore tells us that when Mickey Mouse burst onto the movie scene in 1928 in *Steamboat Willie*, the first synchronized-sound cartoon, his success was so great that his busy schedule demanded he practically live at the Walt Disney Studios. Thirty cartoons later, in the early 1930s, he was one tired mouse, so he moved into a quiet residence in a "toon only" community south of Hollywood. Over the years, many toon stars gravitated to Mickey's Toontown, as it quickly became known. Minnie Mouse, Pluto, Goofy, Roger Rabbit, Chip, Dale, and Gadget have all lived here, and Donald Duck docks his boat, the *Miss Daisy*, on Toon Lake.

One afternoon, while Mickey Mouse and his close friend Walt Disney were relaxing on Mickey's front porch, Walt revealed his idea for a theme park that would appeal to "youngsters of all ages." Mickey suggested that he build it next to the secret entrance to Toontown, and the rest is history. Disneyland opened to the public in 1955, but little did anyone realize as they were drifting through It's a Small World that they were actually right next door to Mickey's Toontown.

In the 1990s, Mickey and his friends decided to open up their neighborhood to non-toons, and, in preparation, all of Toontown received a new coat of ink and paint. The grand opening took place in January 1993.

Legend aside, the development of Toontown was a real challenge: to create a three-dimensional cartoon environment without a single straight line. Yet, as topsy-turvy as it is, Mickey's Toontown is a complete community, with a downtown area, including a commercial zone, a suburban neighborhood (home to everyone's favorite mice), and CenTOONial Park. The best part is that everything is meant to be touched, climbed, and jumped on. Children do just that, while adults relish the attention to detail and the assortment of sight gags. All guests are welcome to relax under a majestic tree in the park, which is just one of the enhancements to enjoy as this cheery place emerges from a year of "re-imagination." Yep, Disney Imagineers have been hard at work and this happy place has been thoroughly refreshed. The bulk of the transformation took place last year, with finishing touches expected to wrap up in early 2023. (All details are subject to change.)

When the pixie dust is settled, this booming toon-tropolis will feature several attractions—including the addition of Mickey & Minnie's Runaway Railway (see page 78), plus opportunities to dine, shop, and play.

Guests enter this colorful zone by walking under the Toontown train depot. You never know just what to expect once inside—but it's all bound to be goofy!

CENTOONIAL PARK: As guests cross the border from Fantasyland to Mickey's Toontown, they enter a sprawling nature-inspired zone dubbed CenTOONial Park. This grassy space is a great place for families to play, relax, and unplug. In the heart of the park stands an interactive fountain that pays tribute to Toontown's most famous residents: Mickey and Minnie! The fountain does double duty as the land's central icon and a focal point for fun. In addition to the usual fountain-y features, this spot sports several interactive water tables. Guests of all ages are encouraged to splish and splash till their hearts' content. At night, this special spray spot comes to life in a "unique spectacle" of color and light.

NEW

Another landmark of note is the majestic "Dreaming Tree." It was inspired by the tree that Walt Disney used to dream under when he was a kid. Toontown's leafy homage to Walt's original tree supplies shade, inspiration, plus a plethora of places for kids to crawl, climb, explore, and—of course—dream.

ROGER RABBIT'S CAR TOON SPIN: `G+` This chaotic, rollicking ride combines the technology of the Mad Tea Party teacups and the tracks of Fantasyland attractions, such as Mr. Toad's Wild Ride. In it, Benny the Cab, Jessica Rabbit, and Roger Rabbit embark on a dizzying chase, which takes guests through the back alleys of the toon

HOT TIP

Mickey's Toontown usually closes about an hour before the pyrotechnics begin on evenings when Disneyland park presents a fireworks show.

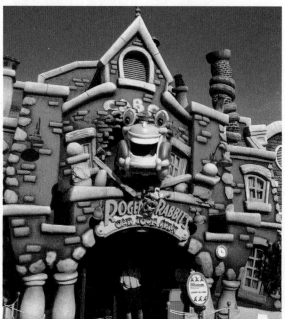

PHOTO BY JILL SAFRO

underworld made famous in the classic feature film *Who Framed Roger Rabbit.*

It seems Jessica Rabbit, who is now a private eye, is on a mission to thwart the evil weasels (while avoiding the dreaded DIP!) and she takes you along for the ride. During the 3-minute adventure, expect to crash into Bullina's China Shop, slide through the Power House, and spin wildly into the Gag Warehouse storage area, where the Weasels are waiting to take aim at your cab.

This "hare-raising" attraction is fun for all ages, but it does have some dark moments that may spook timid tots. Note that the ride vehicles can spin a full 360 degrees as they travel along the track. If the whirling teacups over in Fantasyland make your head spin (or worse), you should probably sit this one out. And please don't eat just before climbing aboard Benny.

MINNIE'S HOUSE: It's hard to miss Minnie Mouse's humble abode. This lavender-and-pink creation has a sweetheart theme for the sweetheart inside. Here, guests can peek at Minnie's living room with its chintz sofa and sophisticated magazines (*Cosmousepolitan* and *Mademousele*) on the coffee table.

There are messages from Goofy and Mickey on the answering machine in the hallway. Guests are invited to create new fashions for Minnie on the computer in her dressing room.

In Minnie's kitchen, a cake in the oven rises when a knob is turned, pots and pans clank out a melody when the stove is switched on, and the dishwasher churns after green door, and green shutters is home to the toon who started it all. Not only is Mickey's face on the mailbox out front, but his welcome mat is in the instantly recognizable shape of three circles—his head and ears.

In the living room stands a player piano and a curio cabinet filled with all manner of memorabilia, including Mickey's baby shoes and a picture of him with his friend Walt Disney, as well as some of Pluto's favorite treasures—a bone and a half-eaten shoe. In the laundry room, the washing machine chugs merrily away, and laundry supplies, such as Comics Cleanser and Mouse 'n' Glo, are at the ready.

a button is pushed. Her Cheesemore refrigerator is stocked with an assortment of dairy products, including Golly Cheeze Whiz, and the shopping list left on the outside of the fridge hints at this mouse's cheeses of choice. Be sure to check out the cookies on Minnie's kitchen table (and be prepared for a sweet practical joke, courtesy of Ms. Mouse).

As you leave Minnie's House, you'll pass the wishing well in her yard. Don't think you're imagining things: It's been known to share a few parting thoughts. Details are subject to change.

MICKEY'S HOUSE: A short path leads from Minnie's backyard to the front door of Mickey's House. The welcoming yellow dwelling with a tile roof, huge

RE-IMAGINATION STATION

Expect lots of swell surprises when Mickey's Toontown re-opens its toon-y gates in early 2023. In addition to the brand-new, kinetic fun fest known as Mickey & Minnie's Runaway Railway and the updated Roger Rabbit's Car Toon Spin (Jessica Rabbit is a detective now!), this bustling burgh invites you to enjoy newly re-imagined versions of the following classic Toontown attractions: Gadget's Go Coaster, Goofy's Playhouse, and Donald's Boat (aka the *Miss Daisy*). For additional info and updates, use the Disneyland app, or visit *disneyland.com*.

PHOTO BY JILL SAFRO

From here, make your way through the greenhouse and into Mickey's backyard, where you may catch a glimpse of Pluto's doghouse and a vegetable garden with mysteriously disappearing carrots. Details are subject to change.

BIRNBAUM'S ★BEST★ MICKEY & MINNIE'S RUNAWAY RAILWAY: Enter a wild and wacky cartoon realm via Mickey & Minnie's Runaway Railway—a fanciful, family-friendly attraction that's on track to chug its way into Mickey's Toontown in early 2023

NEW

(though it could arrive a bit later). Housed inside a spiffy new theater, the "2.5-D" (no glasses required) adventure begins with the premiere of a new cartoon that guests watch in the pre-show area. In it, Mickey and Minnie are preparing for a picnic. When a train driven by Goofy pulls up beside them, it's all aboard for everyone! Thanks to a bit of movie magic, guests are invited to step into the action and enter the zany, unpredictable world of a Mickey Mouse Cartoon Short. The train zigs and zags through nine scenes, while a happy tune underscores the jolly journey. ("Nothing Can Stop Us Now" is a gift that keeps on giving—you will be humming the optimistic earworm long after the ride ends).

In addition to dozens (possibly hundreds?) of Hidden Mickeys, this delightful experience features a bounty of Easter eggs for eagle-eyed Disney fans—including the number 1928 (the year our dear friend Mickey Mouse entered the world).

Mickey & Minnie's Runaway Railway is suitable—and enjoyable—for guests of all ages. The experience can be a tad herky-jerky (especially when the ride vehicle weathers a cyclone). Folks with back or neck issues may want to skip the trip. For updates on this sure-to-be blockbuster's debut (it's wildly popular at Walt Disney World, where it premiered in similar form in 2020), use the Disneyland app or visit *disneyland.com*. Details are subject to change.

Tomorrowland

PHOTO BY JILL SAFRO

When Walt Disney was alive, the future seemed simple: We would all dress in Mylar and travel in flying saucers. The Tomorrowland he created in the '50s was set in the distant year of 1987, part Buck Rogers and part World's Fair. The current incarnation of Tomorrowland retains that spirit and is based on a classic vision of the future, one that looks at it from the perspective of the past. The result is an innocent and hopeful place—imagine, for instance, a planet that renews itself. Visit Tomorrowland today, and you enter a realm more in keeping with the rest of Disneyland than with the sterile, less positive future world often depicted on television and in the movies.

Cross the bridge into this sleek land and enter a visually engaging terrain, where the palette of colors is not otherworldly, but still forward-thinking. Futuristic boulders and dreamlike architecture coexist with apple, orange, lemon, and pomegranate trees that line pathways created from gray, mauve, and burgundy bricks. This landscape aims to fire up the intellect as well as the imagination.

Galileo Galilei, Leonardo da Vinci, Jules Verne, H.G. Wells, and Walt Disney would have felt right at home here. Aldous Huxley probably wouldn't have. Several of Tomorrowland's attractions are also located at Walt Disney World in Florida: Space Mountain, Star Tours—The Adventures Continue, Astro Orbitor, and Buzz Lightyear Astro Blasters (known in Walt Disney World as Buzz Lightyear's Space Ranger Spin). Other classic Tomorrowland attractions include the Finding Nemo Submarine Voyage, the Disneyland Monorail, and Autopia.

A replica of the Moonliner, a Tomorrowland icon from 1955 to 1966, sits on the site of its predecessor. Monorail trains glide to and from the Downtown Disney District, while traditional Disneyland Railroad trains chug their way into the Tomorrowland station, a vibrant reminder that the past is indeed prologue. (The Disneyland Railroad has stations at Main Street, U.S.A., New Orleans Square, and Mickey's Toontown, too).

Attractions described on the following pages were operating at press time, but specifics are subject to change. Check *disneyland.com* for updates.

PHOTO BY JILL SAFRO

ASTRO ORBITOR: Towering high above the entrance to Tomorrowland, this big whirligig with spinning orbs and speeding starships is a fitting symbol for Tomorrowland. Astro Orbitor, modeled on a drawing made by Leonardo da Vinci almost six centuries ago, is the successor to the Rocket Jets, which gave Disneyland guests a lift for 30 years. Each ride vehicle accommodates two passengers (or two adults and one small child), who can maneuver it up and down while spinning clockwise for 1½ minutes, reveling in sweeping views of Tomorrowland, (Main Street's) Central Plaza, the Matterhorn, and Sleeping Beauty Castle.

Note: The minimum age to ride Astro Orbitor is one year. Children under the age of 7 are required to be in the company of an adult.

BIRNBAUM'S ★BEST★ BUZZ LIGHTYEAR ASTRO BLASTERS:

G+ The evil Emperor Zurg is up to no good—and it's up to that Space Ranger extraordinaire Buzz Lightyear and his Junior Space Rangers (that means you) to save the day.

So goes the story line of Tomorrowland's video game–inspired spin through the toy universe. The adventure is experienced from a toy's point of view. Guests begin their 4½-minute tour of duty as Space Rangers at Star Command Action Center. This is where Buzz gives his team a briefing on the mission that lies ahead. Then it's off to the Launch Bay to board the ride vehicles. The ships feature dual laser cannons, glowing lights, and a piloting joystick.

In addition to Buzz and the evil Emperor, you may recognize some other toy faces swirling about—the little

HOT TIP

To maximize your scoring potential at Buzz Lightyear's Astro Blasters, aim for targets that are lit up, moving, or far away. They tend to reward you with the most points.

green, multi-eyed alien toys, best known for their awe of "the claw." The Little Green Men have been enlisted to help in the fight against Zurg.

Once Junior Space Rangers blast off, they find themselves surrounded by Zurg's robots, who are mercilessly ripping batteries from toys. As Rangers fire at targets, beams of light fill the air. For every target hit, you will be rewarded with sight gags, sound effects, and points. The points, which are tallied automatically, are accumulated throughout the journey. Although the vehicles follow a rigid "flight" path (they're on a track), the joystick allows riders to maneuver the ships, arcing from side to side or spinning in circles while taking aim at their surroundings.

PHOTO BY JILL SAFRO

When the star cruiser arrives at Zurg's spaceship, it's showdown time. Will good ultimately prevail over evil? Or has time run out for the toy universe? And will you score enough points to be a Galactic Hero? (Most folks improve their scores with a little practice.)

BIRNBAUM'S ★BEST★ STAR TOURS—THE ADVENTURES

CONTINUE: G+ Inspired by George Lucas's beloved blockbuster series of Star Wars films, this is one of the most enjoyable attractions in Tomorrowland. It offers guests the opportunity to ride on droid-piloted StarSpeeders—the exact same type of flight simulator used by military and commercial airlines to train pilots—and explore the galaxy in a bumpy 3-D adventure. The action here takes place throughout the time period covered by the major Star Wars movies. The best part? There are dozens of different adventures to experience here—multiple visits will likely yield multiple surprises.

This is a rather turbulent trip—seat belts are definitely required. Passengers must be free of back problems, heart conditions, motion sickness, and other physical limitations to ride. Guests under 40 inches tall may not ride. Pregnant women must skip this one. Make sure young children understand the significance of wearing 3-D glasses (and keeping them on) before you board the attraction—it's a concept lost on most tots. Battle scenes and sudden appearances by Star Wars villains have been known to spook little ones.

STAR WARS LAUNCH BAY: Star Wars Launch Bay offers an immersive atmosphere in which to experience both the Light and Dark sides. Housed in the space formerly occupied by Innoventions, Launch Bay features props, videos, and movie memorabilia celebrating Star Wars and the recently reawakened Force. In addition to Light and Dark galleries, guests may meet characters such as everyone's favorite Wookiee, Chewbacca and that menacing Sith Lord, Darth Vader. Details are subject to change at any time. Use the Disneyland app, or check *disneyland.com* for updates.

BIRNBAUM'S
★BEST★ **SPACE MOUNTAIN:** G+ When Space Mountain first opened in 1977, it quickly rocketed to the top of just about everyone's list of favorite attractions—where it remains to this day. While the classic facade and essence of the thrilling attraction remain intact, the experience is decidedly 21st century. Brave voyagers blast off from a realistic

launch port. Once they've shot through a disorienting tunnel, riders may have a close encounter with a meteorite. After that, it's all about screeching through the inky darkness, past spinning stars and whirling galaxies. Add to that an edgy soundtrack (which is impressively synchronized to each ride vehicle), and you have got one out-of-this-world attraction.

If your courage fails you, just ask an attendant to direct you to the nearest escape route (aka "the chicken exit"). Space Mountain is an astronomically popular attraction—get there early and take advantage of Disney's Lightning Lane service if budget allows.

Note: Pregnant women and guests who have weak backs or necks, heart conditions, motion sickness, or any other physical limitations must sit this one out. Kids under age 7 must be accompanied by an adult. Guests must be at least 40 inches tall to experience Space Mountain.

F.Y.I.: *Mercury 9* and *Gemini 5* astronaut Gordon Cooper worked with Disney Imagineers to create Space Mountain. He wanted to give guests a realistic feeling of actual space flight. Mission accomplished!

AUTOPIA: G+ The only attraction remaining from the original Tomorrowland, Autopia was dubbed "The Freeway of the Future" back in 1955. Kids have always loved guiding the small sports cars around the twisting roadways (for them, a top speed of seven miles per hour is thrilling). The Tomorrowland and Fantasyland roadways now comprise a single attraction (yes, there were two Autopias; the one in Fantasyland opened in 1959 to accommodate spillover crowds). Guests travel in restyled race cars through 21st-century terrain, experiencing a series of happy roadside surprises along the way. Featuring a real working gas pedal and steering wheel, each car can seat 2 adults or 3 children and navigates curves and inclines just like the real thing. Don't let the lack of a brake pedal scare you—to slow down or stop the car, simply ease off the accelerator. This attraction is quite popular with those who've not yet reached Driver's Ed age.

Notes: Guests must be at least 54 inches tall to drive solo. Folks who are at least 32 inches tall are also permitted to drive, as long as they are accompanied by someone who is at least 54 inches tall. Kids under age 7 must be accompanied by someone at least 14 years of age. Pregnant women; guests with heart, back, or neck problems; and those sensitive to motion should not ride. Intentionally bumping the vehicle in front of you is not allowed.

PHOTO BY MIKE CARROLL

DISNEYLAND MONORAIL: Who doesn't love the monorail? The first daily operating monorail in the Western Hemisphere was a novelty when it was introduced at Disneyland in 1959. Today, it's still a thrill to watch them glide through the park. The sleek, Mark VII trains were designed to evoke images of their 1959 predecessors. Straddling a concrete beamway, the monorail has rubber tires—which enable it to glide quietly—as well as braking wheels atop the concrete beam and guiding and stabilizing wheels on either side.

The 2½-mile-long "highway in the sky" is a distinctive and integral part of Tomorrowland. The electrically powered ride takes guests around the periphery of Tomorrowland, over to Downtown Disney and its diverting activities, and then back to Tomorrowland.

For a special experience, inform the cast member on the boarding ramp that you'd like to sit up front in the pilot's cabin. It can usually accommodate up to five passengers. If all the seats are taken, you can always wait for the next monorail and try your luck again.

By boarding the monorail in Tomorrowland, you are actually leaving Disneyland Park. If you get off at the Downtown Disney station, be sure to retain your valid park ticket. You will need to show it (and photo ID) to reboard the monorail or pass through Disneyland Park's turnstiles. Know that walking back to the park is an option—as Disneyland is about a 5-minute stroll from the Downtown Disney monorail station.

FINDING NEMO SUBMARINE VOYAGE: Uh-oh. It seems that curious little clownfish has wandered off again. And this time he's done so in Tomorrowland's submarine lagoon. The good news is the subs that used to take guests to the North Pole now provide the perfect means for monitoring the fin-challenged fish and his high-spirited underwater hi-jinks.

The submarine adventure begins as a quiet expedition to observe an undersea volcano. But faster than you can say, "All drains lead to the ocean," our frisky friends from *Finding Nemo* start floating and fluttering in front of a personal porthole. The whole gang's here, including Nemo's overprotective dad, Marlin; the faithful-if-forgetful royal blue tang, Dory; that totally awesome turtle dude, Crush; and more. They're on a quest to catch up with their buddy Nemo, and you're invited along for the slightly frenetic, completely kinetic undersea search. Oh, and remember that volcano you were going to observe? It erupts.

Will you survive the sub-shaking volcanic quaking and find Nemo? Yep. They don't call this "the happiest place on earth" for nothing.

This under-water experience is appropriate for guests of all ages, provided they're claustrophobia-free. Several moments may be too intense for some tots.

HOT TIP

A trip on the monorail yields lovely views of Disney California Adventure park and its neighbor, the Grand Californian Hotel & Spa. However, it does not stop at either place. It's strictly a Tomorrowland Express!

Star Wars: Galaxy's Edge

There's a wondrous new adventure zone in the heart of Disneyland Park—Star Wars: Galaxy's Edge! The new land is set on the planet Batuu, a remote outpost on the far reaches of the galaxy. As the story goes, Batuu was once a busy crossroads along the old sub-light-speed trade routes. Now, thanks to the rise of hyperspace travel, Batuu has pretty much fallen off the radar. It's far from deserted, however. In fact, the largest settlement on the planet, Black Spire Outpost, has become quite the haven for folks who prefer to fly under the radar: smugglers, rogue traders, and space-traveling adventurers. It's also an excellent destination for anyone trying to avoid the First Order.

The land is accessed via pathways connected with Fantasyland, Critter Country, and Frontierland. There are two major attractions here—*Millennium Falcon*: Smugglers Run and Star Wars: Rise of the Resistance. Each invites guests to live out their own Star Wars adventures.

BIRNBAUM'S **★BEST★** **MILLENNIUM FALCON: SMUGGLERS RUN:** Are you eager to jump into hyperspace on the "fastest hunk of junk in the galaxy"? Here's your chance to fly in Han Solo's beloved bucket of bolts, the *Millennium Falcon!*

It seems Hondo (from the animated shows *Star Wars: The Clone Wars* and *Star Wars Rebels*) is now running a "legitimate business" out of a spaceport and he needs extra flight crews to make some runs for him—provided they don't ask too many questions, of course. That's where you come in.

Before entering the cockpit of the legendary starship, you and five fellow crew members are assigned a role. There are three roles (pilot, gunner, and engineer) and one goal: complete the mission without banging up the ship. At the end of the thrilling (and bumpy) flight, your crew will receive a point total—and a few choice words from Hondo himself.

Guests must be at least 38 inches tall to ride this attraction and should be free of motion sickness and any other health issues. Expectant mothers are advised to skip *Millennium Falcon*: Smugglers Run.

BIRNBAUM'S **★BEST★** **STAR WARS: RISE OF THE RESISTANCE:** What happens when Star Wars heroes and villains end up on the same planet? A *massive* battle breaks out!

In one of the most ambitious adventures ever produced by Walt Disney Imagineering, this immersive attraction places you in the middle of an epic battle between the First Order and the Resistance—including a face-off with the infamous Kylo Ren.

The journey takes guests aboard a full-size transport shuttle and a Star Destroyer. It's a thrilling and harrowing adventure—and not for the faint of heart. To ride, guests should be free of health issues (including, but not limited to, pregnancy and motion sickness), and at least 40 inches tall.

Notes: At press time, Rise of the Resistance was a Lightning Lane/Individual Attraction Selection (aka à la carte) attraction. As such, it has a traditional standby line to ride (included with the price of admission) and offers an expedited wait time for a fee (purchased through the Disneyland mobile app). For details, use the app or visit *disneyland.com,* and refer to page 22.

From time to time, access to Star Wars: Rise of the Resistance may require joining a virtual queue. Guests are encouraged to check the Disneyland app on the day of their visit for attraction access status.

Shopping

Until you get to know Disneyland park, you might not expect that anyone would visit just to go shopping. But among Southern Californians, it's definitely a top draw for the Disney-themed merchandise and gift items. Mickey Mouse paraphernalia, such as key chains, mugs, T-shirts, ear hats, and other such souvenirs, is found here in abundance, of course, but there are some surprises, such as character-inspired costumes for youngsters, mobile phone accessories and items for the office, plus upscale items, such as art collectibles, jewelry, products for the home, and custom-made lightsabers.

MAIN STREET, U.S.A.

CANDY PALACE: An old-fashioned pageant in pink and white, this shop is alluring at any time of day, but never more than when the candy-makers are at work in the glass-walled kitchen confecting candy canes, chocolate-covered strawberries, caramel apples, toffee, fudge, and other sweet temptations for anyone with a sweet tooth. The products made on the premises are available for purchase, along with a veritable bounty of chocolates, licorice, taffy, and other tasty treats.

CHINA CLOSET: If you're in the market for kitchenware, mugs, figurines, picture frames, snow globes, or Christmas ornaments, this is the place to go.

CRYSTAL ARTS: Glasses and pitchers, frames, trays, and other mementos can be engraved (for a fee) and monogrammed while you wait, or you can get them unornamented. The shop also sells glass miniatures, bells, and paperweights.

DISNEYANA: Serious collectors and the simply curious alike will discover rare and unusual Disney merchandise here, such as limited-edition art and hand-painted cels inspired by Disney animated classics. Popular pieces have included sculptures from the Walt Disney Classics Collection. This amusing shop is in the Bank of Main Street building, next to the Main Street Opera House.

Note: Disney sketch artists often drop by the shop to sign reproduction artwork, sculptures, or recently published books.

DISNEY CLOTHIERS, LTD.: Disney character merchandise has always been popular, but if you want something a little more stylish, this is where to find it. The spot caters to fashion-conscious shoppers with a love for Disney-themed gear. Almost every item in the selection of men's, women's, and children's clothing and accessories sold here incorporates Mickey and Minnie in some way.

DISNEY SHOWCASE: Specializing in the latest seasonal merchandise (Disney style), this shop also offers hats, shirts, home decor items, park logo merchandise, and assorted souvenirs. Personalization is offered (for a fee).

EMPORIUM: Much like an old-time variety store, this large and bustling shop offers an incredible assortment of wares, and it is home to Disneyland logo selections. Decorative figurines, mugs, home decor, clothing, plush toys, character hats, jewelry, and a variety of souvenirs make up the bulk of the stock.

PHOTO BY JILL SAFRO

PHOTO BY JILL SAFRO

FORTUOSITY SHOP: Merchandise in all shapes and sizes, including trendy fashions and accessories like Mickey Mouse watches and character-laden novelty clocks, beckons from this unique emporium.

MAD HATTER: This hat shop stocks Mickey Mouse ear hats in black and various colors and designs. You can even get your name stitched on the back.

MAIN STREET MAGIC SHOP: Small but well stocked with gags and tricks—and books about how to pull them off—this shop has the wherewithal to inspire budding illusionists. In the market for an invisible pooch? A magic wand? An ice cube with a bug in it? This corner store has it all.

MARKET HOUSE: This Disneyland version of an old-fashioned general store is actually a cleverly themed Starbucks coffee shop. Stop here for fresh-brewed coffee and specialty drinks, plus cookies, cake pops, sandwiches, salads, savory snacks, and much more.

NEW CENTURY JEWELRY: Among the delicate offerings here are 14-karat-gold charms of Tinker Bell, Donald Duck, and Minnie Mouse. The marcasite character jewelry is subtle and somewhat sophisticated.

NEWSSTAND: While no actual news is offered here (No news is good news, right?), this modest stand stocks a small selection of Disney-themed souvenir items.

PLAZA POINT HOLIDAY SHOPPE: A Victorian-era emporium, Plaza Point is holiday central all year long. Festooned with garlands and festive decor, the space celebrates a host of holidays, including (but not limited to): Hanukkah, Lunar New Year, Easter, Halloween, and Christmas. Stop in to discover ornaments, housewares, linens, and accessories—all with a holiday theme.

NEW

PENNY ARCADE: Adjacent to the Gibson Girl Ice Cream Parlor is a virtual Coney Island of food and fun. Freshly made treats fill ornate shelves, and scrumptious salt-water taffy is available in an array of flavors. To add to the classic carnival atmosphere, old-fashioned arcade games that still cost just a penny to play and a Welte Orchestrion line the walls. And for 25 cents, you can have beloved fortune-teller Esmeralda predict your future.

SILHOUETTE STUDIO: Working at the rate of about 60 seconds per portrait, Disneyland's silhouette artists truly are a wonder to behold. Individual and group portraits are available. The Silhouette Studio was on pause at press time, but is expected to return.

PHOTO BY JILL SAFRO

20TH CENTURY MUSIC COMPANY: This little place carries a selection of collector pins and pin lanyards, plus books, classic Disney music, and DVDs.

NEW ORLEANS SQUARE

CRISTAL D'ORLEANS: Glasses and chandeliers, decanters, tiaras, glass slippers, pitchers, and paperweights are typical treasures here. Engraving (and some monogramming) is available for a fee.

GET YOUR EARS DONE HERE

Since Disneyland first opened in 1955, there has been no more coveted souvenir than a pair of Mickey Mouse ears personalized with the lucky owner's name. And never have there been more styles from which to choose. Most hats can be embroidered (for a nominal fee) at both locations of the Mad Hatter (in Fantasyland and on Main Street, U.S.A.), and other select locations. Shops will not embroider company names on hats. (Note that it's possible to get ear hats at World of Disney in the Downtown Disney District and at a shop in Disney California Adventure park, too.)

LE BAT EN ROUGE: Looking to cross a few Disney-themed items off your shopping list? You have come to the right place. Some of the merchandise may have a New Orleans flair, too. Expect clothing, jewelry, and other accessories.

LA MASCARADE D'ORLEANS: A compact and brightly lit showcase for PANDORA products, this shop has a variety of its signature items: necklaces, earrings, rings, and charm bracelets—many with a Disney theme. In fact, some items are Disney Parks exclusives.

MLLE. ANTOINETTE'S PARFUMERIE: This pleasantly fragrant boutique carries classic and chic fragrances for men and women. The parfumerie "blends the essence of French-style elegance with American-style spontaneity." It's in the heart of New Orleans Square.

PIECES OF EIGHT: Wares with a pirate theme are purveyed at this shop beside the Pirates of the Caribbean exit. You will also discover T-shirts, key chains, glasses, and other souvenir items imprinted with the Pirates of the Caribbean logo. In the market for a pirate sword? Look no further. And, for the right price, you may be able to fill a bag with colorful pirate booty. *Arrrrrrrrrrrr!*

PORT ROYAL CURIOS AND CURIOSITIES: Ready to give your treasured Mickey Mouse T-shirt a day off? Stop at this boutique to augment your Disney-oriented closet. Expect to find an assortment of merchandise featuring the nearby Haunted Mansion attraction: shirts, hats, and more. Also on hand: a selection of items with a *Tim Burton's The Nightmare Before Christmas* theme (coffee mugs, bags, dolls, dresses, T-shirts, hats, etc.).

PORTRAIT ARTISTS: Sit for a portrait—done in pastel or watercolor—amidst the quaint charm of a New Orleans *rue* (street). Individual and group portraits are offered. Prices vary.

FRONTIERLAND

BONANZA OUTFITTERS: Oozing rustic ambience, this cozy yet quaint shop offers traditional frontier-wear with a trendy twist. Look for cowboy hats and coonskin caps. They sell a variety of collector pins and Disney-themed merchandise, too.

PIONEER MERCANTILE: Inspired by the paraphernalia of the pioneer period in American history, this shop is home to a vast array of Disneyland merchandise. Expect to find plush toys, shirts, books, bags, towels, and more. There's a large selection of headwear, too. Have a quarter handy? Drop it in the shop's classic Ho-Down machine and watch Woody dance!

WESTWARD HO TRADING COMPANY: This rustic store stocks something for the whole pin-trading frontier family, including pins, lanyards, and other pin-collecting accoutrements. We dig the antler light fixtures—Gaston would likely approve.

CRITTER COUNTRY

THE BRIAR PATCH: Near Splash Mountain, this shop offers hats, toys, character merchandise, and other items.

POOH CORNER: This *hunny* of a spot is home to a candy kitchen filled with sweet treats. Lining its many shelves are other Disneyland logo merchandise and items with a Winnie the Pooh theme. Pooh's pals from the Hundred Acre Wood are also represented. All kinds of Pooh products await, including plush toys, watches, infants' apparel, children's clothing, sleep shirts, and slippers. There is also a sumptuous selection of freshly baked cookies and chocolates.

STAR WARS: GALAXY'S EDGE

BLACK SPIRE OUTFITTERS: Guests who wish to blend in on Batuu can suit up at this boutique. Costumes representing the light and dark side of the Force are available for guests of all ages.

CREATURE STALL: Stop here to adopt an other-worldly pet. Creatures from which to choose include tentacle-beast rathtars, cooing baby tauntauns, tongue-lashing worrt frogs, and growling puffer pigs.

DOK-ONDAR'S DEN OF ANTIQUITIES: The mysterious Dok-Ondar has stuffed this shop with everything from jewelry and ancient tools to rare kyber crystals, statues, and high-end lightsabers.

DROID DEPOT: If you have ever dreamed of owning your own droid, dream no more: Mubo has miniature droids waiting for you to customize. There are two basic models: an R (like R2-D2 or R5-D4) or a BB unit (the ball-droid style similar to BB-8 and the evil BB-9E). Once you choose all your droid pieces, you can piece them together in the assembly area. Then head to the chip station to select a personality circuit. Last but not least, bring your droid to life at the activation center.

SAVI'S WORKSHOP—HANDBUILT LIGHTSABERS: The First Order would not allow the manufacture of lightsabers—so Savi took that task underground. Head here to build your own high-end lightsaber. Colors include Sith red, Jedi blue and green, and Mace Windu purple. Choose wisely.

TOYDARIAN TOYMAKER: Visit this street market to peruse a variety of hand-crafted toys and other playthings crafted by local artisans.

ADVENTURELAND

ADVENTURELAND BAZAAR: The plush and hand-carved jungle animals corralled here include lions, tigers, and hippos. You may also find rain sticks, drums, collector pins, Indiana Jones™ items, and California-themed apparel.

FANTASYLAND

BIBBIDI BOBBIDI BOUTIQUE: Nestled inside Sleeping Beauty Castle, this boutique offers young guests (ages 3 through 12) the chance to be transformed into "little princesses" and princely "cool knights." Makeovers were on pause at press time, but are expected to return. For updates and to make reservations, use the Disneyland Resort app, visit *disneyland.com*, or call 714-781-7895.

Among the wares available for purchase are sparkly crowns, swords, and regal costumes that dazzle the eyes of many a young royal.

DISNEY'S PHOTOPASS

As you wander the parks, Disney cast members are happy to snap your picture (with your camera and/or theirs). After mugging for their camera, you will get a PhotoPass card. It'll link all such photos together for viewing online. You can ogle the low-res images for free (with watermarks) or purchase favorites for up to 45 days after they are taken. Disney's Genie+ service includes unlimited downloads of photos taken on any given day (see page 22 and go to *disneyland.com* for details). Another option is a Photopass+ One Day Package. It includes the whole day's worth of Disney photographer-snapped shots, plus select attraction and dining photos. High-quality prints, plus mugs, shirts, and other items are for sale. To buy or just peruse, use the Disneyland app, or visit *disneyland.com*. It's definitely a splurge, but we think PhotoPass is an excellent way to get images of your whole party.

Note that PhotoPass is included with the purchase of Disney Genie+ Lightning Lane Service. For details, use visit *disneyland.com*, use the Disneyland mobile app, and turn to page 22.

FAIRYTALE TREASURES: Conveniently situated next to the Royal Theatre, this spot is all princesses all the time: Elena of Avalor, Elsa of Arendelle, and more.

IT'S A SMALL WORLD TOY SHOP: A small, whimsical open-air structure near It's a Small World is stocked with Disney-themed toys, dolls, pins, and plush items featuring Disney characters and the It's a Small World attraction (of course!).

LE PETIT CHALET GIFTS: Designed to look like a little bit of Switzerland and as cozy as a warm cup of cocoa on a winter evening, this spot is the repository of traditional Disneyland gifts and souvenirs. Included in the wares are coloring books, autograph books, head-bands, and a variety of hats—many of which can be personalized on the spot (for a fee). The small Swiss shop is situated near the base of the Matterhorn, along the park's parade route. Handy!

MAD HATTER: Always a great place for hats and plush character caps—and Mouse ears, of course (they will embroider them for you for a small fee). The selection of novelty headgear always includes a few surprises.

PIN TRADING, DISNEY STYLE

It's one of the biggest—and most enduring—collectible crazes to sweep through Disney's land—pin trading! These small enamel pins can be purchased through-out Disneyland Resort property, but buying them is only half the fun. The real joy comes when you encounter another pin trader with a worthy swap. To get a head start, bring some Disney pins from home (*shopdisney.com* carries pins, too). Once on-property, keep an eye out for cast members sporting a good selection of pins—they tend to be agreeable to almost any trade. And when negotiating a trade with a cast member, always remember the rules: (1) Only Disney pins may be traded, and (2) Every trade must be an even pin-for-pin exchange.

MERLIN'S MARVELOUS MISCELLANY: A stone's throw from the Disneyland's Sword in the Stone (by King Arthur Carrousel), this whimsically appointed shop has shelves lined with Disney-themed merch: shirts, bags, notebooks, cups, and collectibles, among other things.

NEW

STROMBOLI'S WAGON: Located near Red Rose Taverne, this stand offers a wagonful of wares—everything from plush toys to sunglasses. Some of the items available include key chains, pens, buttons, popcorn, and candy. The shop is named after one of the villains from Disney's 1940 classic, *Pinocchio.*

TOMORROWLAND

AUTOPIA WINNER'S CIRCLE: Racing enthusiasts will enjoy the Autopia-inspired souvenirs and toys offered at this small shop. Soft drinks are sold, too.

LITTLE GREEN MEN STORE COMMAND: Sharp traders know they can find an astronomical assortment of pins and collectibles at this spot. Disneyland's commanding pin destination, the store offers pins, lanyards, and pin-trading accessories, plus souvenirs and toys featuring Disney/Pixar characters.

THE SPIRIT OF REFRESHMENT: There's a red-and-white rocket perched on a 12-foot pedestal near Alien Pizza Planet! Head there to score a fizzy soft drink and admire the two-third's scale, 53-foot high replica of Disneyland's original Moonliner rocket. The Moonliner was part of a futuristic exhibit that opened with Disneyland Park in 1955. A fine mist cools guests in the warm weeks of summer.

THE STAR TRADER: The Star Trader is the repository of everything from T-shirts and jewelry to novelty head-wear, mugs, key chains, candy, and more—many emblazoned with the likenesses of Disney pals and characters from the Star Wars universe.

Entertainment

Disneyland is famous for festive, live entertainment. What follows is typical of the variety that is traditionally available. However, details are subject to change and some offerings may be temporarily suspended, modified, or replaced. For updates, check a park tip board, the Disneyland app, or *disneyland.com*.

PERFORMANCES & LIVE SHOWS

Performers stroll, march, croon, and pluck their way through Disneyland every day—so frequently that all you usually have to do to find them is follow your ears.

MAIN STREET, U.S.A.

ATMOSPHERE BANDS: Look and listen for the musical groups that perform near the Fire House and Sleeping Beauty Castle on select days.

DAPPER DANS OF DISNEYLAND: The official greeters of Main Street, U.S.A., this classic barbershop quartet performs standards in perfect four-part harmony. The colorfully clad performers may be found strolling on the sidewalk, planted by a storefront, or whizzing by on a trolley or a bicycle built for four.

DISNEYLAND BAND: A presence in the park since opening day in 1955, Disneyland's signature musical group specializes in turn-of-the-century band music and Disney tunes, but it can play just about anything. The band performs inside the main entrance when the park opens, in Town Square (at the South end of Main Street), and at other locations.

The Disneyland Band's first performance of the day often takes place in front of the train station, just inside the turnstiles. It's an interactive and magical way to start the day. Kids of all ages simply love it.

FLAG RETREAT: The flag at Town Square is lowered just before sunset each day (times vary). The ceremony is often highlighted by a performance by the Disneyland Band or the Dapper Dans. The band has been known to perform several rousing marches per show. On the band's day off, the Dapper Dans perform a capella renditions of American classics. "The Star-Spangled Banner" makes for a stirring finale. (We always get choked up during this touching ceremony.) It's a rewarding experience that captures the essence of what Walt Disney hoped guests would feel as they experienced Main Street, U.S.A. It's usually presented daily.

MAIN STREET PIANO PLAYER: Piano players are often on hand to tickle the ivories on the snow-white upright piano at the Corner Cafe. Presented daily.

NEW ORLEANS SQUARE

THE BOOTSTRAPPERS: Yo, ho! Yo, ho! A Pirate Band for you! These musical buccaneers wander about New Orleans Square and perform on Tom Sawyer Island.

JAMBALAYA JAZZ: This group plays down-home New Orleans jazz with plenty of soul. Fetch yourself a mint julep (sans alcohol) or a bowl of gumbo, and let the music wash over you like the mighty Mississippi.

ROYAL STREET BACHELORS: Their style is early traditional jazz and blues, with a mellow four-beat sound similar to that once commonly heard in the Storyville section of the Crescent City. The Bachelors can be found performing throughout the Square.

FRONTIERLAND

THE GOLDEN HORSESHOE: Dishing up a "rootin', tootin' good time," this place never takes itself—or its guests—too seriously. The entertainment varies, but it always pairs nicely with the frontier-style grub offered at the counter for lunch and dinner (think fish and chips, chicken tenders, mozzarella sticks, and more). Seating (bar or tables) is on a first-come, first-served basis.

SHOWDOWN AT THE GOLDEN HORSESHOE!: Yee-ha! Dueling piano players challenge one another in a good ol' fashioned showdown. They take turns playing familiar ditties of the Old West and even take requests from the audience. Think you can stump them? Mosey on over to the Golden Horseshoe saloon to give it your best shot. Shows take place throughout the day.

PARADES

No Main Street is complete without a peppy parade, and Disneyland's Main Street is no exception. The usual route runs between Town Square and the promenade in front of It's a Small World—or vice versa. The direction and route can vary, so it's wise to ask at the Information Center at City Hall or the Central Plaza Tip Board. The park traditionally offers an afternoon and an evening parade. For parade updates, visit *disneyland.com*.

 MAIN STREET ELECTRICAL PARADE: Whether you're experiencing the Main street Electrical Parade for the first time or for the first time in 20 years, we guarantee you'll be back for more. This enchanting classic, which made its Disneyland debut in 1972, is back (for a limited time) in all of its sparkling glory. Cue applause!

A mesmerizing mix of shimmering lights (more than half a million of them!) and merry music, the processional features nearly two dozen illuminated floats, plus scores of performers—including beloved Disney character friends. As visually stunning as this show is, it's the delightful score that makes it a truly unforgettable show. The "electro-synthe-magnetic musical sound" of Baroque Hoedown brings a smile to all faces, young and young-at-heart.

 MAGIC HAPPENS PARADE: New to Disneyland, this peach of a pageant celebrates Disney's tradition of magic-making—the awe-inspiring moments at the heart of its storytelling. The daytime spectacular features stunning floats, elaborate costumes and, of course, Disney characters. Look for favorites such as Mickey, Minnie, Goofy, Pluto, Chip and Dale, Anna and Elsa, Moana, Maui, Miguel and Dante, folks from *Peter Pan, The Princess and the Frog, Cinderella, Aladdin,* and *Pinocchio,* to name a few. The inspirational processional—which usually wends its way through the park in the afternoon—was "on pause" at press time. For updates, use the Disneyland mobile app, or visit *disneyland.com*.

WHERE TO WATCH THE PARADES: Some of the best points from which to watch a parade are the platform of the Disneyland Railroad's Main Street depot, Town Square near the flagpole, and the curb on either side of Main Street, U.S.A. If you'd like to avoid crowds, any viewing location other than Main Street may be better for you.

Two other options are the terrace outside the Plaza Inn (but be aware that seating is limited) and the tables in the courtyard of the Carnation Café, where the view may be partially obstructed.

You can also stand on either side of the promenade area in front of It's a Small World whose facade provides a whimsical, only-at-Disneyland backdrop. Wherever you decide to station yourself for the parade, plan to arrive about 30 to 45 minutes early to claim your piece of parade-viewing real estate.

MICKEY'S MIX MAGIC

Everybody get your ears on—and get ready to dance! This rollicking street party is a high-energy celebration of Mickey, Minnie, and the magic of Disney. In it, Mickey Mouse serves as deejay, spinning house-mix versions of classic Disney tunes, while electrifying projections, lights, and lasers wash over Sleeping Beauty Castle, most of Main Street, U.S.A., and the facade of It's a Small World. (Mickey's rockin' playlist includes "I Wanna Be Like You," "Ev'rybody Wants To Be A Cat," "Friend Like Me," "Grim Grinning Ghosts," "Un Poco Loco," and "Let It Go.") An extra pinch of pixie dust—in the form of fireworks— is added on select nights. At press time, this 10-minute nighttime fan-favorite was in the midst of a limited run. Will it be presented during your visit to Disneyland park? Visit *disneyland.com* to find out.

FIREWORKS

BIRNBAUM'S ★BEST★ DISNEYLAND FOREVER FIREWORKS SPECTACULAR: Disneyland Forever is an impressive, nostalgic fireworks extravaganza. The 14-minute spectacle dazzles guests with a combination of pyrotechnics, lights, a stirring soundtrack, and clever special effects projected onto and high above Disneyland park icons.

First presented to mark Disneyland park's sixtieth anniversary, the recently enhanced show takes guests on a wondrous celebration of Disney magic, imagination, and animation. The fan favorite is presented on select nights throughout the year. It features Tinker Bell's flight, Nemo's swim, and appearances by favorite Disney characters thanks to some nifty projection technology. The show's stellar soundtrack features the exit song "A Kiss Goodnight," written by Disney Legend Richard M. Sherman. Check a park Tip Board or the Disneyland app for the schedule. The show is back for a limited engagement and may be replaced at any time. Will it be presented during your visit to the park? Use the Disneyland app or visit *disneyland.com* to find out.

A longtime Disneyland tradition, specially themed fireworks presentations take place throughout the year. Patriotic pyrotechnics fill the sky on the Fourth of July, while a special, spooky spectacular is presented during the Halloween season, and the December holidays feature Believe . . . in Holiday Magic.

Where to Watch: The best area is about midway down Main Street, U.S.A., near Refreshment Corner up to the Castle hub area, but the area near It's a Small World and waterfront in New Orleans Square afford excellent views, too.

Note: The fireworks spectacular is usually presented on select nights. The show may be modified or canceled due to inclement weather, including high winds. All details are subject to change at any time.

Glow with the Show: "Made with Magic" accessories such as MagicBand+ wristbands let guests be part of Disneyland Resort's nighttime spectaculars. Other light-up accessories have included glowing mouse ear hats, Mickey Mouse gloves, and magic wands.

SPECIAL OCCASIONS

Along with plenty of special events in the parks and hotels year-round (some of which require special admission tickets), Disneyland park celebrates three major seasons each year: summer (including the Fourth of July holiday), Halloween (September through October), and the winter holidays (mid-November through early January).

SUMMER: While plenty of folks are on vacation, Disney offers a satisfying slate of atmosphere entertainment and spectaculars from Memorial Day to Labor Day. Expect longer wait times at attractions, and consider using Lightning Lane access if budget allows. (For details about Disney's fee-based, expedited wait time system, see page 22, and use the Disneyland app). Past summers have seen a patriotic, pyrotechnic tribute to the U.S.A. on Independence Day in a rousing (and wildly popular) celebration known as Disney's Celebrate America! A Fourth of July Concert in the Sky.

HALLOWEEN: Halloween Time at the Disneyland Resort brings a palette of fall colors, festively carved pumpkins, Disney characters dressed in Halloween costumes, and trick-or-treat touches, along with an extra-spooky Haunted Mansion transformation inspired by *Tim Burton's The Nightmare Before Christmas* and a spirited fireworks display dubbed Halloween Screams.

WINTER HOLIDAYS: This jolly period generally stretches from November through the first week of January, when the entire park glows with holiday themes. (We've witnessed Yuletide holiday decorations in place as early as October.) Expect the park to be festooned with holiday decor and perhaps even the occasional snow flurry (which is known to make Olaf very happy). The Disneyland Resort officially begins to celebrate the holidays in November, when the merriest attraction on Earth—It's a Small World Holiday—returns for the season.

It's a Small World Holiday celebrates Yuletide customs around the world. The singing Small World dolls add "Jingle Bells" to their repertoire in numerous languages,

and the big clock on the attraction's whimsical facade dons a Santa Claus hat.

Main Street, U.S.A., is decked out in traditional red and green, including hundreds of poinsettias and a huge Christmas tree that's surrounded by oversize holiday packages. Highlights include the chance to meet the man in the red suit, Santa himself. Sleeping Beauty Castle gets in on the fun: Each evening during the holiday season, guests watch the castle transform into a shining, icicle-adorned spectacle. As the snow falls and music fills the air, Sleeping Beauty's Winter Castle glimmers with thousands of twinkling lights, illuminated in stages. On select December nights, a candlelight processional ending at Town Square takes place. Special music is provided by a large choir, and a holiday story is read by a well-known entertainer. **A Christmas Fantasy Parade**, a Disney holiday favorite, takes place throughout the holiday season. The extra-merry, 40-minute processional traditionally includes favorite Disney pals, dancing gingerbread cookies, toy soldiers, colorful floats, and Santa Claus. (Note that all parades at Disneyland Park are dependent on weather conditions and are subject to change or cancellation.) **Believe . . . In Holiday Magic** is Disneyland's festive fireworks show. Set to seasonal music, the 15-minute pyrotechnic spectacular takes place above and around Sleeping Beauty Castle, with excellent vantage points on Main Street, U.S.A., and throughout the park.

Live entertainment and a truly dazzling fireworks show on **New Year's Eve** (no special ticket required) provide a grand finale for this happy holiday season.

For details about seasonal happenings in the park, use the Disneyland Resort app or visit *disneyland.com.*

WHERE TO FIND THE CHARACTERS

Look for Disney characters in Town Square on Main Street, U.S.A. throughout the day. Tinker Bell and her friends may appear at Pixie Hollow. Princesses hold court at Fantasy Faire in Fantasyland, just off Main Street. Winnie the Pooh and his pals are known to congregate in Critter Country. Tiana may appear on or near the *Mark Twain* riverboat. Aladdin and Jasmine have been seen mingling near Snow White's Wishing Well (near the castle) and the Fantasy Faire courtyard. Friends and foes interact with travelers on Batuu (aka Star Wars: Galaxy's Edge).

Cast members at park Tip Boards can help you locate characters, as can *disneyland.com.* This book's *Good Meals, Great Times* chapter explains where to dine with character friends. Another excellent source for character appearance updates and schedules? The Disneyland Resort app. Details are subject to change.

BIRNBAUM'S ★BEST★ Welcome back, Fantasmic! After a 2-year hiatus, the beloved Disneyland nighttime spectacular is once again lighting up the Rivers of America in dramatic, high-tech fashion. The classic show features cutting-edge projection technology and many character-laden scenes (including one in which Aladdin and Jasmine float on a magic carpet while "A Whole New World" fills the air).

An amalgam of music, magic, special effects, and live performances, Fantasmic! is a fan favorite. The show, which lasts about 20 minutes, lights up the Rivers of America on weekends, holidays, and throughout the summer. More than 50 performers put on an unforgettable show in a dazzling display of pyrotechnics, giant props, video, and light.

Fantasmic! is a good vs. evil tale, and it is up to Mickey Mouse to overcome an array of villains. Draped in his red sorcerer's robe, Mickey first appears at the tip of Tom Sawyer Island and uses his imagination to make comets shoot across the sky while the river waters dance about. He materializes in a cone of light, and a shower of sparks dramatically shoots from his fingertips.

Top-notch technology makes Fantasmic! all the more impressive. Mickey works his magic and a film sequence appears in midair, above the Rivers of America. The effect is achieved by projecting digital images onto giant screens of seemingly magical mist.

The illusions build toward a confrontation of good and evil in which Disney villains attempt to disrupt Mickey's wondrous fantasy. Fearsome creatures all have an opportunity,

including an ominous, animated Maleficent, who morphs into a towering, animated, fire-breathing dragon. Villains turn Mickey's dreams into nightmares, and he must overcome them with his own powers of goodness—with a little help from his friends. The Sailing Ship *Columbia* glides through the show with the swashbuckling cast of Peter Pan on board, and the *Mark Twain* riverboat brings along a host of Disney friends.

Where to Watch: The best spots are in front of the Pirates of the Caribbean (be sure you can see the water and have a view of Tom Sawyer Island). Get there early. (Late arrivals can sometimes find a place to watch near the Haunted Mansion, in New Orleans Square.)

If you decide to splurge—and it's offered during your planned visit to the park—consider a Fantasmic! Dining Package. It includes lunch or dinner at a Disneyland eatery and space in a reserved viewing area for Fantasmic! The cost starts at about $50–$75 per adult, $30–$45 per child (ages 3 to 9). Tax and gratuity are extra. For details and to make reservations, visit *disneyland.com*, or call 714-781-3463 (between 8 A.M. and 9 P.M. Pacific Standard Time). We recommend booking exactly 60 days before your desired dining date. For updates and additional information, use the Disneyland mobile app, or visit *disneyland.disney.go .com/dining/disneyland/fantasmic-dinner-packages*.

Notes: Fantasmic! may be performed twice nightly during the summer. If so, the later presentation is usually a bit less crowded. The special effects are quite realistic, and may be too intense for some tots. Details are subject to change.

HOT TIPS

🐭 Tuesday, Wednesday, and Thursday tend to be the least crowded days to visit year-round. If you must come on a weekend, choose Sunday over Saturday.

🐭 Measure your kids before your Disneyland visit so you will know in advance which attractions they may be too short to ride. This can help avoid disappointment later on.

🐭 Wear comfortable shoes. Blisters are the most common malady reported to First Aid.

🐭 Main Street, U.S.A., may open a bit before the rest of the park (usually when Disneyland opens at 9 or 10 A.M.). Take advantage of this to grab a quick snack, shop, or say hello to some Disney characters.

🐭 Avoid attractions such as Star Tours, *Millennium Falcon:* Smugglers Run, Star Wars: Rise of the Resistance, Splash Mountain, the Matterhorn Bobsleds, and the Mad Tea Party immediately after meals (for obvious reasons).

🐭 Check the daily entertainment offerings at one of the park's Tip Boards or by using the Disneyland mobile app and plan your day accordingly.

🐭 Wait times are posted at Disneyland attractions themselves, and on the Information Board at the north end of Main Street, U.S.A. (on the Adventureland side of the street), and on the Disneyland app. The times are updated frequently.

🐭 An attraction may reach its Lightning Lane limit before the end of the day, especially if the park is packed. Be sure to book any must-do early if you don't want to wait in the standby line. Note that fees apply for Disney's Lightning Lane Service. For details, see page 22 and visit *disneyland.com.*

🐭 During busy afternoon hours, go to lower-key attractions, where the waits may be shorter. The afternoon is also prime time for shopping, enjoying an outdoor performance, watching a parade, taking in a show at the Golden Horseshoe, or watching the daily Flag Retreat on Main Street, U.S.A.

🐭 Try to enjoy lunch before 11:30 A.M. or after 2 P.M., and dinner before 5 P.M. or after 8 P.M. to avoid long register lines (which may be shorter toward the left of fast-food counters).

🐭 Try to visit the major attractions—*Millennium Falcon:* Smugglers Run, Star Wars: Rise of the Resistance, Space Mountain, Star Tours, the Indiana Jones Adventure, Big Thunder Mountain Railroad, Finding Nemo Submarine Voyage, Haunted Mansion, the Matterhorn Bobsleds, and Splash Mountain—early or during parades. The lines are often shorter during those periods.

🐭 If you're traveling alone or willing to split up your party, know that Indiana Jones Adventure, Space Mountain, Matterhorn Bobsleds, *Millennium Falcon:* Smugglers Run, and Splash Mountain usually offer Single Rider lines—potentially much shorter than the standby lines.

🐭 For a change of pace food-wise, head over to Downtown Disney District or to one of the hotels on property. They have something for almost every budget and taste—from simple to sublime, ravioli to rack of lamb—as well as buffet meals with popular Disney characters (at the Disneyland resorts only).

🐭 The monorail transports guests from Tomorrowland to the Disneyland Hotel end of Downtown Disney. All guests must disembark, but it's okay to reboard if you'd like to complete the round-trip journey. Keep your park ticket handy—you'll need it to get back on to Disney's "highway in the sky."

🐭 Main Street shops are a good place to escape the midday heat, but try to steer clear of them at the end of the park's operating hours, when they tend to be the most crowded.

🐭 For most attractions, if you're in line up to one minute before the park's closing time, you'll be allowed on. It's a good tactic for popular attractions such as Space Mountain, Peter Pan's Flight, and the Indiana Jones Adventure.

🐭 Avoid the crowds by returning your stroller (and getting your deposit back) before the evening's fireworks presentation comes to an end.

🐭 Break up your time in the park (unless you have only one day). Arrive early, see major attractions until things get busy, return to your hotel for a swim or a nap, then go back to the park. Remember, you must present your valid ticket to re-enter Disneyland Park later in the day.

DISNEY CALIFORNIA ADVENTURE

Fame, fortune, and fun in the sun have lured adventurous spirits to California for centuries. But now visitors have an alternative way to enjoy the glories of the Golden State: through Disney's eyes. In February 2001, The Walt Disney Company officially unveiled its new California Adventure theme park—and it was a work in progress for quite some time. To that end, an ambitious, billion-dollar expansion is complete. Fresh themes and attractions joined the landscape, while some veteran rides and lands were "re-imagined," with new shows and attractions forever on the horizon. The result? A theme park adventure to impress even the most devoted Disneyland Park devotees.

Disney California Adventure sits snugly in the heart of the Disneyland Resort, sharing an entrance esplanade with Disneyland, neighboring Downtown Disney District, and the Disney hotels. But once you set foot inside the park, you're in a world all its own. Regions blend into each other, and no matter where you stand, you are sure to see (or hear whoops and hollers coming from) one of the park's eye-catching icons—Guardians of the Galaxy—Mission: BREAKOUT!, WEB SLINGERS: A Spider-Man Adventure, the majestic Sierra-inspired Grizzly Peak mountain, Pixar Pier's Incredicoaster, and the wildly popular Radiator Springs Racers.

With a small vineyard, several upscale restaurants, scream- and smile-inducing thrill rides, and attractions tailored for every member of the family, the 66-acre theme park has something for everyone to enjoy. California, here we come!

HOLLYWOOD LAND
1. Disney Animation
2. Hyperion Theatre
3. Monsters, Inc.—Mike and Sulley to the Rescue!
4. Disney Junior Dance Party!
5. Mickey's PhilharMagic

GRIZZLY PEAK
6. Soarin' Around the World
7. Grizzly River Run
8. Redwood Creek Challenge Trail

PARADISE GARDENS PARK
9. The Little Mermaid—Ariel's Undersea Adventure
10. Golden Zephyr
11. Jumpin' Jellyfish
12. Goofy's Sky School
13. Silly Symphony Swings
14. World of Color

PIXAR PIER
15. Incredicoaster
16. Pixar Pal-A-Round
17. Toy Story Midway Mania!

18. Jessie's Critter Carousel
19. *Inside Out* Emotional Whirlwind

CARS LAND
20. Luigi's Rollickin' Roadsters
21. Mater's Junkyard Jamboree
22. Radiator Springs Racers

AVENGERS CAMPUS
23. Guardians of the Galaxy—Mission: BREAKOUT!
24. WEB SLINGERS: A Spider-Man Adventure

Getting Oriented

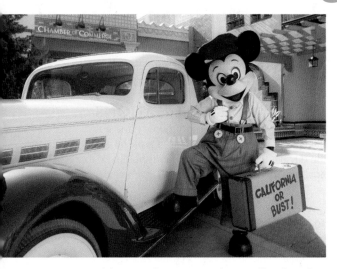

Disney California Adventure is a bit smaller than the nearby Disneyland Park, so most guests have little trouble covering all of it on foot—as long as they wear comfy walking shoes.

The main entrance area is known as Buena Vista Street. East of Buena Vista Street lies Hollywood Land. It's a mock studio backlot where guests can, among other things, say hello to Anna and Elsa, enjoy the lighthearted Monsters, Inc.—Mike and Sulley to the Rescue!, and see Mickey's PhilharMagic.

West of Buena Vista Street is Grizzly Peak, home of the popular Soarin' Around the World attraction and a drenching, white-water rapids ride known as Grizzly River Run. Pacific Wharf is a district dedicated to the cultures, industries, and natural beauty that shaped California, complete with a well-stocked winery.

Pixar Pier (originally known as Paradise Pier) and Paradise Gardens Park have nostalgic rides with a modern twist, located around a lagoon. (If you want to minimize the wait for Toy Story Midway Mania!, get there early.) The World of Color light show takes place right on the local lagoon. The show is best viewed from the Paradise Gardens Park side of the water.

HOT TIP

Attraction wait times and performance schedules may be tracked via in-park Tip Boards and by using the Disneyland app. Temporary closures, if any, will be listed there, too. This info comes in very handy while navigating through the parks.

The new Avengers Campus brings big thrills with WEB SLINGERS: A Spider-Man Adventure and Guardians of the Galaxy—Mission: BREAKOUT!

Finally, the impressively immersive Cars Land offers guests the opportunity to experience all the thrills of a trip to Radiator Springs. That's where to experience Mater's Junkyard Jamboree, Luigi's Rollickin' Roadsters, and the park's extraordinarily popular Radiator Springs Racers.

Guests may park vehicles in either the six-level Mickey and Friends parking structure or the Toy Story parking lot on Harbor Boulevard, which can be accessed from the I-5 freeway.

Parking Fees: Guests arriving in passenger vehicles pay about $30 to park. (The fee for vans and buses is $35; for trucks and buses with extended trailers, $40.) Preferred parking starts at $45. You may leave during the day and return later the same day at no extra fee. Hold on to your parking stub as proof of payment.

Lost Cars: Even if you take careful note of where you parked your car, you might have trouble remembering or recognizing the exact spot when you return hours later. Hundreds more vehicles will likely be parked around yours. If this happens, tell a Disney cast member approximately when you arrived. With that information, parking lot personnel can usually help narrow down a car's general location.

GETTING AROUND

You'll have to depend a lot on your feet—other than the Red Car Trolley ride, there is no transportation in this theme park.

Guests staying at Disney's Grand Californian hotel have their own exclusive entrance into Disney California Adventure park. (This entrance is exclusively reserved for guests of the Grand Californian. A valid hotel key card must be presented to use the private turnstiles.) Guests of Disney's Paradise Pier Hotel will soon have their own entrance to the park, too. (For information about the Paradise Pier Hotel's ongoing transformation, turn to page 46 and visit *disneyland.com*.) All other visitors must enter and exit Disney California Adventure through the park's main entrance, directly across the esplanade from Disneyland park. From there, trams transport guests to parking areas. Since the area is pedestrian-friendly, guests may easily walk from the park along the esplanade to the three Disneyland Resort hotels and the Downtown Disney dining, shopping, and entertainment district.

Park Primer

BABY FACILITIES

Changing tables, baby-care products, and facilities for nursing can be found at the Baby Care Center. (It's next to Ghirardelli Soda Fountain and Chocolate Shop.)

DISABILITY INFORMATION

Many park attractions and nearly all shops and restaurants are accessible to guests using wheelchairs. Services are also available for those with visual or hearing disabilities. Ask about these services at Guest Relations.

FIRST AID

Minor medical problems are handled at the First Aid Center, by the park's main entrance. *In case of emergency, alert a cast member and call 911.*

GUIDED TOURS

For information about or to book a tour, call 714-781-8687, or stop by the park's Chamber of Commerce.

HOURS

Operating hours vary from about 10 A.M. until 8 P.M. to about 8 A.M. until 11 P.M., depending on the date and time of year. For the park's hours during your planned visit, use the Disneyland Resort app, *disneyland.com*, or call 714-781-4636. Guests with hopper tickets may hop to Disneyland starting at 1 P.M. Details are subject to change.

INFORMATION

Chamber of Commerce, near the park's main entrance, is equipped with guidemaps and a helpful staff. Maps may also be available at some of the park's shops. The Information Station, in Carthay Circle Plaza, is an excellent resource for attraction wait times and show schedules.

LOCKERS

Lockers are available near the park's main entrance. Fees range from $7 to $15 per day, depending on size.

LOST & FOUND

The Disneyland Resort's Lost & Found is on the left side of the Disneyland Park entrance. Report lost items there. If you find an item, kindly present it to the nearest cast member.

LOST CHILDREN

Report lost children at the Baby Care Center and alert the closest employee to the problem.

MONEY MATTERS

There are ATMs in the park. Currency may be exchanged at Guest Relations (aka Chamber of Commerce). Cash, credit cards, traveler's checks, and Disney gift cards are accepted for most purchases.

PARK RESERVATIONS

To enter a Disneyland Resort theme park, guests must have valid park admission *and* a park reservation for the day. Park reservations can (and should) be made in advance via the Disneyland app or *disneyland.com*.

PARK RULES

To ensure a safe and enjoyable experience for all guests, visitors are asked to comply with all Park rules, including:

- All bags are subject to inspection.
- Proper attire is required.
- Smoking—including e-cigarettes and all types of vaping—is prohibited.
- Selfie sticks are not permitted in Disney parks.
- Weapons (including toys) are strictly prohibited.
- Marijuana is prohibited.
- Guests under age 14 must be accompanied by a guest age 14 or older to enter the park.

For additional information and a complete listing of Disneyland Resort theme park Rules, visit Guest Relations or go to *disneyland.com/ParkRules*.

SAME-DAY RE-ENTRY

All guests have their picture taken upon initial entry to the park. The photos, which are linked to tickets, make for speedy and convenient re-entry, with the presentation of the respective park ticket. Note that hand stamps are no longer required for re-entry to the park.

SECURITY CHECK

Visitors entering Disney parks are subject to a thorough security check, including a metal detector screening. Bags purses, strollers, etc., will be searched by security personnel before guests may pass through the entrance.

STROLLERS & WHEELCHAIRS

Strollers, wheelchairs, and Electric Conveyance Vehicles (ECVs) can be rented just outside the Disneyland Park entrance. If you need a replacement, present a receipt. Strollers larger than 31 inches by 52 inches and wagons are not permitted. For pricing and other information, use the Disneyland app or visit *disneyland.com*.

PHOTO BY JILL SAFRO

BUENA VISTA STREET

When a young Walt Disney took the train from Kansas City to Los Angeles in 1923, he discovered a bustling metropolis teeming with pedestrian boulevards, shops, restaurants, and shiny red trolley cars. Buena Vista Street, inside the park's main entrance, sends guests back to this era—to an idealized version of a city beaming with optimism and opportunity.

Follow festive Buena Vista Street, which begins inside the turnstiles, to the Carthay Circle Restaurant—a replica of the theater where *Snow White and the Seven Dwarfs* premiered in 1937. (This version of the Carthay Circle houses a popular restaurant. For Carthay Circle details, see page 121.) Or enjoy a trip back in time by hopping aboard a jolly trolley.

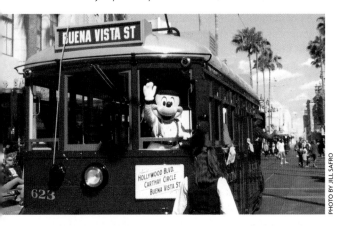

RED CAR TROLLEY: The Red Car Trolley system revives the gone-but-not-forgotten Pacific Electric Railway right here in Disney California Adventure. This jolly trolley transports guests between Buena Vista Street and Guardians of the Galaxy—Mission: BREAKOUT! by way of Hollywood Land. It it stops near the park's main entrance, at Carthay Circle, near the Animation building, and on Sunset Boulevard (just past the Hyperion Theatre.)

HOLLYWOOD LAND

Lights! Camera! Action! The spotlight is on you in the glitzy Hollywood district of Disney California Adventure, where the action unfolds all around you. No movies are actually filmed here, so you will have to keep waiting for your big break. You can think of this place as the "Hollywood that never was and always will be."

Turn onto Hollywood Boulevard and you'll enter Disney's interpretation of the legendary street. And it all fits neatly into a two-block strip. In contrast to the starstruck Hollywood

TICKET PRICES

Although prices[†] will likely increase, the following should give an idea of what you will pay for tickets in 2023. Note that 1-Day tickets purchased in 2023 must be used by 12/30/23. The first day of use of multi-day tickets must be on or before 12/30/23. Multi-day tickets must be used within 13 days of first use or by January 12, 2024, whichever occurs first. For updates, use the Disneyland mobile app or visit *disneyland.com*. All details are subject to change.

	ADULTS	CHILDREN*
1-Day Ticket (1 park)	$104/164	$98/154
1-Day Ticket (hopper)	$164/224	$158/214
2-Day Ticket	$255	$240
2-Day Ticket (hopper)	$315	$300
3-Day Ticket**	$330	$310
3-Day Ticket (hopper)**	$390	$370
4-Day Ticket**	$360	$340
4-Day Ticket (hopper)**	$420	$400
5-Day Ticket**	$380	$360
5-Day Ticket (hopper)**	$440	$420
Enchant Key pass		$649
Believe Key pass		$949
Dream Key pass		$1,399

† One-day prices represent the range in which you can expect to pay. Prices vary based on date. For dates, visit *disneyland.com*.
* 3 through 9 years of age; children under 3 free
** Includes one "Magic Morning" early Disneyland Park admission on Tuesday, Thursday, or Saturday with advance purchase. (Magic Mornings were "on pause" at press time, but expected to return.)

There is a single price (for adults and children) for Enchant Key, Believe Key, and Dream Key passes. Said passes are part of the "Magic Key" pass program that replaced traditional annual passes. There is a limited number of Magic Key passes available and sales may be suspended at any time. For more information on Magic Key passes, use the Disneyland mobile app or visit *disneyland.com*.

Boulevard, the backlot area peels away the sparkly facade and takes a backstage look at Hollywood without its makeup. Alongside soundstage buildings, behind-the-scenes support departments do their unseen, essential work: Props are put into position, klieg lights are set to shine on the scene, and the crew is busy making sure every performer is on their mark before the director yells "Action!"

BIRNBAUM'S ★BEST★ MONSTERS, INC.—MIKE AND SULLEY TO THE RESCUE!: G+ A monster's-eye spin through Monstropolis, this colorful, slow-moving attraction was inspired by the Disney-Pixar animated film *Monsters, Inc.* It invites guests to follow affable monsters Mike and Sulley as they valiantly attempt to deliver Boo safely back to her room—all while dodging trucks, helicopters, and the occasional yellow-suited representative of the Child Detection Agency.

While this thoroughly enjoyable attraction is as family-friendly as it gets, there are some dark moments that may spook sensitive tots. Just a heads up!

DISNEY JUNIOR DANCE PARTY!: A joyful celebration of Disney Junior, this show is most popular with very young guests—who are the most enthusiastic members of the audience. The performance space holds large groups (of mostly tiny) people at a time. All guests are invited to sing, dance, catch bubbles, and laugh themselves silly. Disney Junior favorites such as Vampirina, Doc McStuffins, and Timon—and, of course, Mickey Mouse and Minnie Mouse—join the party, too. This show is presented daily.

PHOTO BY JILL SAFRO

MICKEY'S PHILHARMAGIC: Mickey Mouse and a panoply of his pals (including Donald Duck, Simba, Miguel, Dante, and Ariel) strut their stuff in this snazzy 3-D production. The attraction, which debuted in 2019, has a new scene featuring the Disney-Pixar film, *Coco.*

The presentation is an amalgam of music, effects, and animation. Of course, this being Hollywood Land, the film is by no means ordinary. It's colorful, crisp, and to the delight of many a goggle-wearing guest, three-dimensional. The lively experience unfolds on a massive digital canvas. Special effects and silly surprises take place off the screen, too. Pay attention!

As with many Disney attractions, there are moments of darkness. If you are unsure as to whether your child might find this (or any attractions) unsettling, express your concern to an attendant. They will help you make the right decision. Note that all guests must wear 3-D glasses to enjoy the show.

BIRNBAUM'S ★BEST★ DISNEY ANIMATION: When you look around at all the attractions, themed hotels, and dozens of familiar animated faces that Disney has become famous for, it's almost impossible to remember it all started with a simple sketch of a mouse. This behind-the-scenes exploration invites guests to step into Disney's wonderful world of animation. Here, visitors get an insider's look at the process, the heritage, and, above all, the artistry of this world-renowned art form, along with a possible preview of an animated feature in progress.

Disney Animation: This central area aims to make visitors feel as if they are stepping into an animated film. Sketches and artwork from Disney and Pixar movie classics are projected onto giant screens that encircle the colorful atrium as familiar melodies fill the air. From this central hub, guests progress to several interactive animation-inspired shows and activities.

Anna & Elsa's Royal Welcome: The beloved siblings welcome visitors in the Disney Animation building in Hollywood Land. The colorful experience pays tribute to Arendelle and the revered regal characters from the animated feature *Frozen*.

Anna and Elsa are popular, to say the least. Plan on a bit of a wait to see the regal duo. Try to get there early, or later in the day (after most tykes have run out of steam for the day). And don't forget to have a camera or mobile device powered up and ready to go.

Animation Academy: Do you want to draw a snowman? Or perhaps a famous mouse? Inspired by the animation art in the courtyard, this attraction lets guests take a crack at drawing favorite Disney characters. With step-by-step guidance provided by a Disney animator, you'll use basic shapes and simple techniques to create your own sketch, suitable for framing. Check with a cast member or check the schedule out front to see which character is being drawn during your visit.

Sorcerer's Workshop: Budding animators and artists particularly get a kick out of these three rooms. They are built around interactive exhibits featuring animation special effects. At Enchanted Books, for example, you can take a personality survey (hosted by *Beauty and the Beast's* Lumiere and Cogsworth) to determine the Disney character to which you are most similar.

Turtle Talk with Crush: If ever there were an attraction that left guests smiling and asking, "How do they do that?!"—this is it. The concept is simple enough:

a 10-minute, animated show starring the surfer-dude sea turtle from *Finding Nemo*. The amazing part? The cartoon critter actually interacts with the audience. In doing so, he imparts turtle-y wisdom, answers questions, and cracks more than a few jokes. Dory and friends may join in the fun. You have to see it to believe it. To do that, you may have to wait a bit—the show is popular with guests of all ages. It's totally awesome, dude.

Little humans are encouraged to sit up front, on the floor by the big screen. That'll make it easier for Crush to see them. Grown-up humans can take a load off on the theater's bench-style seating (note that the benches do not have backs). You can collect the wee ones at the conclusion of the performance.

AVENGERS CAMPUS

Avengers Campus brings together Earth's Mightiest Heroes for the common good, and they're calling all recruits to join them! The park's newest neighborhood promises a host of high-flying adventures and close encounters of the Super Hero kind.

BIRNBAUM'S ★BEST★ GUARDIANS OF THE GALAXY— MISSION: BREAKOUT!: **G+** Inside this 183-foot, towering fortress is a collection of treasures, hoarded by one Taneleer Tivan, aka The Collector. Included in this trove are the Guardians of the Galaxy themselves. Your mission is to join forces with Rocket and break the Super Heroes out of their gilded cages.

The storytelling begins even before the ride does, with painted notes from Rocket scrawled throughout the queue area. (The attraction's story line expands on the film *Guardians of the Galaxy*—but even if you've never seen it, you'll have no trouble following along.)

The topsy-turvy ride experience is similar to this attraction's predecessor—The Tower of Terror. (If you have second thoughts about boarding the ride vehicle and following through with this daunting mission, simply ask the attendant to direct you toward the "chicken exit.") Once you take a seat in the gantry lift, the doors close and the room begins its ascent—and thus begins the chaotic and thrilling adventure.

Hang on—the gantry lift takes an immediate plunge (of about eight stories) before shooting up to the 13th floor. At the top (about 157 feet up), passengers can look out at the park below. Once the doors shut, you plummet 13 stories. The drop lasts about two seconds, but it seems a whole lot longer.

Just when you think it's over, the elevator launches skyward, barely stopping before it plunges again. And again. From the time you are seated, the mission takes about 5 minutes.

Note: You must be at least 40 inches tall to experience G.O.T.G.—Mission: BREAKOUT! The attraction is not recommended for pregnant women, or people with heart conditions, back and neck problems, or other medical issues. Though thrilling (and rather scary), the drops are surprisingly smooth. Still, if you are susceptible to motion sickness, sit this one out.

WEB SLINGERS: A SPIDER-MAN ADVENTURE: The World Engineering Brigade, or WEB, is hosting an open house

NEW to show off some nifty new inventions—and you are invited! So are Peter Parker, Lunella Lafayette, Doreen Green, and other familiar faces. When the young inventors start to tinker, a bit of their technological wizardry goes a bit wonky. A self-replicating Spider Bot (which seemed like a great idea at the time) suddenly multiplies and starts to run amok! As the hungry critters devour Peter Parker's lab, he calls on you for help.

Would-be Super Heroes (aka park guests) don 3-D glasses and board 8-person ride vehicles for a frenetic mission to catch or destroy the suddenly sinister Spider Bots. The mission is accomplished with the help of virtual spider webs, conveniently (and somewhat miraculously) shot from guests' wrists. The attraction is fun for the whole family, with no height restrictions. Guests who

are sensitive to motion or have back, neck, or other health issues should skip this web-slinging trip.

At press time, this attraction was available via traditional standby line (included with park admission) or via Individual Lightning Lane Purchase (aka à la carte selection.) For additional information about this attraction (including Lightning Lane status updates), visit *disneyland.com*, or use the Disneyland mobile app. Details are subject to change at any time.

ANCIENT SANCTUM: Doctor Strange, the master of

NEW mystic arts, occupies a special section of Avengers Campus—in the ruins of an ancient sanctum. Surrounded by lush greenery, the doctor demonstrates illusions and sorcery for willing recruits. The quiet, shady enclave is especially atmospheric in the evening, when the trees and glowing ruins pulse with energy and special effects.

GRIZZLY PEAK

The centerpiece of the Grizzly Peak recreation area (which includes the Grizzly Peak Airfield) is a bear-shaped mountain that juts 110 feet above the park floor. The eight-acre wilderness surrounding the Grizzly Peak mountain serves as a tribute to the Golden State's grandeur and natural beauty. The Grizzly Park Airfield area was inspired by California's aviation history. It pays tribute to famous flyers and their precious planes. A huge aircraft hangar, the focus of this section, is the site of a wildly popular attraction known as Soarin' Around the World.

BIRNBAUM'S ★BEST **SOARIN' AROUND THE WORLD:** G+ Up, up, and away! On this smooth, high-flying attraction, you will be suspended in a hang-glider–like ride vehicle 45 feet in the air, above a giant IMAX projection dome, and treated to an aerial tour of majestic landscapes and treasured landmarks. Soarin' has been delighting park guests with its wraparound glory since 2001—but these days, instead of hovering over one state (California), visitors experience a much broader tour. (The original version of the show does return from time to time, much to the delight of Soarin' fans.)

Soarin' Around the World showcases some of the planet's most compelling sights: The Great Wall of China, the plains of Africa, the oceans of Fiji, the Grand Canyon, Egyptian pyramids, and much more. (Disneyland park veterans may notice a familiar mountain peak in the Swiss Alps. Yep, it's the Matterhorn!)

With the wind in your hair and your legs dangling in the breeze, the hang glider feels so real that you may even be tempted to pull up your feet for fear of tapping the rooftops and landscapes below.

The entire flight takes about 5 minutes and employs synchronized wind currents, scent machines, and a musical score set to a film that wraps 180 degrees around you. A Disney California Adventure original, there is a version of this ride in several Disney theme parks around the world. Soarin' is a hit with guests of all ages.

Note: You must be 40 inches tall and free of back problems, heart conditions, motion sickness, and any other physical limitations to ride. Afraid of heights? Skip this flight.

Note: To ride, passengers must be free of back and neck problems, heart conditions, motion sickness, and other physical issues to ride. Pregnant women, guests not meeting the 42-inch height requirement, and kids under age 3 will not be permitted to board. Finally, if you wish to stay dry, bypass this ride.

GRIZZLY RIVER RUN: `G+` Disney legend says that Grizzly Peak was once chock-full of gold—which made it a magnet for miners in search of riches, as is evidenced by the mining relics scattered about the mountain. But the gold rush has come and gone, and the peak has since been taken over by another enterprising group—the Grizzly Peak Rafting Company. They converted the area into a rafting expedition called Grizzly River Run.

Each round raft whisks eight passengers on a drenching tour of Grizzly Peak. The trip begins with a 45-foot climb, and it's all gloriously downhill from there. Fast-moving currents send adventurers spinning and splashing along the river, bumping off boulders and rushing through an erupting geyser field. Because the raft is perpetually spinning as it moves through the water, each rider's experience is slightly different, but one thing's for sure— everyone gets wet. During the expedition, intrepid rafters encounter two major drops. It's the 21-foot drop that earns Grizzly River the distinction of being the world's tallest, fastest raft ride.

REDWOOD CREEK CHALLENGE TRAIL: Lace up your trusty sneakers and test your skills at this rustic adventure zone near the eastern slope of Grizzly Peak. Some highlights include the Cliff Hanger traverse rock climb, Boulder Bear rock formations, and a trio of wooden lookout towers featuring authentic ranger gear, rope bridges and hidden surprises to keep guests on their toes.

Of course, even the most intrepid explorers may need directions. Fortunately, there are handy maps at the trail's entrance—just ask a park ranger. Need a hand to assist you through the course? Just whistle for one of the workers outfitted in ranger gear. They're always happy to help.

There is a special cave hidden here, too. Find it and you will discover which noble creature—bear? salmon? skunk?—is your animal spirit.

Note: Redwood Creek Challenge Trail keeps shorter hours than the rest of the attractions in the park.

PACIFIC WHARF

Inspired by Monterey, California's Cannery Row, this industrial waterfront salutes the cultures, products, and businesses that make the state of California so international in nature. Guests can tour a working bakery and watch local products such as fresh-baked San Francisco sourdough bread being prepared. There are also many tables scattered about, making this a good place to stop and enjoy a rest or a snack.

THE BAKERY TOUR: Soft sourdough bread is featured at this working bakery. While baking tips are shared in the walk-through corridor tour, the famous Boudin-family recipe remains a well-kept secret.

PHOTO BY JILL SAFRO

CARS LAND

Ladies and gentlemen, start your engines—there's a real-life Radiator Springs in this theme park! This 12-acre *Cars*-themed town invites guests to enjoy the following attractions:

LUIGI'S ROLLICKIN' ROADSTERS: Luigi's Flying Tires has, well, flown away. But Luigi fans, fear not! The mechanically inclined Radiator Springs resident has a fun-filled (or is that fun-fueled?) experience for guests to enjoy. The attraction, which sits behind Luigi's Casa Della Tires, takes guests for a silly ride as Luigi's cousins demonstrate dances from their native Italy. It's a "wheel" hoot! Guests must be at least 40 inches tall to ride. The experience involves quite a bit of motion, including spinning. Just a heads-up.

MATER'S JUNKYARD JAMBOREE: This attraction is a tractor-pulling square dance party hosted by everyone's favorite tow truck. As baby tractors pull the junkyard cart (with you in it), the cart gets whirled and twirled

in time to tunes pumped through Mater's junkyard jukebox. Those tunes—all seven of 'em—are original songs performed by Disneyland legends, Billy Hill and the Hillbillies. To ride, guests must be at least 32 inches tall. Don't ride on a full stomach.

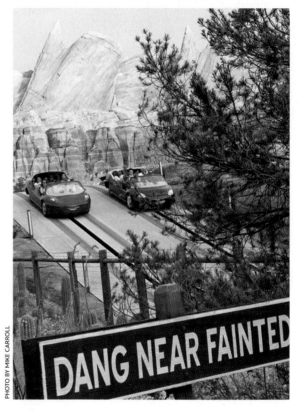

PHOTO BY MIKE CARROLL

BIRNBAUM'S ★BEST★ **RADIATOR SPRINGS RACERS:** Fasten your seat belts—this bona fide "E-Ticket" attraction will set your heart racing as you compete with other speed seekers. Using technology similar to that of EPCOT's beloved Test Track attraction, Imagineers have devised a thrilling experience for guests: a high-speed tour of Ornament Valley, featuring hairpin turns, steep banks, and a head-to-head race to the finish. Sally, Luigi, Guido, Ramone, and other familiar *Cars* friends zoom around this revved-up racetrack.

At press time, this attraction was available via traditional standby line (included with park admission) or via Individual Lightning Lane selection (aka à la carte purchase.) For additional information about this attraction (including Lightning Lane status updates), visit *disneyland.com*, or use the Disneyland mobile app.

Notes: To ride, guests must be at least 32 inches tall and without health conditions. Expectant mothers must sit out this race.

PIXAR PIER

It's all about fun in the sun at Pixar Pier, a colorfully themed neighborhood featuring high-flying adventures with popular Pixar pals. Attractions here line a board-walk amusement pier wrapped around a scenic lagoon.

At night, the district undergoes a dazzling transfor-mation. Thousands of tiny lights illuminate the rides and building facades, creating a magical display—especially as you soar past them on one of Pixar Pier's most thrilling attractions: Incredicoaster. This area used to be known as Paradise Pier.

BIRNBAUM'S ★BEST★ **INCREDICOASTER:** **G+** Like many classic boardwalks, the centerpiece of Pixar Pier is a gleaming roller coaster. A steel structure, Incredicoaster is designed to look and sound like an old-fashioned wooden coaster, but the thrills are as modern as they get. The ride starts at lagoon level, where the long car bursts up the track as if cata-pulted up by a crashing wave. The car goes from zero to 55 miles per hour in 4.7 seconds—before reaching the first hill. Several lengthy drops are combined with an upside-down loop, plus a blasting soundtrack. The result is the longest and fastest roller coaster ride in the entire Disneyland Resort.

Along the way, vehicles travel through bright red tubes that trap guests' screams as they test their vocal cords on the big drops, magnifying all the hoots and hollers and adding to the excitement. Every time you approach a tube, you know you're in for a very big thrill, so brace yourself and be prepared to scream! (Inciden-tally, the previous incarnation of this ride was known as California Screamin'.)

Daredevils should be sure to enjoy this attraction after the sun goes down, when the night sky is speckled with the pier's glowing lights, and the topsy-turvy twists and turns on the roller coaster will prove even more disorientingly exciting—and scary!

Note: Passengers must be at least 48 inches tall and free of back problems, neck problems, heart conditions, motion sickness, and other health concerns to ride. Pregnant guests should skip this attractions

INSIDE OUT EMOTIONAL WHIRLWIND: This attrac-tion may trigger memories of the cherished Flik's Flyers from the now-defunct "A Bug's Land." If that is not enough to get your emotions churning, *Inside Out's* Joy, Sadness, Disgust, Anger, and Fear will get the job done. This simple ride—which tends to be a big hit with fans of Disneyland's Dumbo the Flying Elephant—lasts about a minute and a half.

JESSIE'S CRITTER CAROUSEL: Yee-ha! Get ready to saddle up with one of the 56 cuddly critters on this carousel. Jessie's new ride was inspired by the *Woody's Roundup* TV show in *Toy Story 2*. It features a twirling herd of wilderness creatures such as bunny rabbits, rams, armadillos, turtles, snakes, and one super silly skunk. There are two stationary logs in which guests may ride, too (both logs are inhabited by owls). This attraction is fun for the young and the young at heart. On select nights, Jessie's Critter Carousel closes early to accommodate World of Color (see page 112) performances.

HOT TIP

A number of the cars on Pixar Pal-A-Round remain fixed on the edge as the wheel spins—perfect if you would prefer to take a more tranquil trip. If so, be sure to get in the queue that's marked "non-swinging." (It's to the left of the "swinging" queue.)

PIXAR PAL-A-ROUND: A modern loop-de-loop, this gleaming Ferris wheel, centered by a huge Mickey face, takes guests on a head-spinning trip. If you think this is a run-of-the-mill Ferris wheel, you're in for a surprise: While the wheel turns, most of its cabins swing in and out along the interior edges of the wheel's colossal frame—which creates a dizzying effect. At 150 feet, this is one of the park's tallest attractions, and while it may wreak havoc on sensitive stomachs, thrill-seekers rave over its ride within a ride. For a tamer experience, board a non-swinging gondola. (There may be a longer wait involved.) This attraction closes early on days when World of Color is presented.

Pixar Pal-A-Round is one of only two Ferris wheels that combine fixed and swinging gondolas. The other one is the Wonder Wheel at New York's Coney Island.

Note: Passengers must be free of back problems, heart conditions, motion sickness, and other physical limitations to ride. Afraid of heights? We *highly* recommend skipping this one!

BIRNBAUM'S
★BEST **TOY STORY MIDWAY MANIA!:** G+
This beloved attraction is an energetic, interactive toy box tour with a twist: Guests wear 3-D glasses as they take aim at animated targets with spring-action shooters. The high-tech adventure is rooted in classic midway games of skill. As points are scored, expect effusive encouragement from a colorful cast of characters—Toy Story's Jessie,

Woody, Buzz, Hamm, Wheezy, Rex the Dinosaur, and, of course, the Little Green Men.

Fans of Disneyland's Buzz Lightyear Astro Blasters will no doubt delight in this adventure, which takes the experience of the interactive attraction into a new dimension. As far as skill level goes, there's something for everyone—from first-timers to seasoned players alike. (Most folks up their score with practice.) And don't worry about your accuracy score—it's all about the point total.

Toy Story Midway Mania! is a very popular destination with guests of all ages—make a beeline for it when the park first opens for the day.

PARADISE GARDENS PARK

A colorful celebration of the Golden State (California), Paradise Gardens Park hugs the shores of Paradise Bay, a shimmering lagoon in the heart of Disney California Adventure park. Here you'll find a dynamic lineup of shows and attractions:

SILLY SYMPHONY SWINGS: This attraction pays tribute to some of Walt Disney's earliest animated triumphs—the Silly Symphonies. The specific symphony highlighted here is the 1935 cartoon called *The Band Concert*. Riders take flight in swings, while Mickey and his barnyard band serenade them with a rousing rendition of the William Tell Overture.

As the attraction's momentum picks up, a cyclone reveals itself as guests swirl higher and higher. Avoid it if you fear heights.

Notes: Riders must meet the Silly Symphony Swings height requirement of 48 inches to ride solo. (Guests between 40 and 48 inches may ride in a double swing. Children under the age of 7 must be accompanied by a responsible person over age 14. Those under 40 inches are not permitted to take this flight.) All guests must be free of back problems, heart conditions, motion sickness, and other physical limitations to experience this ride. Silly Symphony Swings closes early to accommodate World of Color performances.

GOOFY'S SKY SCHOOL: G+ At this miniature roller coaster, guests of most sizes climb into crop dusters and follow the same fluky flight path taken by the Goof himself. The planes zip through the farm and crash through a barn, causing quite a ruckus among the chickens. Don't let the size fool you. This roller coaster proves that big thrills definitely can come in small packages. Although guests as young as age 3 are permitted to ride, it may be too turbulent for some.

Notes: Although it's small as roller coasters go, the ride's sudden stops and herky-jerky motion during turns may prove too scary for riders not used to more strenuous coasters. Riders must be at least 42 inches tall and free of back problems, neck problems, heart conditions, motion sickness, and any other physical limitations to take this jolting ride.

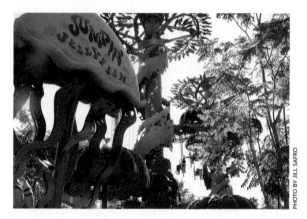

PHOTO BY JILL SAFRO

JUMPIN' JELLYFISH: A dense kelp bed tops this sea-themed attraction, from which riders sitting in brightly colored jellyfish seats are lifted about 40 feet straight up in the air. When you reach the top, hang on to your tentacles! A jellyfish acts as a parachute, and fish and friends float safely back down to the ground. While the trip is a rather gentle one with special appeal for younger riders, it might take a few minutes for guests with the most sensitive of stomachs to get their land legs back. Folks who are highly susceptible to motion may want to save the heavy snacking for after they jump like a jellyfish.

Notes: All guests must be at least 40 inches tall and free of back problems, heart conditions, motion sickness, and any other physical limitations to ride.

On nights when World of Color (see page 112) is presented, Jumpin' Jellyfish closes early to accommodate the evening's performances of the park's popular fountain and light show.

THE LITTLE MERMAID—ARIEL'S UNDERSEA ADVENTURE: In the first theme park attraction to have featured everyone's favorite Disney mermaid, guests are invited to board (continuously moving) clam-mobiles and embark on a jolly journey above and below sea level. (Be sure to take in the 86-foot-long, hand-painted mural in the boarding area.) Along the way, they join Ariel,

Flounder, Sebastian, and all of their aquatic acquaintances and enjoy major musical moments and pivotal plot points from the classic animated feature. It's fun for the whole family.

A wheelchair-access vehicle is available for this "undersea" attraction. Ask a cast member for assistance.

GOLDEN ZEPHYR: Disney Imagineers took the rocket ride to new heights with the launch of Astro Orbitor in Disneyland. But long before those space-age ships took off, riders were taking flights in rocket-shaped swings on boardwalks and amusement piers across America. Disney pays homage to those old-fashioned attractions with rocket ships that take guests for a spin beneath the Golden Zephyr tower. As speed picks up, the rockets lift into the air and fly over the lagoon several times before touching down for a landing. The high-flying ride lasts approximately a minute and a half.

Note: Passengers must be free of back, neck, and heart problems, motion sickness, and other physical limitations to ride. This attraction closes for World of Color presentations (see page 112) and during inclement weather (including high winds). While there is no height minimum, young guests must be able to ride without assistance. Have an unpleasant reaction to heights? Skip this attraction.

HOT TIP

World of Color, this park's nighttime spectacular, is a wildly popular show. Get there early, or reserve a spot in the "virtual queue" early in the day. You can do so via the Disneyland app after you enter Disney California Adventure for the day. If you're lucky enough to snag a spot in the virtual queue, you'll get a notification to enter the viewing area about 45 minutes before the show begins. Details are subject to change.

Shopping

BUENA VISTA STREET

ATWATER INK AND PAINT: Shoppers enjoy the quaint ambience of a 1930s Hollywood-style market house as they peruse collector pins, seasonal merchandise, kitchen gadgets, towels, mugs, dinner plates, flatware, and much more.

BIG TOP TOYS: Teeming with playthings, Big Top Toys sells innovative and interactive toys and games, plus a plethora of plush character merchandise. You may also find Star Wars–themed toys and souvenirs (action figures, lightsabers, and other selections).

ELIAS & CO.: Paying tribute to the Art Deco–style buildings of yesteryear, this emporium features an array of fashion finery for the whole family—it rivals Disneyland Park's Emporium shop in size. It stocks clothing (hats, shirts, shoes, jackets, and more), snacks, accessories, and wristwatches.

   F.Y.I.: Elias was Walt Disney's middle name and his dad's first name.

JULIUS KATZ & SONS: Adorned with old-timey clocks, radios, and assorted memorabilia, this cozy shop is a hotspot for Disney shoppers. Among its wares: kitchen items, mugs, frames, and Christmas ornaments. The store's name was inspired by Julius the Cat, a featured character in Walt Disney's classic Alice Comedies.

HOT TIP

Disney California Adventure occasionally offers special, reservation-only shopping experiences. (Note that valid same-day park admission and D.C.A. reservation are required, too). For additional info, visit *disneyland.com*.

KINGSWELL SHOP: Stop here to peruse, purchase, and personalize mouse ear hats. The shop's name comes from Walt Disney's first California address. When he arrived in Los Angeles in 1923, he rented a room from his Uncle Robert on Kingswell Avenue. It's where the Walt Disney Company was born.

LOS FELIZ FIVE & DIME: In addition to attraction- and California-themed clothing and souvenirs, there is a selection of Disney character items. It's possible to have some items personalized (for a fee).

OSWALD'S: Stop here for autograph books, hats, bags, and souvenirs themed to the park, Oswald the Lucky Rabbit, and more. It's located just inside the park's main entrance. (Fittingly, Oswald was the first Disney character to generate merchandise. Nearly a century ago, there was a pen, a stencil set, and a pin featuring Walt's first animated star.)

TROLLEY TREATS: If the thoughts of "mountains of candy" and "rivers of fudge" make you smile, this is the shop for you. Tasty temptations include caramel apples, toffee, chocolate-dipped cookies, fudge, and seasonal selections such as housemade marshmallows.

PLAY DISNEY PARKS APP

NEW When it comes to visiting a Disney park, the name of the game is fun—and lots of it! And thanks to the new Play Disney Parks App, there's a new layer of digital fun for guests to enjoy in Disneyland Resort theme parks. The free app lets you test your Disney trivia smarts and play games while waiting in lines for several theme park attractions. At press time, that list included Toy Story Midway Mania! (at Disney California Adventure) and Disneyland Park's Space Mountain and Peter Pan's Flight. The app also lets you interact with Disneyland's famous Fortune Tellers: The Great Esmeralda on Main Street, and Fortune Red in New Orleans Square. Perhaps the most impressive feature of the trusty app is its power to transform your smart device into a "Star Wars: Datapad" in Star Wars: Galaxy's Edge. With it, you can decrypt messages in Aurebesh (the native tongue of Batuu), discover hidden items in the land, hack into droids, and much more.

We recommend downloading the app prior to arriving at the parks. And pack an extra battery pack for your mobile device. You'll need it.

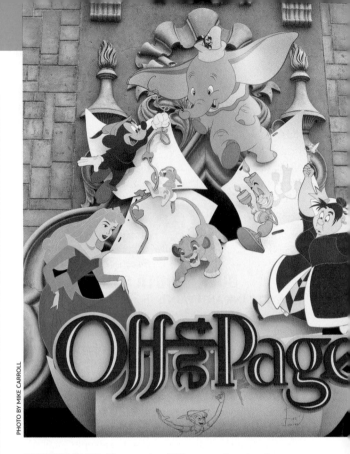

PHOTO BY MIKE CARROLL

Choose from packaged candy or items made fresh in the display kitchen. It's fun to watch the candy makers hard at work—and it's even more satisfying to gobble up their creative confections.

HOLLYWOOD LAND

GONE HOLLYWOOD: A cheerful boutique, Gone Hollywood celebrates Hollywood blockbusters. Expect to find apparel, books, toys, collectibles, and seasonal items—many with a Star Wars or Marvel twist.

OFF THE PAGE: The magic of Disney animation leaps off the page at this shop that showcases collectible Disneyana pieces. Cels, limited-edition prints, books, and figurines are sold here, as are attraction-inspired items. Guests may interact with artists as they sketch classic Disney characters.

DISNEYLAND RESORT BACKLOT PREMIERE SHOP: This open-air shop puts the spotlight on current shows in Hollywood Land. The themes vary, but expect to find items such as T-shirts, hats, toys, snacks, and more. You will find it across from Monsters, Inc.—Mike and Sulley to the Rescue!

GRIZZLY PEAK

HUMPHREY'S SERVICE & SUPPLIES: When you see the large selection here, you know this is a "beary" serious shopping spot (sorry, we couldn't resist). The grizzly bear–inspired merchandise includes hats, souvenirs, toys, pins, items with a Soarin' theme, and glow merchandise. This souvenir shop is across from the park's perennially popular Soarin' Around the World attraction.

RUSHIN' RIVER OUTFITTERS: This outpost is the perfect place to gear up for an outdoor adventure. Expect to find a variety of Rushin' River apparel, headwear, towels, rain ponchos, plush toys, and other items.

CARS LAND

RADIATOR SPRINGS CURIOS: Hit the brakes and make a quick stop at this country-style mercantile. You may be tempted to fill the trunk with the latest park logo merchandise, *Cars*-themed paraphernalia, and other accessories. There is also a substantial supply of items celebrating the revered roadway Route 66.

RAMONE'S HOUSE OF BODY ART: Ramone stocks all manner of items with a *Cars* theme (hey, this *is* Cars Land). Look for T-shirts, hats, toys, and other wares with a Radiator Springs vibe.

SARGE'S SURPLUS HUT: Young (and young-at-heart) racers, rejoice: Sarge has a super supply of clothes and toys that were designed with you in mind. For many *Cars* fans, it's well worth making the pit stop—even if it is just to sneak a peek at the scale model of Radiator Springs. It's super cool.

PIXAR PIER

PHOTO BY JILL SAFRO

BING BONG'S SWEET STUFF: This super sweet spot specializes in sugary treats and colorful merchandise celebrating familiar friends from the film *Inside Out*: plush toys, baseball caps, jammies, shirts, accessories, and mugs. It is located on the boardwalk, across from Pixar Pal-A-Round.

KNICK'S KNACKS: The snow globe snowman (from the classic Pixar short *Knick Knack*) stocks items themed to Disney/Pixar films. Look for items featuring *Finding Nemo*, *Up*, *Inside Out*, *Coco*, *WALL-E*, and more. The shop's on the boardwalk, across from Lamplight Lounge.

MIDWAY MERCANTILE: Conveniently located next to Toy Story Midway Mania!, the shelves at this mercantile are lined with items featuring a *Toy Story* theme. Expect to see spirit jerseys, T-shirts, pajamas, hats, toys, costumes, and other similarly-themed merchandise.

PARADISE GARDENS PARK

SEASIDE SOUVENIRS: A 1930s-style, open-air stand, Seaside Souvenirs offers character items, hats, shirts, toys, sunglasses, and more.

PACIFIC WHARF

GHIRARDELLI SODA FOUNTAIN AND CHOCOLATE SHOP: In addition to a decadent line-up of ice cream treats and soda fountain specialties, Ghirardelli offers a sweet array of their famous chocolates (available in every flavor), plus chocolate gifts and limited edition packaging unique to this location, and an assortment of bulk snacks including chocolate covered almonds and cashews. There's always the possibility of a free sample, too. Sweet!

AVENGERS CAMPUS

AVENGERS CAMPUS SUPPLY POD: A somewhat self-explanatory spot, supply pod specializes in Avengers-inspired treasures such as T-shirts, backpacks, accessories, jackets, and action figures.

NEW

THE COLLECTOR'S WAREHOUSE: The exit lobby of Guardians of the Galaxy—Mission: BREAKOUT! does double duty as a gift shop. It sells souvenirs themed to the attraction (collector pins, shirts, hats, backpacks, action figures, etc.), plus Super Hero shirts, comic books, Marvel DVDs, and toys. This is also the place to buy the photo that's taken of you on the attraction. The shot is snapped just before the ride's big drop, so that look of horror is captured forever!

WEB SUPPLIERS: This "one-stop hero shop" supplies everything arachnid—Spider-Bots (those rascally remote-controlled critters known for causing a commotion at WEB SLINGERS: A Spider-Man Adventure), special Spider-Bot backpacks, spider light goggles, web shooters, and other cutting-edge inventions ostensibly developed by the Worldwide Engineering Brigade (aka WEB). Other merch selections include hats, shirts, keychains, collector pins, notebooks, and a make-your-own spider web kit.

NEW

Entertainment

Disney California Adventure boasts a boisterous lineup of live entertainment. For updates and Disney character greeting locations go to *disneyland.com*. Check a park Tip Board or the Disneyland app for schedules. Details are subject to change at any time.

AVENGERS HEADQUARTERS: Encounter some of Earth's mightiest Super Heroes and watch them spring into action to defend the Avengers command center. You'll find it in the Avengers Campus area of the park.

FIVE & DIME: This singing group travels Buena Vista Street in their jalopy, hoping to get their big break in the music world. A fleet-footed Goofy joins in the jazzy fun.

GUARDIANS OF THE GALAXY AWESOME DANCE-OFF: Gather around as Peter tries to get Gamora to crack a smile by playing his legendary mixtape. Help him out by showing off your own epic dance moves!

MARIACHI DIVAS: Guests are invited to sing along as this talented, Grammy award–winning quintet performs pop music and traditional Mexican folk songs. This act performs during the holiday season.

OPERATION PLAYTIME: A rhythmic squad of *Toy Story's* Green Army Men is on a mission to serve, protect, and entertain! The plastic platoon engages guests with games and percussive shenanigans.

PARADISE GARDEN BANDSTAND: Sit back, relax, and enjoy a variety of live musical acts in a lovely garden setting. Shows usually last about 25 minutes.

BIRNBAUM'S ★BEST★ WORLD OF COLOR: Arrive early and prepare to smile. This 25-minute nighttime spectacular, shown on Paradise Bay, is a kaleidoscopic journey of music, animation, water, special effects, and, of course, brilliant color. The show is best viewed from the esplanade near The Little Mermaid—Arie's Under Sea Adventure.

World of Color is intended for all audiences, but it does feature loud noises, fire, and other effects that may be too intense for some tykes. Guests closest to the water's edge will get spritzed.

An extra-festive version of this show—World of Color Season of Light—may be offered during the holiday season. Check *disneyland.com* for updates.

HOT TIPS

🔲 Favorite characters (including Mickey Mouse) make appearances throughout the day. Check a park Tip Board or the Disneyland app for appearance schedules.

🔲 As a rule, Disney's Single Rider lines involve a shorter wait than the standby line. Soarin' Around the World, however, tends to be an exception to that rule. The good news is the wait time for this attraction tends to dwindle as the day wears on.

🔲 Curious about showtimes or wait times? Stop by the Information Station on Buena Vista Street or use the Disneyland app. Guest Relations kiosks in Cars Land and Paradise Gardens Park can help, too.

🔲 Shops on Buena Vista Street usually stay open about a half hour after the park closes.

🔲 Ready for a break from the park? Head to Downtown Disney District to shop or grab a bite to eat. There are more than a few (relatively) cost-efficient spots to consider (i.e., Wetzel's Pretzels, Napolini Pizzeria, Tortilla Jo's, Jamba Juice, and La Brea Bakery).

🔲 Many attractions have height restrictions—measure the kids before you leave home.

🔲 Radiator Springs Racers has a maniacally devoted fan base. To minimize your wait, get to the park as it opens, and head to this attraction after passing through the turnstile—or take advantage of the Single Rider line. If budget allows, consider booking an à la carte Lightning Lane reservation (fees apply).

🔲 Don't risk water-logging your valuables while riding Grizzly River Run. We recommend using zip-top bags to protect mobile phones and cameras while you ride. Better yet, stash your items in a short-term complimentary locker (conveniently located by the drenching attraction's exit).

🔲 Guests may be allowed to enter before the park's posted opening time, so we always aim to arrive at the gate about 40 to 45 minutes early.

🔲 For a sweet retreat, visit Ghirardelli Soda Fountain and Soda Shoppe in the Pacific Wharf neighborhood of Disney California Adventure. You may even score a free sample. Now that is sweet!

GOOD MEALS GREAT TIMES

Dining at the Disneyland Resort is definitely an adventure—and not just in Adventureland. There's more to any meal in a theme park, Downtown Disney, District, or a Disneyland Resort hotel than just food. Disney friends such as Mickey, Minnie, Goofy, Tigger, Pooh, Chip and Dale, or Donald Duck might pass by your table to say hello. A colorful parade or a romantic paddle wheeler could drift by. Or you just might find yourself surrounded by twinkling stars (in the middle of a sunny day!) as you savor some Cajun cooking in an elaborate bayou setting.

In this chapter, the Disneyland Resort restaurant section is divided by location (Disneyland park, Disney California Adventure park, the Disney hotels, and the Downtown Disney District). Within the theme parks, eateries are arranged by area, and then by category—table service or fast-food and snack facilities, including food courts; individual eatery listings are alphabetized within each respective category.

If you're hankering for something to do after dinner, or you just need to take a break from the theme parks, you will find plenty of suggestions at the end of the chapter. Downtown Disney, the property's dining and entertainment district, is party central. Or for a more relaxed atmosphere, chill out in a lounge at one of the Disneyland Resort hotels.

Dining
In Disneyland Park

One of the most popular noshes in Disneyland is the burger, followed closely by churros (decadent sticks of deep-fried dough rolled in cinnamon and sugar) and ice cream. But healthy-minded eaters will be happy to find fish, grilled veggie skewers, salads, grilled chicken, and vegetable gumbo, plus fresh fruit and smoothies. Disneyland's table-service restaurants (Blue Bayou, Café Orleans, River Belle Terrace, and Carnation Café) provide full-course meals and lighter fare, plus a welcome break from long lines and the California sun. All details are subject to change.

Main Street, U.S.A.
TABLE SERVICE

CARNATION CAFE: On the west side of Main Street, near Town Square, this indoor/outdoor cafe is exceptionally pleasant, especially in springtime, when its planters are bursting with seasonal flowers. Stroll into the courtyard dining area that's filled with umbrella-shaded tables and surrounded by a cast-iron fence; from your table you'll hear the melodies from any passing parade. Breakfast choices include Mickey-shaped waffles; pancakes; oatmeal; breakfast sandwich (served with potatoes); and a breakfast skillet (including Mickey-shaped egg bites, potatoes, applewood smoked bacon, and sliced smoked sausage), along with coffee, tea, and orange juice.

Lunch and dinner feature comfort foods, including fried pickles with dipping sauce, "Walt's chili," baked potato soup, and wedge salad. Popular entrées include braised short rib, cheeseburgers, patty melts, and chicken-fried chicken. There are special selections for kids, too. Finish off the meal with a housemade dessert (apple pie à la mode, perhaps?) and specialty coffees. This cafe is one of four restaurants at Disneyland park that offers table service for lunch and dinner. (River Belle Terrace, Blue Bayou, and Café Orleans are the others). **BLD/$–$$**

HOT TIP

For a jolt of java, head to Market House (aka Starbucks) or Jolly Holiday Bakery Cafe on Main Street, U.S.A. The iced and hot specialty coffees are sure to please. Specialty cold brew drinks are offered at various park locations, including Oga's Cantina in Star Wars: Galaxy's Edge.

RESTAURANT PRIMER

The eateries in this chapter have been designated inexpensive (lunch or dinner under $15), moderate ($15 to $36), expensive ($36 to $60), and very expensive ($60 and up). Prices are for an entrée, a soft drink, and either soup, salad, or dessert for one person, excluding tax and tip. Some prices may be higher during peak-attendance times throughout the year. The letters at the end of each entry refer to the meals offered: breakfast (B), lunch (L), dinner (D), and snacks (S).

Cash, credit cards, traveler's checks, and Disney gift cards can be used at all of the eateries described on the following pages. (Foreign currency may be exchanged at City Hall in Disneyland Park, at Chamber of Commerce in Disney California Adventure Park, and at the Disneyland Resort hotels.) Disneyland Resort hotel guests can charge meals from most theme park eateries to their rooms.

While only a few Disneyland Park restaurants (Blue Bayou, River Belle Terrace, Café Orleans, Carnation Café, and Plaza Inn [breakfast only], plus Lamplight Lounge, Wine Country Trattoria, and Carthay Circle Restaurant in California Adventure) accept reservations, you can book a table at most Downtown Disney spots and at the Disney resort hotels. Unless otherwise noted, make reservations up to 60 days ahead via *disneyland.com,* or the Disneyland app.

FAST FOOD & SNACKS

JOLLY HOLIDAY BAKERY CAFE: A festive tribute to Disney's *Mary Poppins*, the Jolly Holiday is at the far end of Main Street. There is always a steady supply of pastries here, including cookies, cupcakes, and Mickey-shaped macarons. Specialty coffee drinks are available all day (hot and iced). Also on the seasonal menu are breakfast sandwiches, yogurt parfait, and (after 10:30 A.M.): soups, salads, and sandwiches. Kids' meals are available as well. **BLDS/$–$$**

GIBSON GIRL ICE CREAM PARLOR: A perennially popular place, with a polished-wood soda fountain, the parlor serves up a delightful array of scoops and toppings in paper cups, handmade waffle cups, and plain or chocolate-dipped cones. Choose from 9 flavors, including rainbow sherbet and no-sugar-added vanilla and chocolate swirl. We are quite fond of the Firehouse Dalmatian Mint Sundae (hold the cherry). Don't be daunted by the (usually) long line; it moves rather quickly. (It helps to commit to your treat order *before* jumping into the queue.) **S/$**

LITTLE RED WAGON: This wagon, near the Plaza Inn, is a throwback to the delivery trucks of the early 1900s, with ornate beveled and gilded glass panels. Step right up and order your freshly hand-dipped corn dogs, the specialty of the wagon. A selection of soft drinks and chips is also served. **LDS/$**

MAIN STREET FRUIT CART: Parked between Disney Clothiers Ltd. and Market House, this old-fashioned cart is stocked with fresh fruit, chilled juices, bottled water, and other soft drinks. Other snack options may include pickles, hummus, and fresh veggies. It's the perfect pit stop for a (relatively) healthy snack. **S/$**

WHERE TO DINE WITH CHARACTERS

Meals with Disney characters take place daily at Disneyland Park's Plaza Inn (breakfast with Minnie Mouse and her friends) on Main Street, U.S.A.; Storytellers Cafe (breakfast with Mickey Mouse) and Napa Rose (breakfast with princesses) in the Grand Californian Hotel; and Goofy's Kitchen at the Disneyland Hotel (breakfast and dinner with Goofy and friends). For additional information and to make reservations, visit *disneyland.com* or use the Disneyland mobile app.

HOT TIP

Do you spend a lot of time visiting the Disneyland Resort each year? If so, we recommend the purchase of a Magic Key pass. It could net you a 10 to 15 percent discount (depending on the type of pass) at many eateries and shops property-wide. Note that passes are limited and may not always be available for purchase or renewal.

MARKET HOUSE: Visit this Victorian-style market for a fresh-baked or brewed treat. It sells sweet and savory snacks and a cornucopia of tea and coffee concoctions, courtesy of Starbucks. Breakfast wraps and sandwiches, fresh fruit, and pastries are served all day. **BLDS/$**

PLAZA INN: On the east side of Main Street's Central Plaza, this eatery is the one Walt Disney was most proud of, and with good reason. Tufted velvet upholstery, gleaming mirrors, and a fine, ornate floral carpet elevate this cafeteria above similar eateries. Two ceilings are stained glass framed by elaborate painted moldings. Sconces of Parisian bronze and Baccarat crystal are mounted on the walls, and two dozen basket chandeliers hang from the ceiling.

The setting, including front-porch and terrace dining (with heat lamps to keep guests toasty at night), creates a lovely backdrop for the food—pasta; seasonal fish; fried chicken served with mashed potatoes and mixed vegetables; pot roast served with fresh veggies and mashed potatoes; salads; and desserts.

An extremely popular character breakfast is held here daily, from park opening until 11 A.M. Minnie Mouse and her pals make appearances. A fixed-price buffet features omelets, eggs, Mickey-shaped waffles, sausage, bacon, yogurt, fresh fruit, pastries, and more. **BLDS/$–$$**

REFRESHMENT CORNER: Better known as Coke Corner, this eatery at the northern end of Main Street is presided over by a ragtime pianist who tickles the ivories periodically throughout the day while visitors nibble hot dogs, chili cheese dogs, or chili in a sourdough bread bowl. Mickey-shaped pretzels (stuffed with cream cheese), chips, soft drinks, and coffee are sold, too. **LDS/$**

Adventureland

PHOTO BY JILL SAFRO

FAST FOOD & SNACKS

BENGAL BARBECUE: This alfresco stand is a popular place to munch on a skewered snack of bacon-wrapped asparagus, or chicken, beef, grilled pork belly, or veggies. It's possible to have skewers served on a bed of rice with citrus slaw. Other choices include pickles, pineapple spears, tiger tails (bread sticks baked with garlic, herbs,

and cheddar cheese), and housemade hummus served with vegetables. There is a large indoor seating area in which to savor your skewers. **LDS/$**

TIKI JUICE BAR: Located at the entrance to Walt Disney's Enchanted Tiki Room, this thatched-roof kiosk sells fresh Hawaiian pineapple spears and juice, but the biggest draw here is the Dole Whip soft-serve—a frozen, non-dairy, pineapple treat. **S/$**

TROPICAL HIDEAWAY: An alfresco courtyard behind the Tiki Room, this enchanting hideaway has two counters from which to order sweet and savory selections. The menu offers steamed bao buns (lime chicken, pork, and spicy veggie), fruit, chips, and (frozen non-dairy) Dole Whip desserts. (In addition to traditional pineapple, this spot sells raspberry, orange, and other specialty Dole Whip flavors.) Diners are entertained by talented Tiki Bird, Rosita—who tells tales and cracks one-liners worthy of the nearby Jungle Cruise attraction. **LDS/$**

TROPICAL IMPORTS: A close neighbor of Bengal Barbecue, this stand offers whole fresh fruit, pineapple spears, cheese, pickles, assorted chips, bottled water, and soft drinks. This is also the place to get your fortune told by Shrunken Ned (for 50 cents). **S/$**

Critter Country
FAST FOOD & SNACKS

CRITTER COUNTRY FRUIT CART: This modest peddler's cart is filled with refreshing selections, including fresh fruit, dill pickles, chilled bottled water, and soft drinks. (It's handy if you need some fortification after taking the big Splash Mountain plunge.) **S/$**

HARBOUR GALLEY: This tiny place, tucked into the shanties that line the docking area for the *Columbia*, offers sourdough bread bowls filled with New England clam chowder or broccoli and cheddar cheese soup; tuna salad sandwiches; kids' "power packs" (snack packs with mini yogurt smoothie, fruit, and whole grain "fish" crackers, and lowfat milk or water); soft drinks (including frozen lemonade); and fresh cut fruit. **LDS/$**

HUNGRY BEAR RESTAURANT: A rustic, waterside classic, this alfresco locale serves fried green tomato sandwiches, classic cheeseburgers, plant-based cheeseburgers, honey-spiced chicken sandwiches, french fries, and onion rings. For youngsters, there are hamburgers,

DINING PACKAGES

The Disneyland Resort offers "dining and a show" experiences—pairing nibbles and sips with reserved viewing for the Main Street Electrical Parade (in Disneyland), World of Color, and Fantasmic! Here are two recent offerings:

1. Plaza Inn (at Disneyland Park): A table-service lunch package comes with reserved seating for the Main Street Electrical Parade. Cost for lunch is about $45 for adults, $25 for kids.

2. World of Color Dessert Party (at Disney California Adventure): At this soirée, guests enjoy sweet treats and cheeses as they view the evening's presentation of World of Color from a dedicated water-front area. The package includes unlimited soft drinks and two alcoholic beverages (for guests 21 years of age and older). The cost is $89 per guest.

Space is limited for these special experiences, so reservations are recommended. For details on these and other dining packages, or to make reservations up to 60 days in advance, visit *disneyland.com*, or use the Disneyland app. Reservations require a credit card guarantee. Cancellations must be made at least 24 hours ahead to avoid paying the full price.

chicken nuggets, or mac and cheese (kids' meals come with applesauce, fruit, and a choice of milk or water). Hungry Bear's dessert options include strawberry fruit bars, ice cream sandwiches, and funnel cakes topped with powdered sugar. **LDS/$**

New Orleans Square
TABLE SERVICE

BLUE BAYOU: The lure of this popular dining spot is as much the atmosphere as it is the menu. Occupying a terrace alongside the bayou in the Pirates of the Caribbean attraction, the eatery is perpetually moonlit—stars shine through Spanish moss draped languidly over the big, old live oaks. Off in the distance, an old settler rocks away on the porch of a tumbledown shack.

The menu features starters such as chicken gumbo and house salad with crumbled blue cheese and candied pecans. Entrée options may include sustainable catch

of the day, Cajun cauliflower, jambalaya, chicken with rice, Monte Cristo sandwich (at lunch only), plus filet mignon. A sweet finish to the meal may come in the form of 8-layer chocolate and hazelnut cake or crème brûlée. Specialty beverages include (alcohol-free) Louisiana lemonade and mint juleps, plus beer, wine, sparkling wine, and cocktails. Kids' menu selections may include a "Chef's beefy specialty," chicken breast, and pasta with marinara sauce. All children's meals are served with vegetables and fresh fruit with a choice of low-fat milk or bottled water.

The busiest periods are from about noon to around 2 P.M. and from about 5 P.M. until 9 P.M. Reservations are recommended. **LD/$$-$$$**

CAFE ORLEANS: An authentic Cajun-Creole spot, Café Orleans offers sumptuous starters such as a ratatouille crostini, chicken gumbo, plus seasonal soup and salad. Among the entrées, look for shrimp and grits with andouille sausage; roasted half chicken; farro risotto; and two versions of the venerable Monte Cristo sandwich. For dessert, there's praline cheesecake. The children's menu offers roasted chicken, Mickey's cheesy macaroni, and sautéed shrimp. Guests may enjoy their meal inside or outside overlooking Tom Sawyer Island, the *Columbia* and the *Mark Twain* resting on the Rivers of America. Reservations are suggested. **LDS/$$-$$$**

FAST FOOD & SNACKS

FRENCH MARKET: Situated beside the old-time train depot in New Orleans Square, this eatery is a destination in its own right. On a pleasant day, nothing beats sitting on the open-air terrace, savoring a Cajun breakfast croissant (while supplies last), herb-roasted chicken, seasonal soups and stews (served in bowls fashioned from hollowed-out loaves of sourdough bread), po'boys (sandwiches), Cajun-style chicken Caesar salad, or jambalaya (seafood or vegetarian). Dessert can come in the form of colorful Mardi Gras cake. Coffee, tea, and soft drinks are served. Kids' selections such as baked chicken, macaroni and cheese, and pasta with marinara sauce are available. Dixieland jazz music is played periodically throughout the evening; the Royal Street Bachelors hold forth with such spirit that you could listen for hours. **LDS/$-$$**

MINT JULEP BAR: Beside the New Orleans Square train station, this window-service bar serves Mickey-shaped beignets, hot chocolate, hot tea, and coffee. The alcohol-free mint juleps taste a bit like lemonade

HAPPY BIRTHDAY, DISNEY STYLE

For starters, it is always a good idea to inform Disney cast members when you are celebrating a special occasion, no matter where you are at the Disneyland Resort. But it also helps to plan ahead. Mickey-shaped cakes can be delivered to many full-service restaurants. Each one serves 4 to 6 people and costs about $45 (plus tax and tip). They can be "added on" when making a reservation via *disneyland.com* or the Disneyland app.

Finally, be sure to pick up (and wear!) a special Happy Birthday button. The buttons are complimentary and available at City Hall in Disneyland Park, at the Chamber of Commerce in Disney California Adventure, and at select shops within the aforementioned theme parks.

SWEET TREATS

Sweet teeth may be satisfied at a plethora of places in Disneyland Park. After passing through the turnstiles, make a beeline for Jolly Holiday Bakery Cafe, Gibson Girl Ice Cream Parlor, or Candy Palace. By all means, try a churro (fried dough rolled in cinnamon and sugar) from a food cart. Finally, no trip to the "happiest place on earth" is complete without savoring the classic frozen pineapple treat known as the Dole Whip. The line at the Tiki Juice Bar is often very long, but for many a Dole Whip aficionado, it's well worth the wait.

spiked with mint syrup (definitely an acquired taste); regular lemonade is also on tap. Seasonal specials are often on the menu. Enjoy your snack at one of the tables on the French Market's terrace. **BS/$**

ROYAL STREET VERANDA: Across from Café Orleans, this spot has sourdough bread bowls overflowing with creamy clam chowder (with a slightly spicy kick), and steak or veggie gumbo, and assorted beverages. Check out the wrought-iron balustrade above the Royal Street Veranda's small patio. The initials at the center are those of Roy and Walt Disney (this balcony belonged to an apartment that was being built for Walt himself). **LDS/$**

Frontierland
TABLE SERVICE

RIVER BELLE TERRACE: The terrace, between Golden Horseshoe Saloon and the Pirates of the Caribbean, offers one of the best views of the Rivers of America and of the passing throng—and the food is wholesome and hearty. Walt Disney himself used to dine here most Sundays. Start your meal with crispy cornmeal catfish and shrimp, loaded potato bites, warm pimento cheese dip (served with bread and veggies), or a salad (chopped or wedge). Choose from entrées such as buttermilk fried chicken sandwich, grilled cheese, sweet and sticky pulled pork sandwich, or open-faced blackened catfish sandwich. The dessert menu includes house-made pudding and seasonal monkey bread. Kids' selections include roasted chicken, tofu, and mac and cheese. Lunch and dinner may include a ticket for same-day, premium viewing of Fantasmic!—as part of a Dining Package. (For details about Fantasmic! dining packages, visit *disneyland.com.*) With a lovely interior, it's just as pleasant to dine inside as it is out. **LD/$$–$$$**

FAST FOOD & SNACKS

RANCHO DEL ZOCALO RESTAURANTE: Big Thunder Mountain Railroad's neighbor, this eatery features south-of-the-border specialties. Several of the usual Mexican dishes, including street tacos and burritos, along with selections such as fire-grilled chicken, cauliflower tacos, chips and salsa, and tostada salad with chicken or beef

PHOTO BY JILL SAFRO

are sure to hit the spot. For dessert, sample some sweet cinnamon crisps. **LDS/$$**

F.Y.I: Rancho del Zocalo is in an area of Frontierland that was once called "El Zocalo," or "town square." The eatery's name translates to "Ranch of the Square."

PHOTO BY JILL SAFRO

GOLDEN HORSESHOE: Head to this (dry) saloon for chicken tenders, fish and chips, mozzarella sticks and fries with marinara sauce, and salad with grilled chicken. Wash it down with a soft drink. The kids' menu offers chicken tenders. Cap off the meal with an ice cream sundae, bowl of ice cream, or an ice cream float. Seating is on a first-come, first-served basis. Disneyland purists may remember that the Golden Horseshoe Revue was one of Disneyland's original 18 attractions and was the world's longest-running stage show (July 17, 1955– October 12, 1986). Walt Disney was a big fan and had his favorite box right next to the stage. **LDS/$**

SHIP TO SHORE MARKETPLACE: Nestled near the shores of the Rivers of America, this satisfying snack stand sells turkey legs, corn on the cob, chimichangas, pickles, fresh fruit, cheese, frozen lemonade, soft drinks, coffee, and hot cocoa. **S/$**

GOT I.D.?

The legal drinking age in the state of California is 21. However, just being 21 is not enough to get you served—you have to prove it. To do so, you must present a government-issued photo ID. If your driver's license doesn't have a photo, bring it and an official photo ID (a passport is ideal). Otherwise, you'll have to stick to soft drinks.

STAGE DOOR CAFE: Are you in the mood for one of Disneyland's famous hand-dipped corn dogs? Head here. This small stand, which adjoins the Golden Horse-shoe Stage, also serves fish and chips, chicken tenders, fries, mandarin oranges, funnel cakes, and soft drinks. Grab a seat at an outdoor table. **LDS/$**

Fantasyland
FAST FOOD & SNACKS

EDELWEISS SNACKS: Next door to the Matterhorn, this chalet-style kiosk can supply a quick pick-me-up in the form of chimichangas, jumbo turkey legs, corn on the cob, chips, and soft drinks (including frozen beverages). Souvenir sippers are sold, too. **S/$**

TROUBADOUR TAVERN: Located beside the Fantasyland Theatre, this spot has been known to dispense baked potatoes, caramelized apple-filled hand pie, jumbo turkey legs, kids' power packs (with fruit, carrots, crackers, and more), frozen treats, and soft drinks. This spot may not be open in all of 2023. **BLS/$**

RED ROSE TAVERNE: This eatery, with its gables, pointy roof, and wavy-glass windows, could easily have been relocated to Fantasyland from that small provincial town in Disney's *Beauty and the Beast*. The menu includes cheeseburgers, chopped salad (with or without chicken), grilled cauliflower sandwich, flatbread (plain or pepperoni), "grey stuff" (sweet treat), fries, and soft drinks. Kids' selections include hamburgers and chicken breast nuggets served with packaged yogurt smoothie, fresh fruit, and lowfat milk or bottled water. **LDS/$**

HOT TIP

Mickey's Toontown was in the midst of a yearlong "re-imagination" phase as this book went to press. Will there be tasty nibbles to enjoy as this land emerges from its cocoon? You can count on it! For updates, visit *disneyland.com* or use the Disneyland app. Note that Toontown is expected to reopen in early 2023, but that may change.

Tomorrowland
FAST FOOD & SNACKS

ALIEN PIZZA PLANET: Similar to *Toy Story's* Pizza Planet (minus the arcade), this brightly hued dining destination specializes in pizza, plus pasta, salads, snacks, and soft drinks. The claw-free environment pleases diners with slices of freshly prepared cheese or pepperoni pizza, chicken fusilli, Caesar salad, mixed green salad, and garlic bread. The set-up is classic cafeteria-style—fill a tray as you slide past the serving stations. Little aliens may order space-ghetti with meatballs or kid-size pizza. Situated near the Space Mountain entrance, this food court overlooks the Moonliner. Soft drinks, milk, coffee, and cocoa are served. **LDS/$$**

GALACTIC GRILL: This is one of Disneyland's largest dining areas. For breakfast there's a choice of breakfast burritos, sandwiches, and French toast sticks. At lunch and dinner, choose from burgers, cheeseburgers, fried chicken sandwiches, veggie wraps, and chopped salads. Kids' selections include burgers and mac & cheese. For dessert, there are ice cream sandwiches, strawberry fruit bars, and Mickey ice cream bars. Coffee, tea, milk, juice, and other soft drinks are served. Menu items are subject to change. **BLD/$-$$**

HOT TIP

Relatively well-balanced dining options are available throughout the Disneyland Resort—and kids' meals are no exception. Children's meals tend to include a small entrée, side dish, and drink, and are served in youngster-pleasing shapes and sizes. All kids' meals come with a healthy side and a choice of low-fat milk or water. Toddler meals are available in some spots, too. If you don't see a kids' menu, just ask!

TOMORROWLAND FRUIT CART: Fruit may not sound especially futuristic, but it's a healthy way to snack today and tomorrow. Stop here for fresh fruit, pickles, soft drinks, and more. **S/$**

Star Wars: Galaxy's Edge
FAST FOOD & SNACKS

DOCKING BAY 7 FOOD AND CARGO: Chef Strono "Cookie" Tuggs has docked a food freighter loaded with fresh supplies and he appeases appetites with an array of savory offerings. Kids' selections are available. **LDS/$$**

MILK STAND: Vendors at this stall offer travelers a drink that's a favorite among residents of Batuu—and Luke Skywalker himself (though for many Earth residents, it's definitely an acquired taste). The plant-based (non-dairy) frosty beverage comes in blue or green. **S/$$**

RONTO ROASTERS: To find this stand, just follow your nose—aromas of spit-roasted specialties fill the air. The menu features the Ronto Wrap (grilled sausage and roasted pork), plant-based sausage wraps, and Meiloorun Juice. The aforementioned spit, incidentally, is operated by a pit-master droid. **BLDS/$$**

KAT SAKA'S KETTLE: Pop over to this stand for Outpost Mix—a sweet and savory popcorn-based treat. **S/$**

OGA'S CANTINA: Come to the cantina to quench your thirst and rub elbows with revelers from around the galaxy (guests pack into this place like proverbial sardines). As folks quaff spirited beverages such as the Jedi Mind Trick, Bad Motivator IPA, or Toniray wine, they're treated to bold musical entertainment courtesy of droid DJ R-3X, a former Starspeeder 3000 pilot. Non-alcoholic specialty drinks are served, too. Guests of all ages are welcome to enjoy Oga's hospitality, but valid ID is required for alcohol. Reservations are highly recommended. **S/$-$$$**

In Disney California Adventure Park

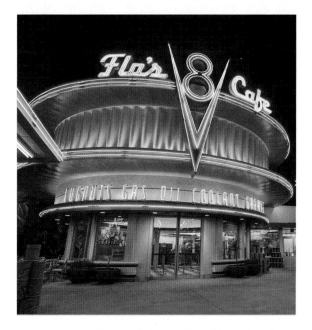

With a winery and an elegant bay-side eatery, the tastes at Disney California Adventure park are clearly grown-up. But fast-food spots and snack stands also supply theme park fare with an entertaining flair—retro Hollywood decor or a seaside boardwalk setting. Just don't gorge before experiencing thrill rides.

Full-service eateries—including Lamplight Lounge, Carthay Circle Restaurant, and Wine Country Trattoria—accept reservations. Use the Disneyland mobile app or visit *disneyland.com* to book a table. Details are subject to change.

Buena Vista Street
TABLE SERVICE

CARTHAY CIRCLE RESTAURANT: The original Carthay Circle Theatre was one of the best known and revered movie palaces in Hollywood history. It also happens to be where Walt Disney's *Snow White and the Seven Dwarfs* made its dazzling debut. The theatre has been re-created at Disney California Adventure. But don't go expecting to catch a flick—this version of Carthay Circle Theatre is actually an upscale restaurant. Menu items such as cheese-stuffed arepa, California ahi poké, braised short rib ravioli, cedar roasted duck breast, pomegranate glazed pork chop, and warm dark chocolate truffle cake earn Carthay Circle rave reviews. Reservations are recommended. Walk-ins may be accommodated in the lounge area. **BLDS/$$$–$$$**

FAST FOOD & SNACKS

CLARABELLE'S HAND-SCOOPED ICE CREAM: Cones and sundaes are among the frosty treats served here. The specialty of the house is hand-dipped ice cream bars. Simply select your bar flavor, milk or dark chocolate for dipping, and a topping. Sweet! Clarabelle offers spirited treats such as hard floats, too (for guests ages 21 and older and willing to prove it). **S/$**

FIDDLER, FIFER & PRACTICAL CAFE: Named for everyone's favorite trio of house-building pigs, this is a great spot to quell hunger pangs and enjoy your favorite Starbucks beverage. Breakfast items, pastries, salads, sandwiches, and snacks are served all day. **BLDS/$**

MORTIMER'S MARKET: Stop here for "the freshest fruit in town." In addition to produce, there are other healthy snacks and soft drinks from which to choose.
   F.Y.I.: Mickey Mouse was almost named Mortimer. Fortunately, Lillian Disney talked her husband into naming him Mickey. **S/$**

Hollywood Land
FAST FOOD & SNACKS

AWARD WIENERS: All-beef dog, Bacon Street Dog, and Uptown Chili dogs are the specialties here. Plant-based Philly dogs and asada (grilled meat) fries round out the menu. A "power pack" snack box may be ordered for wee ones. A nearby seating area provides shaded tables (across from Disney Junior Dance Party!). **LDS/$–$$**

FAIRFAX MARKET: Inspired by the historic Farmers Market in Los Angeles, this stand serves assorted whole fresh fruits, fresh vegetables with ranch dip, dill pickles, hummus with snap peas and tomatoes, chips, apple sauce, and soft drinks. **S/$**

SCHMOOZIES: Smoothies made with ice cream or yogurt are the specialty of the house: Strawberry Banana Sensation, Mango Madness, and Make Mine Mocha, to name a few. Seasonal lemonade, iced cold brew coffee, ice cream topped with espresso, and bottled water are also available. **S/$**

Avengers Campus
FAST FOOD & SNACKS

PYM TEST KITCHEN: Ant Man and The Wasp used

NEW PYM Particles to shrink or supersize menu items in this futuristic food factory. Start the day with Ever-expanding Cinna-Pym Toast (pictured above), eggs two ways with bacon and crispy potato bites, or a plant-based folded omelet. Later in the day, sample some Caesar salad and savory sandwiches such as Not So Little (fried) Chicken, Pym-iny (salami), and PB&J with banana and candied bacon on Pym Particle bread. Kids selections include PB&J, pasta with plant-based meatballs, and sandwiches (ham and provolone or fried chicken). Other menu items of note: ginormous soft pretzels and a "celestial sized" candy bar. Wash it down with some Proton PB&J Punch, cold brew coffee, or a fizzy soft drink. **BLDS/$–$$**

PYM TASTING LAB: Connected to PYM Test Kitchen,

NEW this casual lounge offers a full bar, wine, craft beers, non-alcoholic sips, and creative concoctions such as the Molecular Melt-down (beer cocktail with ice cream and mini marshmallows) and Honey Fusion (beer with gin and a honey straw.) Enjoy any of the aforementioned beverages with fare from PYM Test Kitchen or the solo selection on the Lab menu: snack molecules (a mix of mini pretzels, honey-roasted peanuts, and sweet-and-spicy popped sorghum). **S/$–$$**

SHAWARMA PALACE: You ever tried shawarma? The

NEW Avengers invite you to enjoy their go-to New York City shawarma spot—which has opened a second location right here in Disney California Adventure park. There's a breakfast wrap with sausage and egg, plus New York's Tastiest (chicken shawarma wrap) and a falafel and cauliflower wrap. Bottled soft drinks are also served at this stand. **BDLS/$$**

Grizzly Peak
FAST FOOD & SNACKS

SMOKEJUMPERS GRILL: Paying tribute to the brave souls who parachute into forest fires, this spot serves items such as cheeseburgers (with or without bacon), veggie burgers, chicken sandwiches, grilled chicken salad, waffle fries, and onion rings. For dessert, there are shakes (vanilla or chocolate) topped with whipped cream. **LDS/$**

Pacific Wharf
FAST FOOD & SNACKS

WINE COUNTRY TRATTORIA: On the lower level of the mission house at the Golden Vine Winery, this bright spot offers Mediterranean fare that blends well with the wine list. (Wines are available by the glass or bottle.) Menu favorites include Caprese salad, roasted vegetable lasagna, fried calamari, pasta, salmon, and steak. There is a children's menu, too. Outdoor dining in the plaza features a fountain surrounded by herbs and flowers, conjuring images of Napa Valley. Inside, the dining room is reminiscent of an Italian villa, with plastered walls, terra-cotta tiles, and arched doorways. Reservations are recommended. **LDS/$–$$$**

PHOTO BY JILL SAFRO

COCINA CUCAMONGA MEXICAN GRILL: Come here for street-style Mexican cuisine, inspired by family favorites of Mexico and Southern California. Street tacos are the stars of the menu: steak, chicken, pork, and plant-based. Augment your meal with frijoles charros (chorizo and bacon stewed pinto beans) or lime-cilantro rice. Kid-friendly tacos are offered, as are soft drinks, beer, margaritas, and other spirits. **LD/$–$$**

GHIRARDELLI SODA FOUNTAIN: San Francisco's famous sweet-maker also calls Disney California Adventure home. Stop by this soda fountain for a banana split, chocolaty treat, or root beer float. There's no better place to please a sweet tooth. (And there's always the possibility of a free sample.) The coffee is tops, too. **S/$–$$**

LUCKY FORTUNE COOKERY: This walk-up eatery serves chicken specialties, pork ramen, and more. Sides include chicken wings and chicken or vegetable pot stickers. There are selections for kids, too. **LD/$–$$**

MENDOCINO TERRACE WINE TASTING: Take a break beside a hand-carved stone fountain and sip local varietals and international beers in this alfresco lounge at the Golden Vine Winery. Cheese cups and Bavarian pretzels complement the potent potables quite nicely. The extensive sipping menu includes reds, whites, rosés, ports, sparkling wines, bottled beer, and cider from around the world. Sparkling apple cider and other soft drinks round out the menu. **S/$$–$$$**

PACIFIC WHARF CAFE: Guests visiting this extension of Boudin's display bakery have the chance to sample some of the country's finest sourdough bread (from a secret family recipe dating back to 1850). Soups such as New England clam chowder or loaded baked potato are served in sourdough bread bowls for lunch and dinner. Other options include shrimp rolls, mac & cheese, sandwiches, salads, and sourdough baguettes. **LDS/$–$$**

Pixar Pier
TABLE SERVICE

LAMPLIGHT LOUNGE: A lovely waterside retreat, Lamplight is a breezy celebration of storytelling—with a spotlight on the folks who bring Pixar stories to life. The California casual gastro-pub offers a panoramic perspective of Pixar Pier's amusements and the Paradise Bay lagoon. The area is quite festive in the evening, when the boardwalk is aglow with twinkling lights. Lamplight's

BABY NEEDS

Babies. They're a needy lot. Fortunately, most of the requisite supplies can be found somewhere at Disneyland—if you know where to look. Formula and jarred food are sold at Baby Care Centers in the theme parks and all the three Disneyland Resort hotels. Most restaurants offer kids' menus with toddler-friendly food (mac and cheese, chicken tenders, and the like).

If your baby is partial to a specific formula or food, consider shipping a box of it to your hotel before you leave home. (Note that a delivery fee may be charged to your room for each parcel handled by Front Desk personnel.) Keep in mind that there are several grocery/convenience stores near Disneyland property. If you have a car, it is worth the trip (a Guest Relations clerk can help with directions). Selections are more varied, as are the prices. Stash perishables in an in-room mini fridge. Some additional points of interest regarding baby diners at Disneyland Resort:

• Most table-service eateries have high chairs and booster seats for little ones. Request them when you make your reservation. Quick-service spots offer high chairs on a first-come, first-served basis. Ask a cast member for assistance if you need help finding or transporting one to a table.

• To make your dining experience a little less harried, consider feeding your baby before you arrive at a restaurant for your meal.

• Stroller use inside restaurants is not permitted due to fire safety codes. Kindly park it outside the eatery. Safety codes require that tots be included in restaurant reservations, too.

• Be it a fast-food or table-service restaurant, take (quiet) toys to keep youngsters busy.

• If you'd like a comfortable, distraction-free spot to nurse an infant, head to a Baby Care Center in Disney California Adventure or Disneyland park. They have rooms with rocking chairs.

• In addition to bottle warmers and microwaves (for select use only), theme park Baby Care Center vending machines offer formula, baby food, juice, diapers, wipes, sunscreen, pacifiers, and over-the-counter medication—all available for purchase with a major credit card.

• If you're headed for a long day in a park, pack simple, healthy snacks for hungry toddlers. And look for the Disney check symbol on menus (it marks somewhat healthier options).

brunch menu includes crab & potato cake Benedict, burgers, chilaquiles, frittatas, and avocado toast. For lunch and dinner, savor small and large bites. Items of note include lobster nachos, tuna poke, crab and tuna rolls, potato skins, chicken ratatouille, Scotch egg salad, grilled salmon, cheddar burgers, and more—plus a delightful dessert of warm fluffy doughnuts with dipping sauces. "Budding artists" may enjoy pasta, mini burgers, chicken tenders, and PB&J presented sushi-style. Also served here: soft drinks, beer, wine, and a slew of signature cocktails (with and without alcohol). Reservations are recommended. **Brunch LD/$$$**

LAMPLIGHT LOUNGE—BOARDWALK DINING: This al fresco, waterside gem is easily confused with its nearby indoor counterpart, Lamplight Lounge. This spot offers equally impressive cuisine, but it has its own menu and does not accept reservations. Use the Disneyland app to join the mobile walk-up list and you'll be notified when your table is ready. Once that happens, settle in for tasty temptations such as Angus sliders, pork belly with Brussels sprouts, tuna poke bowls, and the perennially popular lobster nachos (warm lobster with black beans, cheddar and Monterey Jack, pico de gallo, serrano chiles, and chipotle crema). Kids' selections include mini burgers and corkscrew pasta with creamy cheese sauce and cheddar fish crackers (served with fruit and veggies with hummus).

The Lounge has a nice selection of alcohol-free drinks, including Goofball Island (fruit punch, lemonade, and raspberry purée) and Mint to Be (limeade with watermelon and berry puree with fresh mint and soda water), plus a full bar, craft beers, local and imported wines, and a variety of specialty cocktails. **LDS/$$–$$$**

FAST FOOD & SNACKS

ADORABLE SNOWMAN FROSTED TREATS: Frozen treats are ostensibly doled out by the not-so-abominable snowman from *Monsters, Inc.* The non-dairy soft-serve (lemon, mango, and more) offerings come in cones or cups. A duo of spiked treats and bottled water round out the menu. Helping guests cool off during a day of fun in the sun makes the snowman feel warm and fuzzy. **S/$**

ANGRY DOGS: It seems Anger, from *Inside Out*, is channeling his rage into cooking. Head to his snack stand for hot dogs and other blazing bites. **LDS/$**

JACK–JACK COOKIE NUM NUMS: Among the various num nums that Jack-Jack is willing to share (for a price) are warm chocolate chip, shortbread, and gluten-free blackberry-jam-filled cookies—which may be washed down with milk or bottled water. **S/$**

POULTRY PALACE: Chicken drumsticks box (three seasoned drumsticks with coleslaw), jumbo smoked turkey legs, corn-on-the-cob, and bags of chips are served at this waterside walk-up window. **LDS/$–$$**

SEÑOR BUZZ CHURROS: Stop at this stand for Caliente Churros (spicy), Cinnamon Super Galaxy Churros (with cinnamon and sugar), and soft drinks. **S/$**

Paradise Gardens Park
FAST FOOD & SNACKS

BOARDWALK PIZZA AND PASTA: This eatery serves Italian dishes, including pizzas, pastas, and salads. Kids' meals include spaghetti with turkey meatballs, cheesy macaroni, pizza, and turkey meatball sandwiches. Wee ones enjoy the bread sticks with marinara sauce side dish. For dessert, consider cheesecake, tiramisu, or fruit. Meals may be enjoyed alfresco, on the shaded patio. As an added treat, live entertainment is often provided at the nearby Paradise Garden Bandstand. **LDS/$**

CORN DOG CASTLE: Corn dogs, deep-fried to a golden brown and served on a stick, reign supreme. Also served: deep-fried cheddar cheese sticks and soft drinks. **LDS/$**

PARADISE GARDEN GRILL: Despite its name, this spot offers little from the grill. Though the menu changes seasonally, it has been known to serve burritos, tacos, and plant-based chili relleno (stuffed pepper). Beer, wine, and soft drinks are served year-round. **LDS/$**

Cars Land
FAST FOOD & SNACKS

COZY CONE MOTEL: Sally's cozy motel has been converted to a colorful eatery in Radiator Springs. Here guests may find items such as bacon mac and cheese cones, soft-serve ice cream cones, pop "cone," and chili "cone" queso. Soft drinks of note include Ramone's Pear of Dice Soda and Fillmore's Fuelin' Groovy all Natural Lemonade. **LDS/$**

MOBILE ORDER MAGIC

Quietly introduced a few years back, Mobile Ordering has surged in popularity and many a Disneyland Resort quick-service eatery has jumped aboard the bandwagon. While you can still place an order with a cheery cast member, you may opt to order and pre-pay for your vittles with the Disneyland mobile app.

If you've made it this far in this book, chances are you have already downloaded the app. If not, be sure to do so *before* you find yourself exploring Disneyland with your stomach growling.

When it's time to enjoy a meal or snack, open the Disneyland app on your smartphone. Hit the plus sign (+) on the home page. Then tap "Order Food." (You will be asked to sign in at some point, so make sure you know your user name and password for the app.)

After you hit Order Food, a list of available restaurants will pop up, along with possible pick-up times. Choose your eatery and select a pick-up time. Now it's time to place your order! You can even customize certain menu items to your taste. After you have reviewed your details, pay for your order using a credit card, debit card, Disney Gift Card, Disney Rewards Redemption Card, Apple Pay, or stored payment method. (If you qualify for a discount as an eligible Magic Key holder or Disney Vacation Club Member, it will automatically be applied to your total bill.)

As it gets close to your pick-up time, make your way toward the restaurant. When your order is ready, find the Mobile Pick-up sign, grab your grub, and chow down. *Mangia!*

For a complete list of Disneyland Resort eateries that currently offer Mobile Order service, use the Disneyland app or visit *disneyland.com*.

FILLMORE'S TASTE-IN: Guests here fuel up on snacks such as pickles, whole fruits, cheese, assorted chips, and soft drinks. It's the perfect place for a speedy and refreshing pit stop. **S/$**

FLO'S V8 CAFE: Inspired by classic roadside diners, Flo serves comfort food along the lines of fried chicken, turkey club sandwiches, Cobb salad, cheeseburgers, plant-based burgers, steak fries, and shakes (vanilla, chocolate, or strawberry). There's indoor and outdoor seating. **LDS/$–$$**

In the Disneyland Resort Hotels

DISNEYLAND HOTEL

The diverse dining possibilities at the Disneyland Hotel range from grand to Goofy. To make reservations up to 60 days in advance, use the Disneyland mobile app or visit *www.disneyland.com*.

THE COFFEE HOUSE: Order bagels, muffins, pastries, fruit, yogurt, cold cereal, sandwiches, and coffee in this small but busy shop. As the name indicates, this place specializes in fresh-brewed coffee—with everything from a simple cup of decaf to a cafe mocha and ice-blended latte. Outside seating only. Expect long lines in the morning. **BLS/$**

GOOFY'S KITCHEN: This whimsical dining room features popular meals and happy encounters with Goofy and other Disney characters. Service here is buffet/ family-style, so fill your plate as high and as often as you please. Just be sure to clean that plate!

Highlights at brunch include Mickey Mouse–shaped waffles, made-to-order omelets, and Goofy's famous peanut-butter-and-jelly pizza (a favorite with youngsters and Birnbaum editors alike). Dinner offers a carving station, catch of the day, macaroni and cheese, pizzas, salads, breads, fruit, and desserts. Don't forget a camera—Disney characters provide prime photo ops. Reservations are required. (Same-day reservations may be secured via *disneyland.com* or the Disneyland app up to 20 minutes in advance, based on availability.) **BD/$$–$$$**

TANGAROA TERRACE TROPICAL BAR & GRILL: Stop here and travel back in time. The retro-tiki design was inspired by the Tahitian Terrace restaurant—a longtime Adventureland staple. The fare at this casual counter-service restaurant, however, is decidedly modern. The breakfast menu has featured Tangaroa Toast (brick toast with bananas Foster, whipped cream, and toasted coconut), Japanese pancakes, scrambled egg breakfast platter, loco moco burrito, acai chia bowl, and avocado toast. All-day items include a poke bowl, pork gyoza, panko-crusted long beans, salads, Hawaiian platter, ramen, Hawaiian cheeseburgers, and other tropical specialties. The kids' menu includes teriyaki bowls and cheeseburgers. There is a small grab-and-go selection, too (mostly fruit and assorted pastries). **BLDS/$–$$**

> ### HOT TIP
> Looking for a java jolt before a day in the parks? If so, grab a satisfying cup o' Joe (and/or a light breakfast) at Downtown Disney's La Brea Bakery Express, Ralph Brennan's new quick service location, or Starbucks.

DISNEY'S PARADISE PIER HOTEL

At press time, this hotel was beginning an extensive refurbishment and theme change. While its lounges and eateries are being refurbished, there's a small market just off the lobby where guests can get takeaway nibbles and beverages. When the dust settles, the new Pixar-themed resort will feature several special nosh spots. Until then, guests are encouraged to enjoy the myriad of eateries available at the Disneyland Hotel, Grand Californian Hotel, Downtown Disney, Disneyland Park, Disney California Adventure, and in the surrounding Anaheim area. For updates about this hotel, use the Disneyland Resort app, or visit *disneyland.com*.

DISNEY'S GRAND CALIFORNIAN HOTEL & SPA

The restaurants at this resort offer a taste of (and a bit of a twist on) California cuisine. To make reservations visit *disneyland.com*, or use the Disneyland mobile app.

NAPA ROSE: This popular, nationally recognized, award-winning restaurant features a seasonal, upscale menu of market-fresh, wine country–inspired dishes flavored by fruits of the sea and vine (the eatery is named after California's famous valley of vineyards). A striking, 20-foot, stained-glass window offers views of Disney California Adventure park while the open kitchen gives

HOT TIP

Napa Rose's adjoining lounge offers scrumptious nibbles, as well as an impressive wine list. This inviting space was on pause at press time, but is expected to return.

HOT TIP

Storytellers Cafe and Napa Rose offer guests a choice of complimentary valet or self parking with restaurant validation—3 hours for Storytellers Cafe and 5 hours for Napa Rose.

a view of California cooking. The morning meal, aka, Disney's Princess Breakfast Adventure, invites guests to see Disney royalty while they enjoy their breakfast.

The offerings evolve as new items are introduced, but favorites include grilled diver scallop with roasted carrots, wine country pot pie, housemade rabbit sausage, braised beef pot roast, filet mignon, and market fish of the day. The dessert menu offers delectable creations: tangerine crème brûlée tart, winter pear cake with pomegranate sorbet, and single origin chocolate with hazelnut crunch and praline ice cream. Kid-friendly entrées and desserts are served. The California wine list is one of the most extensive on-property.

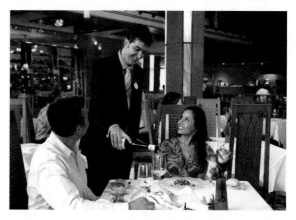

The character breakfast is presented Monday through Thursday from 8 A.M. until noon. The 3-course "Princess Breakfast Adventure" starts at about $125 (plus tax and gratuity) for all guests age 3 and older. This breakfast experience includes a special keepsake. Reservations are suggested. **BD/$$$$**

HEARTHSTONE LOUNGE: A great site for a late bite, this lounge offers hearty fare until about midnight each day. The menu has offered avocado toast with burrata, blistered shishito peppers, burgers, cheese & charcuterie, artisanal pizza, desserts, and, of course, an extensive selection of beer, wine, cocktails, and mocktails. It's a great way to cap off a Disneyland day. **LDS/$**

GCH CRAFTSMAN BAR: The hotel's Arts and Crafts motif

NEW extends to this alfresco eatery, located near the Redwood Pool. In fact, the structure of the venue resembles that of the original garage at Pasadena's Gamble House—the landmark building that inspired the design of Disney's Grand Californian Hotel. The signature clinker brick, stone columns and shady trellis set the stage for outdoor dining amid plush, residential-style patio seating. Dishes of note include black truffle-charred cauliflower grilled cheese sandwich, Maine lobster quesadilla, avocado toast, steak salad, and artisanal pizzas. Oh, they have a hot dog of the month, too! Kid's meals are available, including hamburgers and Power Packs (yogurt, fruit, carrots, crackers, and more). The dessert menu is simple-but-sweet: classic ice cream sundaes. Beer, wine, specialty cocktails (with or without alcohol), and soft drinks are served. The extensive wine list is quite impressive. Reservations are highly recommended. **LDS/$$–$$$**

STORYTELLERS CAFE: It's hard to imagine a time before computers and smartphones (especially for the youngest members of the group), when children were exposed to new cultures and histories only through the stories of others. This eatery salutes tales set in the state of California, like "The Celebrated Jumping Frog of Calaveras County" and *Island of the Blue Dolphins*, through murals that act as backdrops to the chefs at work in the exhibition kitchen. In the morning, the stage is set for a festive, character-hosted buffet known as Mickey's Tales of Adventure Breakfast or Brunch. Mickey Mouse and other Disney characters engage guests throughout the meal. The buffet offers a feast of breakfast options, with bagels and smoked salmon, Mickey-shaped waffles, French toast, eggs Benedict, sausage, and a selection of fresh fruit. The brunch buffet (offered every Friday through Sunday) includes all breakfast offerings, plus crab cakes, cheese-filled crepes,

PHOTO BY JESSICA WARD

grilled and chilled asparagus, beignets, and more. The dinner buffet features artisanal pizzas, pastas, salads, soups, seafood, and chicken.

Breakfast costs $49 per adult; $29 per child; brunch, offered on Friday, Saturday, and Sunday, runs about $51 per adult and $29 per child; dinner—which does not include character visits—costs $44 per adult and $24 per child. Prices quoted exclude tax and gratuity and are subject to change. **Brunch BD/$$$**

GCH CRAFTSMAN GRILL: The splish-splash of the waterfall and kids soaring down the slide at the resort's Redwood pool set the mood for this elegant casual dining spot. Recently refurbished and renamed (it used to be known as Whitewater Snacks), this spot is open for all meals (though hours vary). The snack bar serves coffee, muffins, and made-to-order breakfast selections in the morning. House-made sandwiches, poke bowls, skewers, burgers, and hot dogs are among lunch and dinner options. Grab-and-go items that may be available throughout the day: arugula salad, Caesar salad, fresh fruit, yogurt, cereal, chips, donuts, cookies, candy, soft drinks, beer, and wine. Details subject to change. **BLDS/$–$$**

PHOTO BY JESSICA WARD

HOT TIP

If you don't have a restaurant reservation, be prepared for a long wait at mealtimes. It's next to impossible to snag a table at Disneyland Resort hotels or Downtown Disney full-service spots with any spontaneity.

Avoid getting caught with a growling stomach—reserve table-service meals far in advance! Restaurants may be bookable up to 60 days ahead. To do so, simply visit *disneyland.com*, or use the (free) Disneyland Resort mobile app.

In Downtown Disney District

FAST FOOD & SNACKS

BALLAST POINT BREWING COMPANY: Complete with an on-site brewery, Ballast Point pairs its award-winning beers with a menu of SoCal cuisine—pub snacks, salads, wraps, and entrées that feature local, sustainable, and seasonal ingredients. Kids' entrées include grilled cheese, quesadilla, and chicken breast. In addition to the aforementioned brewery, this sleek space houses a tasting room, kitchen, and outdoor beer garden. Brunch is served until 2 P.M. on Saturdays and Sundays. **Brunch LDS/$$–$$$**

BLACK TAP CRAFT BURGERS & SHAKES: A casual destination, Black Tap has a relaxed atmosphere that's a bit reminiscent of an old-time American luncheonette. Guests may dine in- or outdoors, enjoying burgers, guac and chips, chicken wings, sandwiches, fries, salads, fried pickles, and crispy Brussels sprouts. Shakes (of the classic and "crazy" varieties), beer, wine, and soft drinks round out the menu. **LDS/$$**

DIN TAI FUNG: The world-renowned purveyor of exquisite, hand-crafted soup dumplings (among other delectable dishes) is setting up shop at the Disneyland Resort. Once the "creative space" opens, hungry guests may enjoy authentic, family-style Chinese cuisine near Downtown Disney's new lawn pavilion. The menu may also include pot stickers, buns (pork, shrimp, veggie, etc.), soups, noodles, wontons, shumai, and wok fried rice, plus dessert buns and wraps. For updates on this new Disneyland eatery, visit *disneyland.com*. **LDS/$$**

LA BREA BAKERY CAFE: Many of this spot's offerings—breakfast treats and classic sandwiches—are built on La Brea's legendary, freshly made bread. Also available are traditional breakfast selections, blackened fish tacos, pastas, roast chicken, salads (with organic greens), soups, and coffees. There is indoor seating (at a counter) and a covered patio with table service. **BLDS/$–$$**

NAPLES RISTORANTE E BAR: Dine inside or out at this contemporary Italian trattoria. A spacious terrace provides views of the Disney landscape, plus a lovely setting for lunch or dinner. The menu includes wood-fired pizzas, gnocchi, lasagna, chicken parmesan, penne pasta, and seared salmon. There's an outdoor bar, too. For reservations, call 714-776-6200. **LD/$$$**

PASEO AND CENTRICO: Michelin-starred Chef Carlos Gaytan is bringing his inclusive vision of Mexican cuisine to the Downtown Disney District. Set in the spaces previously occupied by Catal & Uva Bar, the restaurant and central courtyard bar and dining area promises guests a "multi-sensory journey to the heart of Chef Gaytan's homeland," Mexico. Reservations are recommended. Details are subject to change. **LDS/$$–$$$**

RALPH BRENNAN'S JAZZ KITCHEN: Sample some home-style New Orleans specialties at this thoroughly refreshed and revitalized cafe while listening to jazz. Gumbo, jambalaya, chicken, and fresh pasta dishes are house favorites. Reservations are suggested; 714-776-5200. **LDS/$$–$$$**

SPLITSVILLE LUXURY LANES™: Some go expecting just to bowl, not realizing that Splitsville's kitchen turns out impressive casual fare such as freshly rolled sushi, grilled salmon, chicken Alfredo, seared ahi tuna, and sliders. They've also got spicy veggie bowls, pizzas, cheeseburgers, fish 'n' chips, sandwiches, loaded fries, chicken tenders, nachos, and salads. Many menu items are gluten free. Super-sized desserts include sundaes, brownies, "giant cake," and root beer floats. There is a full bar. Reservations are suggested, but walk-ins may be accommodated. **LDS/$$–$$$**

TORTILLA JO'S: A table-service Mexican restaurant and open-air cantina, this spot offers culinary traditions including freshly prepared tamales, street tacos, carnitas, fajitas, salads, burritos, made-to-order guacamole, lime-marinated ceviche, and more. Combination platters are available. Breakfast—which is served on Saturday and

Sunday from 10 A.M. till noon—features entrées with a Mexican flair: breakfast burritos, steak and eggs, breakfast enchiladas, huevos rancheros, etc., plus bottomless mimosas. Reservations are recommended; 714-535-5000. The adjacent Taqueria serves classic Mexican quick-service selections. **BLDS/$$–$$$**

FAST FOOD & SNACKS

CRAZYSHAKE WINDOW: In the mood for a mega shake? Mosey over to this window for monumental milkshakes and other chilly treats. **S/$–$$**

JAMBA JUICE: Craving a cool, tropical smoothie? Perhaps one with protein or a berry blast? They've got that and more (including breakfast sandwiches, berry bars, soft pretzels, turkey sausage wraps, Belgian waffles, chickpea veggie crisps, brownie bites, etc.) **S/$**

HEARTHSTONE LOUNGE: Though primarily a drinking spot (featuring beer, wine, cocktails, and mocktails), this lounge offers appetizers, a variety of artisanal pizzas, and desserts. Kids' meals are served, too (chicken fingers or grilled cheese served with seasonal fruit and a choice of lowfat milk or water.) **S/$–$$**

KAYLA'S CAKE: Come to this confectious kiosk for hand-crafted premium macarons. And get ten percent off your purchase by using the coupon at the back of this book. Sweet! **S/$**

LA BREA BAKERY EXPRESS: Nestled within La Brea Bakery, this counter offers breakfast selections such as granola yogurt parfait, fruit cup, and bagels. The lunch and dinner menu offers tomato bisque (served in a cup or bread bowl), sandwiches, salads, and "Nancy's fancy gelato." Specialty coffee drinks (including espresso and cappuccino) are brewed all day. **BLDS/$–$$**

NAPOLINI PIZZERIA: Adjacent to the popular Naples Ristorante e Bar, this quick-service destination specializes in freshly prepared pizzas (with a large assortment of topping possibilities), hearty sandwiches, fresh salads, and gelato. **LD/$$**

SALT & STRAW: All of the ice cream at Salt & Straw is handmade with local, organic, and sustainable ingredients. It's all super yummy, too. What flavors are they serving today? Visit *saltandstraw.com* to find out. Oh and you can also order ice cream from the website and have it shipped to your home. How cool is that?! **S/$**

RALPH BRENNAN'S QUICK SERVICE: This recently refurbished counter spot has offered gumbo ya ya bowls, freshly made (and deliciously decadent) beignets (fried dough) topped with powdered sugar, non-alcoholic mint juleps, coffee, tea, and assorted soft drinks. Details are subject to change. **LDS/$–$$**

SPRINKLES CUPCAKES: "The world's first cupcake bakery," as dubbed by Food Network, the Beverly Hills-based Sprinkles serves said signature cupcakes (red velvet, salty caramel, chocolate marshmallow, etc.), slow-churned ice cream, and cookies at Downtown Disney. Note that gluten- and sugar-free cupcakes are served here, as is water, soda, and organic milk. **S/$**

STARBUCKS: The familiar coffeehouse is situated beside Downtown Disney's World of Disney store. In addition to a full menu of coffee drinks, there are teas, smoothies, pastries, oatmeal, yogurt, breakfast sandwiches, paninis, protein boxes and bowls, packaged coffee, and more. It's a very popular spot—build in a little extra time to get that java jolt. **BLDS/$**

TAQUERIA AT TORTILLA JO'S: Are you craving tacos and cerveza? Get your fill at this festive courtyard adjacent (logically) to Tortilla Jo's. Taqueria invites you to indulge in customizable burritos, nachos, bowls, and tacos. Side orders include chips (with guac, salsa, or nacho cheese), beans, and rice. Wash it down with a margarita, beer, or soft drink. *Salúd!* For dessert, consider cookies, brownies, fruta fresca (aka fresh fruit), and more. Kids' meals are available, too. **LDS/$–$$**

WETZEL'S PRETZELS: Whether you prefer pretzels salty or sweet, Wetzel's can satisfy. Snackers enjoy the Sinful Cinnamon, Pepperoni Twist, Cheese Meltdown, and many more. Also served: hot dogs encased in pretzels (full- and bite-sized), fresh lemonade, frozen lemonade, and assorted fountain beverages. Buy one, get one free with the coupon at the back of this book! **S/$**

HOT TIP

Would you like to save money at the Downtown Disney District? Visit *disneyland.com* to see if there are any special offers available for the day(s) you plan to visit—and use the coupons at the back of this book. You're welcome!

Restaurant Roundup

There are more dining choices than ever before at the Disneyland Resort. We've picked some favorites, based on food quality, restaurant atmosphere, and overall value. Use these Birnbaum's Bests to help you decide where to grab a quick bite or have a hearty meal.

BIRNBAUM'S
★BEST★

BEST RESTAURANTS FOR FAMILIES

TABLE SERVICE:

Goofy's Kitchen . . . . Disneyland Hotel (p. 126)
Blue Bayou . . . . Disneyland Park (p. 117)
Storytellers Cafe . . . . . Grand Californian Hotel (p. 128)
Plaza Inn . . . . Disneyland Park (p. 115)

QUICK SERVICE:

Royal Street Veranda . . . . Disneyland Park (p. 118)
Rancho del Zocalo . . . . Disneyland Park (p. 118)
Refreshment Corner Cafe . . . . . Disneyland Park (p. 116)
Pacific Wharf Cafe . . Disney California Adventure (p. 123)
Flo's V8 Cafe . . . . . . Disney California Adventure (p. 125)

BEST RESTAURANTS FOR ADULTS

Napa Rose . . . . Grand Californian Hotel (p. 127)
Carthay Circle . . . . . Disney California Adventure (p. 121)

RUNNERS-UP:

GCH Craftsman Bar . . . Grand Californian Hotel (p. 128)
Lamplight Lounge . . . Disney California Adventure (p. 123)
Wine Country Trattoria . . . Disney California Adventure (p. 122)
Ralph Brennan's Jazz Kitchen . . . Downtown Disney (p. 129)

BEST CHARACTER MEAL

Goofy's Kitchen . . . . Disneyland Hotel (p. 126)

RUNNERS-UP:

Napa Rose . . . . Grand Californian Hotel (p. 127)
Plaza Inn . . . . Disneyland Park (p. 115)
Storytellers Cafe . . . . . Grand Californian Hotel (p. 128)

BEST SNACKS

Jolly Holiday Bakery Cafe . . . . . Disneyland Park (p. 114)
Salt & Straw . . . . Downtown Disney (p. 130)
Tropical Hideaway . . . . Disneyland Park (p. 116)

BEST LOUNGE

Trader Sam's Enchanted Tiki Bar . . . .
Disneyland Hotel (p. 132)

RUNNERS-UP:

Lamplight Lounge . . . .
Disney California Adventure (p. 123)
Tangaroa Terrace Tropical Bar & Grill . . . .
Disneyland Hotel (p. 126)

BEST QUICK SERVICE

Flo's V8 Cafe . . . . . Disney California Adventure (p. 125)

BEST SANDWICHES

La Brea Bakery . . . . Downtown Disney (p. 129)

BEST PIZZA

Naples Ristorante e Bar . . . . . . Downtown Disney (p. 129)

Entertainment
Disney Hotels

The Disneyland Resort has more to offer than theme park attractions. There's plenty to do at Disney's three hotels and in the Downtown Disney dining, shopping, and entertainment district. Whether you're seeking a break from the parks or a place to party the night away, the following options are sure to please.

Note: For more information on theme park entertainment, refer to the *Disneyland Park* and *Disney California Adventure* chapters of this book.

LOUNGES

DISNEYLAND HOTEL: The **Tangaroa Terrace Tropical Bar & Grill**, with its alfresco seating and South Seas vibe provides a pleasant meeting place. The counter-service spot features a full bar, plus a nice selection of nibbles. (Food is available inside, while drinks are served from a window out on the terrace.) The always boisterous **Trader Sam's Enchanted Tiki Bar** mixes drinks and light bites with a bit of Disney magic.

HOT TIP

Trader Sam's Enchanted Tiki Bar hosts brave adventurers daily from about 11:30 A.M. until 1 A.M. (or later). Young explorers may enjoy nibbles and "no booze brews" until about 8 P.M.— after that, this lounge is strictly for guests age 21 and older (with valid government-issued photo ID to prove it). After 8 P.M., minors may enjoy some South Seas ambience on the Tangaroa Terrace side of the shared lanai.

F.Y.I.: Trader Sam is the legendary explorer-turned-Lost & Found-operator at Disneyland park's Jungle Cruise attraction. He recently got the bartending bug (which he initially thought was a big mosquito) and began slinging cocktails at this super-immersive drinkery. Kungaloosh!

DISNEY'S GRAND CALIFORNIAN HOTEL & SPA: The lounge adjoining the elegant **Napa Rose** restaurant usually offers an extensive selection of wines by the glass (and bottle) and a soothing atmosphere. Guests may order a savory snack here, too. This spot was on "temporary pause" at press time, but is expected to re-open.

Inside the handsome **Hearthstone Lounge**, you can sip a specialty drink or an after-dinner cordial opposite a roaring fireplace. If so inclined, you may even enjoy your beverage on a comfy couch in the majestic lobby, where live piano music is always a possibility.

Guests staying at Disney's Grand Californian hotel may also opt to relax and unwind at a the new **GCH Craftsman Bar** near the resort's Redwood Pool.

DISNEY'S PARADISE PIER HOTEL: At press time, this hotel was in the midst of a major makeover. For updates, visit *disneyland.com*.

SPA SERVICES

DISNEY'S GRAND CALIFORNIAN HOTEL & SPA: A spa escape is as welcome a diversion as they come— especially when it's a visit to the world-class pampering palace known as **Tenaya Stone Spa**. Treatments include all manner of massage, facials, body wraps, manicures, pedicures, and more. There are services specially tailored for couples and teenaged guests.

For a complete list of Tenaya Stone Spa services or to book an appointment, go to *https://na.spatime.com/dlr92802/4802218/home*. To reach the spa by phone, call 714-635-2300.

LIVE ENTERTAINMENT

DISNEY'S GRAND CALIFORNIAN HOTEL & SPA: As a tribute to the early 1900s storytelling tradition, entertainers tell tall tales in the hotel's main lobby during the evening hours. A piano player adds to the pleasant atmosphere.

Downtown Disney District

Easily accessed by foot (from the Disneyland Resort hotels or parks) or monorail (from Disneyland Park's Tomorrowland), this entertainment district offers a nice break from the theme park hustle and bustle during the day and a busy place to mix and mingle in the evening hours. Many Downtown Disney venues serve double (sometimes triple!) duty as dining, playing, and shopping destinations.

Shops usually open early and don't close until late in the evening. Performers generally hit the stage post-dinner and wrap by midnight. Note that some venues were "on pause" and others were under construction as this book went to press, but are expected to return. For updates, visit *disneyland.com*.

LOUNGES & ENTERTAINMENT

BALLAST POINT: Featuring a modern, on-site brewery, Ballast Point pairs its award-winning beers with a lineup of Southern California-inspired cuisine—salads, small plates, flatbreads, and entrées featuring local, sustainable and seasonal ingredients. In addition to the aforementioned brewery, this sleek venue houses a tasting room, kitchen, and outdoor beer garden. You'll find Ballast between Black Tap Craft Burgers & Shakes and Wetzel's Pretzels. **LDS/$$–$$$**

BLACK TAP CRAFT BURGERS & SHAKES: A colorful burger and beer joint, Black Tap has a casual atmosphere reminiscent of a classic American luncheonette, with a distinctly New York vibe. Guests may sit in- or

outdoors, enjoying burgers, chicken wings, sandwiches, salads, fried pickles, crispy Brussels sprouts, and more. Shakes (classic and "crazy" varieties), beer, wine, and soft drinks round out the menu. **BLDS/$**

OUTDOOR PERFORMERS: Downtown Disney boasts an eclectic lineup of free, live musical entertainment. From calming classical to rousing rhythm and blues, professional musicians create a party-like atmosphere every day. For details and entertainment schedules, follow @Disneylandtoday on Twitter. Text DTDNOW to DPARK (37275) to receive up to three updates via text per week, or visit *disneyland.disney.go.com/ destinations/downtown-disney-district*.

RALPH BRENNAN'S JAZZ KITCHEN—FLAMBEUX'S JAZZ CLUB: The sounds of jazz set the tone for the relaxed atmosphere at this restaurant's lounge. Bands and singers entertain with live jazz every evening. A smooth soundtrack provides music when the stage is dark. Special tickets may be required for certain performances. To inquire about ticket prices and reservations, visit *rbjazzkitchen.com*, or call 714-776-5200. This venue may not operate in all of 2023.

SPLITSVILLE KINGPIN STAGE: Step up to Splitsville's patio to enjoy cocktails, dining, and live music (the later is provided by a rotating lineup of talented local musicians.) Entertainment is usually offered from about 6 P.M. until 10 P.M. (possibly later).

SHOPPING

CALIFORNIA SOLE: Housed in the space previously occupied by the Sanuk store (relax, Sanuk fans, you can still snag sidewalk surfers at this spot), California Sole sells a variety of comfy footwear for the whole family. Look for brand names such as the aforementioned Sanuk, plus Vans, Havaianas, OluKai, and more. Also available: colorful socks and jewelry.

NEW

CURL SURF: You have to figure that anybody who spent not one but 17 years as a champion water-skier has to know quite a bit about trends in beachwear and water-sport equipment. See for yourself at this high-end surf shop by Sammy Duvall. Among the assortment of wares you'll find are sunglasses, jewelry, watches, and shoes.

THE DISNEY DRESS SHOP: Get dolled up, Disney style! The shop carries an assortment of dresses and accessories with a decidedly Disney design. Each item pays homage to a beloved character or attraction: Alice in Wonderland, Minnie Mouse, Snow White, the Haunted Mansion, It's a Small World, and more. Such fetching, fashion-forward accessories as jewelry, handbags, and hats are available, too. This spot is sure to please your inner Dapper Dana.

DISNEY HOME: If you're like the merry multitudes who would happily call Disneyland home, you're in luck: This shop lets Disney devotees add pixie-dusted touches to their actual homes. Many items vary seasonally, but Disney Home always offers fans a variety of Disney-themed treasures: glasswear, linens, kitchen goods, and more. Here's to the happiest home on earth!

DISNEY PIN TRADERS: Do we really need to spell out what this spot specializes in? Didn't think so.

THE LEGO STORE: Hundreds of the world's most famous building brick sets and products are for sale here. There's a play area, too. The shop hosts workshops and LEGO Club meetings for LEGO enthusiasts of all ages. You'll find it across from Disney Pin Traders.

MARCELINE'S CONFECTIONERY: Named for Walt Disney's boyhood hometown in Missouri, Marceline's offers candies, pastries, and other sweet treats. It's fun to watch the candymakers at work.

PANDORA JEWELRY: Known for its customizable bracelets, PANDORA also offers gold and silver necklaces, rings, earrings, and charms—many featuring accents like gemstones, cultured pearls, Murano glass, and cubic zirconia.

SEPHORA: A black-and-white motif provides the backdrop for the colorful palette of products in this cosmetics mecca. Sephora's own line of makeup is complemented by a selection of beauty products and designer fragrances.

SPRINKLES: "The world's first cupcake bakery," as dubbed by Food Network, the Beverly Hills–based Sprinkles serves said signature cakes, slow-churned ice cream, and cookies in the Downtown Disney District. You can order Sprinkles treats from home, too—just visit *sprinkles.com*.

SUNGLASS ICON: Stop at this shop for premium peeper protectors—custom-fit shades are the stock-in-trade at this shop. All the big-name designers are represented.

WORLD OF DISNEY: The shelves are stacked sky-high at this newly refurbished, souvenir seeker's go-to. With areas dedicated to plush toys, dolls, home decor, clothing, and collectibles, there's something for everyone here. The place is busy most evenings and weekends—especially after the parks close for the day.

WONDERGROUND GALLERY: Notably distinctive and eclectic, Wonderground is a work of art in and of itself. The contemporary venue showcases unique art collections and works from a new generation of artists, interpreted through various mediums, styles, and forms.

FUN & GAMES

SPLITSVILLE LUXURY LANES™: Boasting bowling, bars, finger food, upscale menu offerings, and more, Splitsville offers something for just about everyone—however, some areas are zoned exclusively for folks over age 21 (with valid government-issued photo ID to prove it). The venue features 30 bowling lanes, a high-end kitchen, specialty drinks, live music—and billiards! For details, visit *www.splitsvillelanes.com*.

SPORTS & RECREATION

Southern California's combination of warm, sunny weather and invigorating ocean breezes has created a population of outdoor and exercise enthusiasts. Athletes flex their muscles on golf courses and tennis courts; atop surfboards, bikes, and in-line skates; on hiking and jogging trails; or 15 feet underwater, mingling with shimmering schools of fish.

As part of Orange County, California, Anaheim is within easy distance of the county's 35,000-plus acres of parkland and several hundred miles of bike trails. Hiking paths and fishing streams crisscross 460,000 acres of mountain terrain in Cleveland National Forest. Just 15 miles south of Anaheim, prime Pacific Ocean beaches—perfect for basking in the sun or catching the ultimate wave—await the wayfarer. In fact, 42 miles of glistening sand and sleepy seaside communities are within an hour's drive of Anaheim.

Those who delight in spying on Mother Nature can catch glimpses of California's gray whales as they migrate to Mexico for the winter, or ospreys, blue herons, and swallows returning to the area in the spring. A team of Orange County's most entertaining creatures, hockey-playing Ducks, can be spotted from September through April (and later, if they make a run for the Stanley Cup). Even Angels have been sighted, gracing the bases at Angel Stadium, late March through September (and possibly through October).

No doubt about it, the sporting opportunities in and around the city of Anaheim, California, are quite bountiful indeed.

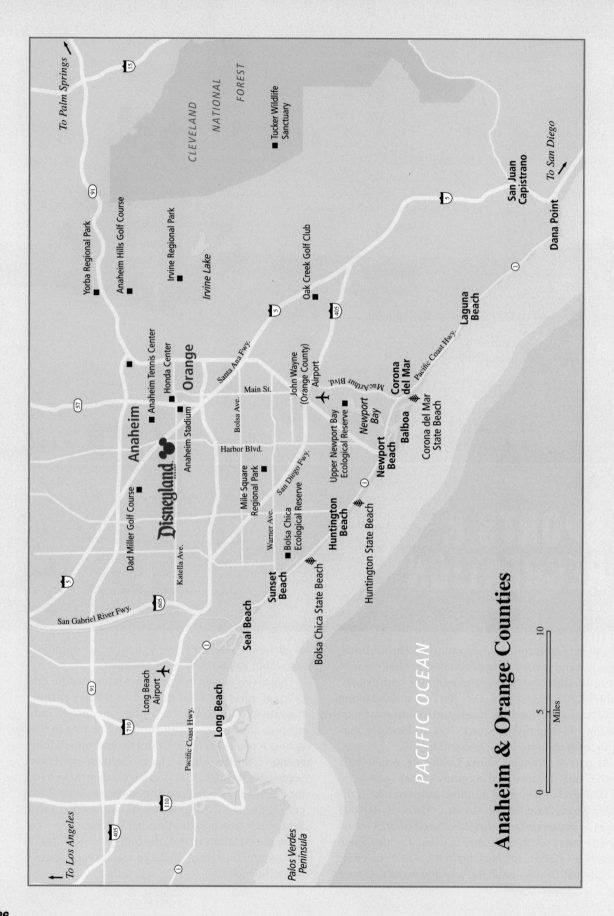

Anaheim & Orange Counties

Eye on the Ball

GOLF

ANAHEIM HILLS GOLF COURSE: This challenging championship course is a hilly, par-71, 6,245-yard layout nestled in the valleys and slopes of the scenic Anaheim Hills. Greens fees range from about $23 to about $63 based on time of day and demand. Golf clubs are available to rent for about $30. Reservations are recommended (it's best to call seven days ahead for both weekend and weekday play). All details are subject to change at any time. The Anaheim Hills Golf Course is open for business 365 days a year, from 6 or 6:30 A.M. until sunset. 6501 Nohl Ranch Road, Anaheim; *www.anaheimhillsgc.com*; 714-998-3041.

DAD MILLER GOLF COURSE: "Dad" Miller made a historic hole in one on this course (on the 116-yard 11th hole) when he was 93 years old, and it's still a favorite with older guests, who appreciate the flat, walkable terrain and park-like setting. But if you're a tad on the younger side, don't let that keep you from playing here. This par-71, 5,892-yard golf course is one of the busiest in California—partly because of its convenient location in the northwest corner of the city, but also because it's just right for the strictly recreational golfer. The cost to play changes daily, based on demand. Guests 60 and older can play standby for $21 Monday through Friday. Golf carts cost about $13 for 18 holes, $8.50 for nine holes.

Reservations are suggested and may be made up to a week in advance. The course is open 365 days each year, from 6 A.M. till 8 P.M. 430 N. Gilbert St., Anaheim; *www.dadmillergc.com*; 714-765-3481 (pro shop and reservations).

TENNIS

ANAHEIM TENNIS CENTER: This public facility has all the perks of a private tennis club—an inviting clubhouse, a well-stocked pro shop, computerized practice machines, lockers, and showers. The staff will make an effort to pair you with a suitable partner, as long as you make your request in advance.

There are 12 fast, hard-surface courts, all lighted for night play. Singles rates range from about $15 per hour (depending on the time of day); doubles rates are about $20 per hour, depending on time of day. Use of a ball machine is about $25 per hour; they are separated from the courts, but this area is still a good place to practice forehand and backhand strokes.

Playing hours usually begin at 7 A.M. and end at 9 P.M. Monday through Friday, and start at 7 A.M. and end at 6 P.M. on weekends and holidays. Racquets are free for those taking lessons. Locker and shower facilities are free of charge (if you want towels, you must supply them yourself). A one-hour private tennis lesson with the resident pro costs about $65 to $88; call for rates for semi-private or group lessons. Drop-in pickleball rates run about $8 per person. Reservations (which may be booked up to three days in advance for nonmembers) are suggested, especially for court times after 5 P.M. The tennis center is about three miles from the Disneyland Resort. 975 S. State College Blvd., Anaheim; 714-991-9090; *www.anaheimtenniscenter.com*.

HOT TIP

For additional information about these and other Orange County area golf courses and tournaments, visit *www.playocgolf.com*.

RISE & EXERCISE

DISNEY'S GRAND CALIFORNIAN HOTEL & SPA: Rise and shine—and exercise! Guests registered at one of the three Disneyland Resort hotels (The Disneyland Hotel, Paradise Pier, and Disney's Grand Californian) can enjoy an early morning group workout session (for a fee) at Disney's Grand Californian Resort & Spa.

For additional information, or to make a reservation, go to *https://na.spatime.com/dlr92802/4802218/home*. Details are subject to change. Here is a sampling of some recent offerings at Tenaya Stone Spa:

Awakening Yoga: Guests (age 18 and over) may wake up with a 45-minute session overlooking Disney California Adventure park. Designed for folks at all levels, the class incorporates various types of yoga meant to improve mental awareness and start the day off right. It takes place on select mornings at the Eureka Fitness Center (at Disney's Grand Californian Hotel) at 6:30 A.M.

Power Walking: Kick off the morning with a power walk through Disney California Adventure before the park opens for the day! Each 45-minute session costs $25 and begins at the Grand Californian's private entrance to the park. For details or to make a reservation, visit *https://na.spatime.com/dlr92802/4802218/home*

Aqua Fitness: Bathing-suit up for this floating workout in the Fountain Pool near the Tenaya Stone Spa. It combines cardio, strength, and core exercises—all done on a paddleboard in the pool. Each 30-minute class starts at 9:30 A.M. and costs $25 per person.

Aqua Yoga: If you've ever thought, "I would love to practice yoga while on a paddleboard floating in a swimming pool," you're in luck: 30-minute sessions are offered at 10:30 A.M. on select days. Each Aqua Yoga session costs about $30. *Namaste.*

SPECTATOR SPORTS

FOOTBALL

Los Angeles Chargers
(August–January)
SoFi Stadium
1001 Stadium Dr., Inglewood
800-745-3000 (Ticketmaster)
www.chargers.com

Los Angeles Rams
(August–January)
SoFi Stadium
1001 Stadium Dr., Inglewood
800-745-3000 (Ticketmaster)
www.therams.com

BASEBALL

Los Angeles Angels of Anaheim
(March–October)

Angel Stadium of Anaheim,
2000 E. Gene Autry Way., Anaheim
714-940-2000 (information)
888-796-4256 (tickets)
www.mlb.com/angels

Los Angeles Dodgers
(March–October)

Dodger Stadium
1000 Vin Scully Ave., Los Angeles
866-363-4377
www.mlb.com/dodgers

HOCKEY

Los Angeles Kings
(September–April)
Staples Center, 1111 S. Figueroa St., Los Angeles
800-745-3000 (Ticketmaster)
www.nhl.com/kings

Anaheim Ducks
(September–April)
Honda Center, 2695 E. Katella Ave., Anaheim
877-945-3946 (information)
800-745-3000 (Ticketmaster)
www.nhl.com/ducks

BASKETBALL

Los Angeles Clippers
(September–April)
Staples Center
1111 S. Figueroa St., Los Angeles
213-204-2900
www.nba.com/clippers

Los Angeles Lakers
(September–April)
Staples Center
1111 S. Figueroa St., Los Angeles
310-426-6000
www.nba.com/lakers

Los Angeles Sparks
(May–September)
Staples Center
1111 S. Figueroa St., Los Angeles
877-447-7275
sparks.wnba.com

Surf & Sun

BEACHES

Orange County's public beaches cover 42 miles of coastline—some dramatic, with high cliffs and crashing waves; others tranquil, with sheltered coves and tide pools. In summer, the water temperature averages 64 degrees but can get as high as 70; in winter, it's a nippy 57 to 60 degrees.

Beaches are usually open from around 6 A.M. to 10 P.M., with lifeguards on duty in the summer. Bicycles, in-line skates, and roller skates are available for rent in some locations. Access is free, but there is usually a fee to park. For additional beach information, go to the Surf and Sand section of *www.orangecounty.net*.

BALBOA/NEWPORT BEACH: The Balboa Peninsula juts into the Pacific Ocean, creating lovely beaches—Newport on the mainland, Balboa on the peninsula—that are long and horseshoe-shaped, pleasant and sandy, and popular with families, surfers, and sightseers. Visit *www.ocbeachinfo.com* for water quality and environmental information.

The largest small-craft harbor in the world, Newport Harbor shelters more than 9,000 boats. For a choice view, drive south along the peninsula on Newport Boulevard to Balboa Boulevard; turn right on Palm Street, and you will find parking for the popular Balboa Pier and Fun Zone; *www.balboaferriswheel.com*.

Throughout the fall and winter, the 1,000-acre Upper Newport Bay Nature Preserve and Ecological Reserve teems with great blue herons, ospreys, and many other wild winged creatures. The park's partially subterranean Peter and Mary Muth Interpretive Center, located at 2301 University Drive (at Irvine Avenue), has exhibits on bird life, the watershed, and the history of Newport Bay (closed Mondays).

During migratory season (October through March), the Newport Bay Conservancy leads free walking tours, pointing out birds, as well as fossils, marsh plants, and fish. On Saturday mornings, year-round, the conservancy

also offers a 2-hour guided kayak tour of the Back Bay for $25 per person, ages 8 and up.

The reserve is open daily 7 A.M. to sunset. To obtain updated information about guided tours and various special events year-round, as well as directions to specific parts of the reserve, contact Newport Bay Conservancy: 949-923-2269 or *www.newportbay.org*.

CORONA DEL MAR STATE BEACH: Secluded Corona del Mar State Beach is a favorite for swimming and snorkeling; and the lookout point above the beach is a great place to watch the sun set. There are picnic tables, grills, fire rings, a snack bar, and showers. For information, visit *www.orangecounty.net* (Surf and Sand section), or call 949-644-3151.

HUNTINGTON BEACH: The self-proclaimed "Surf City, U.S.A." (and home to the International Surfing Museum) hosts competitions year-round (winter is best for wave height). Surfboards and wet suits may be rented or purchased; *www.surfcityusa.com*.

Huntington City Beach is a 3.5-mile stretch of sand fronting the town and is a popular place for swimming, bodysurfing, and beach volleyball. The pier provides an ideal spot for fishing and a good vantage point for observing the passing scene. For surf information, call 714-536-9303; *www.hbonline.com*.

Bolsa Chica Wetlands, 1,449 acres of Pacific Ocean marshland a mile north of Huntington Beach pier on Pacific Coast Highway, harbors fish and wetland birds. The Interpretive Center is open 9 A.M. to 4 P.M. daily with three marine life exhibits. To get there, cross the bridge from the beach parking lot and follow a trail through the marsh; 714-846-1114; *www.bolsachica.org*.

LAGUNA BEACH: More than 20 different beaches and coves line this seven-mile coastline, popular with surfers, kayakers, body boarders, and snorkelers. Laguna is one of the best spots in Orange County to scuba dive, though you need a wet suit year-round.

Laguna Sea Sports (925 N. Coast Hwy.; 949-494-6965; *www.beachcitiesscuba.com*) offers full rentals, guided beach dives, classes, general information, and more; there's a pool on the premises, and it's only two blocks from the beach. Main Beach (which is located in the middle of town) offers basketball and volleyball.

HOT TIP

For a scenic 45-minute walk, follow the harbor-hugging pathway around Balboa Island. For a mini-expedition, head to Little Balboa Island—it can be completed in about 20 minutes.

A short walk away, Heisler Park has scenic picnic areas, beaches, cliff-top lookout points, benches, and charcoal grills; stairs lead to tide pools. Serious hikers like to head for the Aliso and Wood Canyons Wilderness Park (*www.ocparks.com*), the Crystal Cove State Park (*www.crystalcovestatepark.org*), or the Laguna Coast Wilderness Park. Watch the sun set from Laguna Art Museum or Laguna Village; *www.visitlagunabeach.com*.

FISHING

In Orange County, you can cast for bass, catfish, and trout in tranquil lakes; troll the Pacific for bonitos, barracuda, halibut, and more; and hand-scoop grunions (license required) off the beach.

GRUNION ALERT: One scenic place to try your hand—literally—at catching grunion (provided that you have a license) is at Cabrillo Beach in March, June, July, and August, when the tiny fish come ashore to lay eggs in the sand and then head back out to sea on outgoing waves. (Grunion catching is illegal—even if you have a fishing license—in April and May.)

Grunion are quite slippery, and you are required to catch them exclusively with your hands; fortunately, they also shimmer in the moonlight, so they're fairly easy to spot. The best time to go grunion fishing is about an hour or two after high tide on the second through fifth nights after a new or full moon. Park gates close at 10 P.M. Be sure to observe all parking rules. For details, visit *www.wildlife.ca.gov*, or call 831-649-2870.

SPORTFISHING: Fishing boats set out from Davey's Locker at Balboa Pavilion in Newport Beach (949-673-1434; *www.daveyslocker.com*) and from Dana Wharf Sportfishing at Dana Point Harbor (*www.danawharf.com*; 888-224-0603). Reservations are suggested. Fishing licenses, which are legally necessary for deep-sea sportfishing, must be purchased in advance via *www.wildlife.ca.gov/Licensing/fishing*. Licenses cost about $18 per day.

PARKS

IRVINE REGIONAL PARK: Located in Santiago Canyon near Irvine Lake, this peaceful place has hiking and equestrian trails that wind through 491 hilly acres and centuries-old sycamores and oaks. The oldest county park in California, it offers bike trails, the Orange County Zoo, playgrounds, a small waterfall, creek, and picnic facilities. Zoo admission is $2 for guests age 3 and up. There is a $3 to $5 parking fee per vehicle year-round (the parking fee is usually about $7 on major holidays). 1 Irvine Park Rd., Orange; 714-973-6835; *www.ocparks.com*.

MILE SQUARE REGIONAL PARK: It's one square mile in area—hence the name. Besides five miles of winding bike trails, the park has a walking course, a nature area, and picnic areas and shelters. Bicycles may be rented here on weekends and holidays. 16801 Euclid Street, Fountain Valley; *www.ocparks.com*; 714-973-6600.

ENC TUCKER WILDLIFE SANCTUARY: This 12-acre sanctuary in the Santa Ana Mountains' Modjeska Canyon is an oasis of diverse flora and fauna. Naturalists can answer questions, and there are hiking trails, a small natural history museum, and a sensory garden. A donation is suggested (and appreciated). 29322 Modjeska Canyon Rd., Modjeska Canyon; *www.encenter.org*; 949-645-8489.

YORBA REGIONAL PARK: These 140 acres in the Santa Ana Canyon cradle four lakes (with connecting streams), picnic areas, playgrounds, hiking trails, equestrian activities, horseshoe pits, model sailboating, volleyball courts, baseball fields, and biking trails (bike rentals are offered on weekend days). Visitors can walk or ride a bicycle into the park without charge; parking costs about $3 to $5 ($7 on holidays). 7600 E. La Palma Ave., Anaheim; *www.ocparks.com*; 714-973-6615.

WHALE WATCHING & DOLPHIN CRUISE

Whale watching and dolphin cruises leave from Newport Beach daily throughout the year. You may see giant blue whales, finback whales, gray whales, humpback whales, minke whales, and dolphins. Birnbaum's readers net a discount on weekday (about $14 per person) and weekend (about $22 per person) cruises with promo code disney18. Other types of cruises are available as well. Call 949-673-1434, or visit *www.daveyslocker.com*.

AN OFFICIAL DISNEY PARKS COOKBOOK SAMPLER

Good food is part of our memories. In the early 1940s, Walt Disney enjoyed taking his two young daughters to Griffith Park in Los Angeles, but he found much of the time, he was sitting on a bench eating popcorn while they rode a merry-go-round. Soon, he and his team started to work on his ideas for a "Mickey Mouse Park," a place where parents and kids could go together for fun. Walt's dream, of course, became a reality in 1955—with a name change to Disneyland—and with a selection of food that went far beyond popcorn.

Disneyland dining is an ever-growing part of the vacation experience, with more and more restaurants and festivals arguably as entertaining as the theme park attractions themselves. There are longstanding favorites, like casual dining at a cafe on Main Street, U.S.A. or a (very) fancy meal at the award-winning Napa Rose at Disney's Grand Californian Hotel & Spa. There are also seasonal highlights, like the small plates offered at the annual Food & Wine Festival at Disney California Adventure park, each with

Golden State–grown ingredients such as avocados, citrus, strawberries, peppers, garlic, and artisanal cheese.

It's a real balancing act to offer something for every palate, with cuisine as varied as all the guests who visit the resorts. That's why a little bit of everything is featured in the *The Official Disney Parks Cookbook*, a new book by Pam Brandon, author of *Delicious Disney* (and many others). A special selection of those recipes is included here, with instructions that make it easy to enjoy the dishes at home. Some are fuss free; others take a little time. Some are classics; others are new adventures. Please enjoy this sampling from Disney's official recipe collection. *Bon appetit!*

"IT IS MY WISH TO DELIGHT ALL MEMBERS OF THE FAMILY."

—WALT DISNEY

Moogan Tea

Oga's Cantina • Star Wars: Galaxy's Edge at Disneyland
Serves 2

MOOGAN SPICE SYRUP
(Makes 1¼ cup)
- **1 teaspoon vanilla extract**
- **1 cinnamon stick, broken into small pieces**
- **½ cup packed brown sugar**
- **½ cup granulated sugar**
- **1 cup water**

CHRISTOPHSIAN SUGAR–CINNAMON MIXTURE
(Makes 1 cup)
- **1 cup plus 1 teaspoon sugar, divided**
- **½ cup water**
- **½ teaspoon orange extract**
- **½ teaspoon vanilla extract**
- **½ teaspoon ground cinnamon**

MOOGAN TEA
- **1¼ cups prepared unsweetened iced tea**
- **1 cup chocolate milk**
- **¼ cup Moogan Spice Syrup (recipe included below)**
- **½ cup heavy cream**
- **1 ounce Falernum**
- **1 tablespoon Christophsian sugar–cinnamon mixture for garnish (recipe included below)**

FOR MOOGAN SPICE SYRUP
Combine all the ingredients in a small saucepan over medium heat. Cook until the sugar has dissolved, then let sit for at least 4 hours to let the flavors infuse. Strain into a clean bottle and refrigerate until ready to use. Keeps for 1 to 2 weeks.

FOR CHRISTOPHSIAN SUGAR–CINNAMON MIXTURE
1. Combine 1 cup of the sugar with the water and orange extract in a small nonstick saucepan. Cook over medium heat without stirring for about 10 minutes, until the mixture develops a thick consistency and a golden amber color.

2. Add the vanilla extract and the remaining 1 teaspoon of sugar. Stir vigorously until the mixture turns pale and puffy and recrystalizes, about 5 to 10 minutes.

3. Stir a few more seconds to help dry it out, then remove from heat.

4. While still warm, crumble or crush the sugar into fairly small pieces and store in an airtight container.

5. To prepare for the tea, mix 1 tablespoon of Christophsian sugar with the ground cinnamon.

TO ASSEMBLE

1. Combine the iced tea, chocolate milk, and Moogan Spice Syrup in a small pitcher and refrigerate until ready to serve.

2. In a small bowl, beat the cream until it forms stiff peaks, then add the Falernum and beat until just mixed in.

3. To serve, fill two tall glasses half full with ice and divide the tea mixture between them.

4. Top with the flavored whipped cream, and sprinkle a little of the Christophsian sugar–cinnamon mixture on top.

KEEP IN MIND

Please remember that the Disney parks are constantly changing and growing, and the printed recipes you hold in your hands are our best effort at accuracy at the time of printing. If given an opportunity to update these recipes at a future date, we will refine and expand our materials to even better enhance your experience.

These recipes have been adjusted from larger quantity versions used in Disneyland Resort kitchens. The flavor profiles may vary a bit from the restaurant's version, but they all yield yummy results—we happily tested and tasted them.

Always use caution in the kitchen—especially when handling sharp objects and hot contents. And be sure to supervise junior chefs and kids who are nearby.

Enjoy!

Napa Rose Lavosh

Napa Rose • Disney's Grand Californian Hotel & Spa
Serves 6–8

- **1 cup extra-virgin olive oil**
- **2 large cloves garlic, smashed**
- **2 teaspoons finely chopped parsley**
- **coarse salt, to taste**
- **freshly ground black pepper, to taste**
- **1 package lavosh (This flatbread can be purchased in Indian and other specialty food markets.)**
- **1 cup grated Parmigiano-Reggiano cheese**

1. In bowl, mix olive oil, garlic, and parsley; season with salt and pepper.

2. Brush lavosh with olive-oil mixture and sprinkle with cheese.

3. Bake at 350ºF for 8 minutes, or until golden brown and lightly crisp. Serve warm, or cooled, as a cracker, with appetizers.

Walt's Chili and Beans

Carnation Café • Main Street, U.S.A. at Disneyland

Serves 6–8

CHILI

- ¼ cup olive oil, divided
- ¾ pound beef stew meat
- 1 small onion, diced
- 1 medium green pepper, diced
- 4 cloves garlic, minced
- 1 pound ground beef
- 1 tablespoon ground cumin
- 1½ tablespoons chili powder
- 1 tablespoon onion powder
- ¾ teaspoon cayenne pepper
- 3 tablespoons tomato paste
- 2 plum tomatoes, diced
- 1 (28-ounce) can diced tomatoes
- 2 tablespoons beef base
- 1½ cups water
- 1 (14½-ounce) can pinto beans, rinsed and drained
- coarse salt, to taste

GARNISH

- ½ cup sour cream
- 1 cup shredded cheddar cheese
- 2 small tomatoes, diced

FOR CHILI

1. Heat 2 tablespoons of the oil in large Dutch oven, over medium heat for 5 minutes. Add stew meat and sauté for 10 minutes, until meat is browned on all sides. Remove stew meat from pan and set aside.

2. Add the remaining 2 tablespoons of oil to pan, heat for 3 minutes over medium heat.

3. Add onions and green pepper. Sauté 8 to 10 minutes, until soft. Add garlic and sauté one minute longer, until garlic is fragrant.

4. Add ground beef. Cook, stirring occasionally to break up large chunks of beef, for 10 to 12 minutes, until beef is no longer pink. Drain excess fat.

5. Return stew meat to the Dutch oven with ground beef mixture. Add ground cumin, chili powder, onion powder, cayenne pepper, tomato paste, diced plum tomatoes, diced can tomatoes, beef base, and water.

6. Bring chili to a simmer. Cover and simmer over low heat for 3 hours, until stew meat is tender.

7. Add pinto beans. Simmer for 10 minutes, until beans are warm.

8. Season with salt, as needed.

TO SERVE

Garnish with sour cream, shredded cheddar cheese, and diced tomatoes.

Napa Rose • Disney's Grand Californian Hotel & Spa
Serves 6

CHIVE WHIPPED POTATOES
- 3 russet potatoes, peeled and quartered
- coarse salt and freshly ground pepper, to taste
- ¼ cup snipped chives
- ½ cup heavy cream
- 2 tablespoons unsalted butter
- 2 tablespoons sour cream
- 1 tablespoon freshly squeezed lemon juice

HOT TIP
Before juicing a lemon, roll it back and forth on the counter with your palm using firm pressure. This will soften the membranes inside the fruit and make it easier to juice.

LEMON, LOBSTER, AND VANILLA SAUCE

- 2 minced shallots
- 1 tablespoon clarified butter
- 1 cup white wine
- 1 cup chicken stock
- ⅛ teaspoon vanilla extract (or use 1 vanilla bean, split)
- 1 small pinch of saffron
- 3 tablespoons diced tomatoes
- 1 tablespoon chopped fresh thyme
- 1 tablespoon freshly squeezed lemon juice
- 6 tablespoons unsalted butter, softened
- 1 lobster, steamed, cracked, with meat removed

SAUTÉED SEA OF CORTEZ ROCK SCALLOP WITH SAUCE OF LEMON, LOBSTER, AND VANILLA

- 12 large rock scallops or diver scallops
- ¼ teaspoon salt
- 2 tablespoons clarified butter or olive oil
- 1½ cups Chive Whipped Potatoes (recipe included below)
- 1½ cups Lemon, Lobster, and Vanilla Sauce (recipe included below)

FOR CHIVE WHIPPED POTATOES

1. Place potatoes in a saucepot with enough cold water to cover potatoes by at least 3 inches. Place on burner set to medium heat and bring to a boil. Simmer for approximately 20 minutes or until tender.

2. Drain off all excess water and transfer potatoes to a mixing bowl. Smash or pass potatoes through a ricer. Season with salt, pepper, and chives. Add heavy cream, butter, and sour cream until potatoes are nice and moist. Add lemon juice; taste, and adjust seasoning if necessary.

FOR LEMON, LOBSTER, AND VANILLA SAUCE

1. Sauté shallots in clarified butter in saucepan over medium-high heat.

2. Add white wine and reduce by about 70 percent, until about ⅓ cup remains. Add chicken stock, vanilla extract, and saffron, and reduce by half, until about ⅔ cup of liquid remains. Add tomatoes, chopped thyme, and lemon juice.

3. Remove saucepan from heat and slowly whisk in unsalted butter. Add lobster meat. Mixture should resemble a creamy lobster and saffron stew. Taste and add salt or a few drops of lemon juice, if necessary.

TO ASSEMBLE

1. Place scallops on a towel and season with salt. In a large sauté pan over medium-high heat, melt 2 tablespoons butter. Make sure pan is very hot, then add seasoned scallops with their flat sides down.

2. Sauté for 4 minutes, or until golden brown. Using kitchen tongs, turn scallops over and brown the opposite sides. If they are cooking too quickly, reduce heat.

3. For each serving, place the Chive Whipped Potatoes in the center of the plate and set 2 scallops on top of the potatoes. Then with a spoon, pour the Lemon, Lobster, and Vanilla Sauce evenly all the way around the scallops.

McIntosh Apple Charlottes

Napa Rose • Disney's Grand Californian Hotel & Spa
Serves 12

MCINTOSH APPLE CHARLOTTES
- 3 tablespoons unsalted butter
- ½ cup brown sugar
- 1 pinch salt
- 5 large McIntosh apples, peeled, cored, and chopped
- ½ lemon, juiced and zested
- ¼ teaspoon vanilla
- 1 tablespoon apple brandy
- 12 ½-inch-thick slices brioche

CRUMB TOPPING
- ½ cup all-purpose flour
- ¼ cup unsalted butter, softened
- 2 tablespoons brown sugar
- ¼ cup chopped pecans
- ⅛ teaspoon ground cinnamon
- ⅛ teaspoon ground nutmeg
- ½ teaspoon vanilla extract
- Whipped cream or vanilla ice cream, for serving

FOR MCINTOSH APPLE CHARLOTTES

1. Preheat oven to 350°F.

2. Heat butter, sugar, and salt in a medium skillet over medium heat for 3 to 5 minutes. Add apples, lemon zest, and vanilla; sauté for 5 minutes. Add apple brandy and lemon juice and remove from heat.

3. Grease a 12-well muffin tin with butter.

4. Roll brioche slices with rolling pin until ⅛ inch thick. Place into greased muffin tin to form 12 bowls. Pour apple mixture into centers of brioche bowls.

5. Bake for 8 to 10 minutes, or until the edges are golden brown.

6. Cool for 30 minutes, then carefully remove from muffin tin.

FOR CRUMB TOPPING

1. Preheat oven to 300°F.

2. Combine flour and butter with a pastry blender or 2 knives to form a coarse meal. Add brown sugar, pecans, cinnamon, nutmeg, and vanilla extract; mix until dough forms.

3. Break dough into small pieces on a sheet pan. Bake for 15 to 20 minutes, until golden brown.

4. Sprinkle on top of warm charlottes. Serve with whipped cream or vanilla ice cream.

HOT TIP

When zesting a lemon, use light pressure with the zester so as not to dig too deeply into the rind. The white layer beneath the outer rind can be bitter tasting.

NAPA REDS & WHITES

Just behind the check-in podium at Napa Rose is the restaurant's showcase wine cellar. Containing roughly 1,000 bottles of wine—the majority from California's Napa Valley region—the wine cellar is a visual spectacle. One wall features a display of magnums while the counters hold the roughly 90 varieties of wine available by the glass on any given day. One need not be a wine connoisseur to enjoy a glass here, though. Simply inform one of the trusty on-staff sommeliers of your tastes and they will be happy to provide a recommendation.

PB and J Rolls

Lamplight Lounge • Pixar Pier • Disney California Adventure
Serves 4

PEANUT BUTTER ROLLS
- **8 slices wheat bread**
- **¾ cup creamy peanut butter, divided**

JELLY DRIZZLE
- **¾ cup strawberry or grape jelly**

FOR PEANUT BUTTER ROLLS

1. Cut crusts off bread. Flatten bread with rolling pin until bread can bind after being rolled.

2. Spread 1½ tablespoons of peanut butter evenly on each slice of flattened bread, leaving a small border on all sides—the peanut butter will spread as you roll.

3. Starting with long side of bread, gently roll up each bread slice into a spiral. Cut each roll into 4 even pieces.

4. Place 8 pieces of rollups onto each plate, seam-side down.

FOR JELLY DRIZZLE

1. Place plastic quart-size freezer bag into small cup, folding back first few inches of bag over top of cup. Spoon jelly into bag, gently shaking bag to move jelly to bottom of bag. (Note: If jelly is too thick to drizzle, add small amount of warm water to jelly in small bowl and mix to desired consistency before adding to bag.)

2. Once filled, lift bag from cup and squeeze out excess air from bag and seal bag with a few twists to top of bag. Cut bottom corner of bag with scissors.

3. Holding right below the twisted top of bag with one hand and guiding with free hand, gently squeeze to drizzle jelly over each peanut butter roll with zigzag motion.

COOK'S NOTE:

A squeezable bottle of jelly is an easy option. Simply squeeze, in zigzag motion, desired amount of jelly over each peanut butter roll.

INDEX

COUPONS

sunglass hut

10% OFF
SELECTED STYLES

Subject to terms and conditions on reverse side.

BALLAST POINT
BREWING COMPANY

BREWERY AND KITCHEN
10% OFF FOOD
(Excludes alchohol)

Subject to terms and conditions on reverse side.

RECEIVE 10% OFF
ENTIRE PURCHASE

Made to order for that delicious crunchy, crispy bite!

Subject to terms and conditions on reverse side.

california churro
A 50/50 COMPANY

RECEIVE 10% OFF
ENTIRE PURCHASE

The most unique churros—you are definitely in for a treat!

Subject to terms and conditions on reverse side.

RECEIVE 10% OFF
IN-STORE PURCHASE

Redeem this coupon at California Sole
Downtown Disney for 10% off your entire purchase!

Subject to terms and conditions on reverse side.

10% OFF
ENTIRE PURCHASE

Premium brand surf apparel,
women's fashion, swimwear, accessories,
and goods for the entire family!

Subject to terms and conditions on reverse side.

COUPONS

BUY ONE DOG, GET THE SECOND DOG FREE

Subject to terms and conditions on reverse side.

jamba

15% OFF
ENTIRE PURCHASE

Subject to terms and conditions on reverse side.

KAYLA'S CAKE

Inspired Artisan Delicacies

10% OFF
ENTIRE PURCHASE

Delectable French macarons and cake in a jar. Visit our kiosk in the Downtown Disney® District near the World of Disney store.

Subject to terms and conditions on reverse side.

SCORE 10% OFF
ENTIRE PURCHASE

"The World's Greatest Soccer Store" located in the Downtown Disney® District.

Subject to terms and conditions on reverse side.

10% OFF
BOWLING

Subject to terms and conditions on reverse side.

BUY ONE PRETZEL, GET THE SECOND PRETZEL FREE

Subject to terms and conditions on reverse side.